Herold Hamm

# COLORADO
## WITHOUT MOUNTAINS

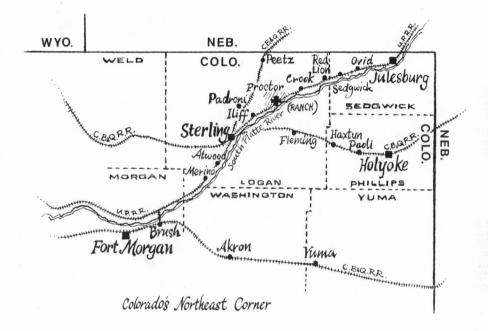

Colorado's Northeast Corner

Endorsed by the Colorado Centennial-
Bicentennial Commission

THE LOWELL PRESS / Kansas City, Missouri

# COLORADO
# WITHOUT MOUNTAINS

by Harold Hamil

Illustrated by James R. Hamil

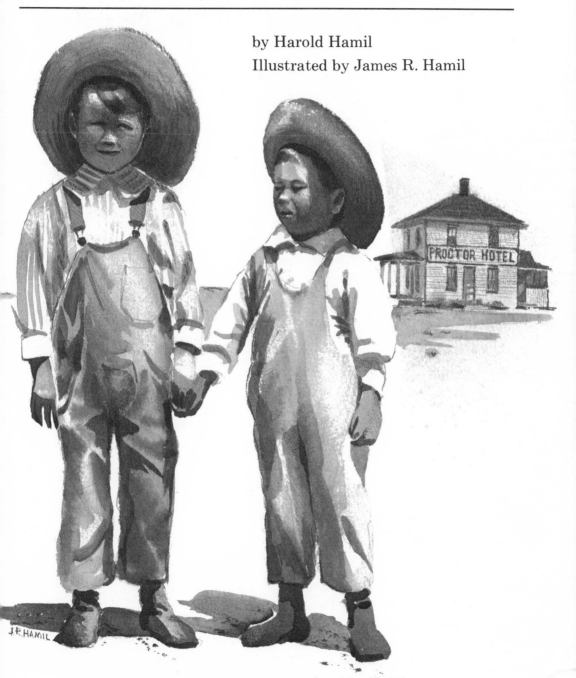

PROCTOR HOTEL

J.R.HAMIL

## A High Plains Memoir

**Library of Congress Cataloging in Publication Data**

Harold Hamil 1906–
COLORADO WITHOUT MOUNTAINS

1. Logan Co., Col.—History.
2. Ranch Life—Logan Co., Col.
3. Hamil, Harold.
4. Logan Co., Col.—Biography.
I. Title.

F782.L8H35            978.8'75'03            76-21134

L.C. 76-21134
ISBN 0-913504-33-5

FIRST EDITION

Copyright 1976   Harold Hamil

Printed in the United States of America

TO
James Newton and Ada Gertrude—their love,
their faith, their courage,
and their uncommon common sense.

# To THOSE WHO COACHED AND CHEERED

One of my grandfathers, pushed and goaded by members of his family for at least 30 years, finally sat down and wrote out his recollections of the Civil War as he saw it from the standpoint of a foot soldier in Sherman's army. This amounted to three printed pages. My mother, under similar pressure over a somewhat shorter period, eventually came up with a 36-page review of her years in Colorado. I have written much more extensively. I like to think it was my own idea and that nobody made me do it. Nevertheless, I must concede that I never would have finished if there had not been a lot of coaching and cheering from the sidelines.

At about the time James Michener made his tour of the South Platte country in preparation for writing "Centennial," two of the persons he listed as important suppliers of background information—Isabel Blair and the late Otto Unfug—urged me to have my Logan County memoirs in book form by 1976, Colorado's centennial year. Col. William Blair, husband of Isabel, was extremely helpful. He read drafts of some chapters, supplied maps and other information that helped with my descriptions of the Proctor vicinity and Spring Valley Ranch. He had lived there before I came on the scene.

When I retired from Farmland Industries in 1971, Mrs. Lisa Warmack, who had been my secretary for 15 years, admonished me to "write that book," backing her order with a promise to help. She typed the finished manuscript of every chapter and straightened out my syntax in a few places. For her help and confidence I am most grateful.

My brothers, David and Donald, and my sister Edna, helped stir my memory of some events and took the time to read early drafts of some chapters. And through it all I had the support of my wife, Mabel, and my son, Jim, whose sketches add a touch of reality that I appreciate.

Three Kansas City friends deserve a special accolade. Each, on learning I was writing a book, asked in terms that reflected more than polite curiosity, to see some of the early chapters. Bits of manuscript were passed to each of them as I went along, and each offered encouragement as well as constructive criticism. They are James E. Campbell, attorney, James McQueeny, public relations man, and John Spore, former editor of military journals and once my colleague on the Hastings, Neb., *Tribune*.

I got advice from several publishing houses—including four university presses—but not a single offer to join me in the venture until I got to Arthur and Payson Lowell of the Lowell Press in Kansas City. It has been a pleasure to work with them and their associates.

Harold Hamil

Kansas City, Missouri
August 1, 1976

# CONTENTS

# 1. WHY THIS BOOK WAS WRITTEN

## ... And to Some Extent, How

Often in my boyhood I wondered if the fates had been fair in their choice of a place for my growing up. The high plains of eastern Colorado seemed to lack many things that were available to children in other parts of the world. I longed to be near a large body of water, near a lake perhaps like the one I had glimpsed from a train as I rode into Chicago with my mother. I envied the children whose lives were depicted in school books and the *Youth's Companion*. They seemed always to live near placid ponds on which they could sail toy ships. They went to the seashore in summer, waded in the shallows and built houses with wet sand. They were close to steep hills down which a sled would zoom when the snow was on in winter.

Our irrigation ditches—dry and weed-grown for most of the year—and the meandering trickles that were the South Platte River most of the time were no match for Tom Sawyer's Mississippi. Skating among the cattails of the Big Slough seemed a far cry from what Hans Brinker could do on the endless ribbons of clear ice in Holland. And the hillsides in our neighborhood that might have been steep enough for some rather tame coasting were usually swept clean by the winds that came with the snow. Our wind-shorn cottonwoods and willows were sad substitutes for the towering trees that showed up in pictures of the countryside in eastern states. I had seen and walked among giant trees on a visit to Tennessee when I was about four years old, and they had become a part of the good life so far as I was concerned.

The catalogs from Sears Roebuck, Montgomery Ward and

3

the Denver Dry Goods Company pictured a variety of veloci-
pedes, handcars and bicycles with which children seemed able
to propel themselves about with exciting speed. Our appeals for
the right to order just one of these vehicles met with a
discouraging explanation that such things were for boys and
girls who lived in cities and towns with paved streets and
sidewalks. There was no place for them on the rough and rutted
roads that were a trial sometimes for heavy horse-drawn
wagons.

While the snowy peaks of the Rocky Mountains were within
150 miles, they seemed as remote, almost, as the Atlantic
Ocean. They were out of sight, out of reach and out of mind. In
grade school we sang about Colorado as the land where the
columbine grew, but I went through high school without ever
seeing the state flower in any form, pristine or otherwise. We
were Coloradoans with no proprietary interest in the mineral
wealth that distinguished the state in its beginning or in the
scenic and climatic attractions which began to take over as the
gold and silver started running out. When I was ready to break
ties with home, I suffered the usual heaviness of heart, but none
of it came from the fact that I was turning my back on Pike's
Peak, Estes Park, Denver, Boulder or other glamorous parts of
one of our most glamorous states. I was a plainsman with no
particular pride in the fact and so completely detached from
the mountainous part of my state as to feel more reason to
apologize than boast when new-found acquaintances started
drawing me out with envious comments on the place of my
origin.

As the years passed, I began to sense that there may have
been more privilege than penalty in having started life in a
somewhat raw and isolated community of eastern Colorado.
Our family's circumstances, while modest by current standards, were relatively good. There was no critical shortage of
material things, although we sometimes thought so. Our house
was spacious and comfortable for its time. The ranch of which it

was a part was equipped far beyond the level of a typical agricultural unit of the period. There was room to move around, and a variety of places for growing boys to let off energy and satisfy their expanding curiosity. We were, to be sure, beyond the direct influence of many currents and movements that were shaping the society of the new twentieth century. But we were close enough that we could sense the ebb and flow of events. As a matter of fact, there was probably some advantage in our sideline position. We could observe and evaluate without feeling the pressures that often force quick and erroneous conclusions on those who are at the heart of the action. We came in contact with relatively few people, but we appreciated every individual for his very presence. We learned to accept foibles and weaknesses while looking desperately sometimes for enough redeeming features to make a person bearable. Our segment of the world was very small, but we learned to know it well, and in so doing we may have learned something about accommodating ourselves to the bigger segments with which eventually we would come in contact.

In the early 1960's, I began drawing on boyhood experiences in my writing for publications of Farmland Industries, Inc. Readers seemed to like what I wrote about my beginnings on a Colorado ranch. I retired from Farmland in 1971 with commitments to scores of these readers and many Farmland associates that I would assemble and rework some of those reminiscent pieces and see if I could come up with a book. Portions of some of the following chapters, therefore, include material lifted directly from *Farmland News* and its predecessor, *The Cooperative Consumer*.

I have not tried to write history in the conventional sense, yet there may be some in what I saw, what I did, how I felt and what I heard others say and what I saw others do in a period to which historians will refer frequently for as long as our civilization survives. I have checked a few names and dates, and I have reviewed incidents with others who observed them.

5

Mainly, though, I have drawn on a memory that is clear on some events as far back as the third year of my life, 1908-09.

I shared with adults around me their first view of an automobile. I watched grown men sit behind a steering wheel, grip it hesitantly and then hastily slide out of the seat to wait for a mustering of new courage before trying to drive one of these things. I heard men question the desirability of this new form of locomotion and saw horses tear up buggies in rearing protest against sharing narrow roads with a vehicle that made noises and spouted fumes. I saw one of the first airplanes to visit our county, a flimsy contraption of wood, wire and fabric, that spent ten hours with the mechanic for every 15 minutes it was in the air.

I saw the first fences come to vast prairie spaces and watched the turning of virgin sod with plows pulled by eight-horse teams, by oxen, and, on at least two occasions, by a steam traction engine. I heard talk of filing on homestead land and "proving up" of homestead land, and, with my parents, I visited homesteading families, in simple frame shacks, sod houses and dugouts.

I followed the outbreak of World War I through the flaming red headlines of the Denver *Post*. I observed the agricultural prosperity of that era, then watched farmers give up in disgust and banks close in the early 1920's, when prices of wheat, livestock and land suddenly dipped in what turned out to be a sort of preview of the Great Depression.

I was not reading much in the spring of 1912, when the *Post* carried a succession of dramatic pictures of the sinking of the Titanic. But what really came home to me at that time was that ships were sending messages through the air, without wires. Some eight years later, I sat in a corner of the local banker's home and heard through the crackling headphones of his crystal radio set the playing of a tune that we had been singing in the high school assembly at Sterling. I hadn't thought much about "Look for the Silver Lining" as a song, but

6

if it was good enough to broadcast through the air, it had to be pretty good. Or so I seem to have concluded. Most certainly I remember it much more from that one hearing than from several occasions when I joined my schoolmates in trying to sing it.

Some of the following chapters include brief flights into personal philosophy or opinion. I offer no apologies; these seem almost inevitably a part of the reflections of one who spent many of his adult years in pursuit of answers and explanations. And so this book.

# 2. THE SOUTH PLATTE

## . . . Little River with Big Responsibilities

The South Platte River rises in the high country of central Colorado. Its founding waters include drainage from some of the state's highest peaks, and its main stem does a 180-degree swing through that giant glen of the Rockies known as South Park.

On a course that is roughly north by northeast, it breaks out of the mountains a few miles southwest of Denver. In the heart of the city it picks up Cherry Creek, flowing in from the southeast, and between Denver and the vicinity of Greeley it is joined by several mountain-fed tributaries, the last of which is the Cache La Poudre. Near the mouth of the Poudre the river makes a decisive turn away from the mountains and heads almost straight east. After some 50 miles in this direction it veers northeasterly and, except for a few minor twists, it holds this course until its crossing into Nebraska just a few miles west of the point where Colorado's northern and eastern boundaries meet. It was along this final stretch in Colorado that I learned to know the South Platte better than I have known any other river.

The South Platte is small as rivers go, but it is Colorado's busiest. While it would seem already to be brutally overworked, it is under constant study by engineers, irrigationists and sanitarians with hopes of making it still more useful. Its normal flow is now supplemented by water from the western slopes of the Rockies, but in most seasons it is little more than a few exhausted rivulets where it crosses into Nebraska.

Within the South Platte basin live far more than half the

people of Colorado. For them the river and the saturated sand on which it flows are a source of water for domestic use and irrigation and a collector of runoff and sewage. It figures far more prominently in the history and economy of Colorado than does the much longer river bearing the state name. Colorado's first major gold rush was to the place where Cherry Creek flows into the South Platte, and the state's population continues to concentrate in that vicinity.

The importance of the river to the state as a whole was the least of our concerns as we grew up beside it. We were vaguely conscious that it came by way of Denver, Brighton, Fort Morgan, Brush and other places to the west and south and that it lost its identity when it joined the North Platte about 125 miles downstream. It was our river, the only one we knew, and our pride was pricked by the occasional jibes of visitors at the way it seemed to sprawl over a lot of territory without carrying much water.

Except in flood seasons, the water that did flow was clear and enticing. We often removed shoes and stockings and let the ripples break around our ankles and shins as we dug our toes into the clean sand. Sometimes we removed all our clothing after finding an isolated hole where the water was two feet or more in depth. If one wanted really to swim in the South Platte, though, he did it only in seasons of high water, at the risk of getting tangled in fence wire or being struck by floating debris. If all one wanted was a cooling bath, one could take it near the head of an irrigation ditch where diversion structures sometimes backed up the water to a depth of four to six feet.

Riding through the river in search of cattle or on any other mission in hot weather, we were tempted to drink from the sparkling shallows. I can recall no occasion, though, when this was a satisfying experience. The water was warm from exposure to the sun, and its tastes were strange and varied. There were those who insisted, in all sincerity, that water flowing over sand and exposed to the air would rid itself of any impurities. This we

9

believed to the extent we didn't hesitate to stoop and sip, even though we knew that Denver and other upstream cities flushed their streets and sewers into the river and that some of the water had been in and out of irrigation systems a half-dozen times before reaching our stretch of the river.

If we had had our choice, I suppose we would have preferred a river that was confined to a single channel and deep enough to provide good swimming holes and places for boating. But what we had was a series of shallow channels spread out over a course that was as much as a half-mile wide in places and showing relatively little water except for those few times when the mountain snowmelt and local rains combined to cause flooding.

When channels started filling on those occasions, the deep and muddied water, dropping at a rate of five to seven feet to the mile, became a destructive force. It wiped out fences, bridge

approaches and the diversion gates and fills of the irrigation ditches that lace the valley from Denver to the Nebraska line.

For young people it was fun to watch the old river assert itself. We rode our horses to the edge of the flood, looked on the swirling water and made token bets on how much would be left of the nearby bridges when the water went down.

The configurations of the channels were bound to change during a period of high water. The beds of some would be washed to new depths, while deposits of sand would leave others high and dry until the next flood or until the management of an irrigation ditch went in with teams and scrapers to restore access to flowing water.

The channels, wet or dry, wound through a maze of spits and islands, the more stable of which were anchored by heavy growths of wild roses, willows and cottonwoods. In the wake of

*The South Platte*

high waters that came when upstream trees were shedding their seeds, cottonwoods would sprout like sown wheat. Enough of these had grown to sufficient size in my day that they marked the line of the river along a valley that was treeless except for the plantings around farm and ranch homes.

The overgrown river area was like a strip of African jungle to plains-bred youngsters exploring it on summer days. The trees and bushes shut off the incessant winds at ground level, making it easier to hear the whispering of the cottonwood leaves 20 or 30 feet above. The insect life and, to some extent, the bird life were different from what one saw and heard in the neighboring hay meadows, alkali flats and sandhills. The rasping soliloquy of the cicada came from countless tree trunks. Magpies swept low over open spaces, kildeers strutted on the wet sand. And here and there a red-winged or yellow-headed blackbird sang from a perch in the undergrowth. The moist air was heavy with the smell of cottonwood sap and wild rose.

Now and then a carp could be spooked from a hole along a bank and sent squirming into shallow water for easy catching. Ducks and geese landed on the river in the fall, and in those few years when the dryland corn made a decent crop the ducks stayed in the neighborhood for weeks, shuttling between the river and these new-found feeding grounds. There were prairie chickens in the hay meadows adjacent to the river in the days of my earliest recollections, but they had disappeared by 1920. For several days one fall a private car of the Union Pacific sat on the siding at Proctor while important men from Omaha hunted along the South Platte.

Old-timers recalled that before there were fences to keep cattle out of the river, only a few scattered trees had been visible. They supported the story with reference to a battered old cottonwood between Iliff and Proctor that everybody called "Lone Tree." For a youngster just beginning to fit words to situations there was something puzzling about a "lone tree" that seemed to have the company of a lot of other trees, some of which stood almost as tall as it did. Adults explained that the neighboring trees were much younger even though they had grown almost to the height of the old cottonwood. I confirmed this a few years later when I rode on horseback to the vicinity of "Lone Tree" and compared its scarred and bleeding trunk with the smoother and smaller trunks of the trees around it. The old tree not only had survived the herds of cattle that roamed the area in the 1870's, the 80's and the 90's; it probably had been exposed to the movement of vast herds of buffalo through the river. It was in the annals of the neighborhood that the buffalo had chewed away at young trees and sprouts exactly as the cattle had, and that no white man had ever seen as many trees along the South Platte as were there in the opening decades of the twentieth century.

There were places along the edge of the valley from which one could trace the line of trees from horizon to horizon, a distance of a dozen miles or more. This was especially true in the spring when the greening willows and cottonwoods stood out against the dull grays and browns of bare fields and pastures. Because vistas were long and unobstructed from most any point in the valley or along its edges, the South Platte was an overwhelming presence. One lifted his eyes and there, in a panorama measured in miles, was some reminder of the river and its containing valley. It's generally that way in the Great Plains; there seems little to see, yet one never looks without seeing much.

We always thought of the valley of the South Platte in terms of the flat and relatively narrow strip that lay just a few feet above the level of the river bed. But this accounts for only a fraction of the vast topographic gash that is the total mark of the river's diagonal course from southwest to northeast through Logan County. From our house, on the northwest, or left, edge of the valley floor, we looked across the line of trees that marked the river and across several miles of ascending waves of sandhills to a friendly meeting of earth and sky some eight to ten miles away. Beyond the rounded tops of those farthest hills were high flatlands drained by the headwaters of the Frenchman River. From a comparable spot on the opposite side of the valley floor one could look to the north and west over a more gently rising expanse to a more distant horizon. This is hard land, in contrast to the sand of the other side, and there is almost geometric exactness in the water courses, or draws, that originate three, five, or thirty miles from the river and head toward it in a southeasterly direction. Beyond the steep breaks that accent the horizon, beyond the heads of the longer draws, lie the tablelands that divide the South Platte watershed from that of Lodgepole Creek, which starts near Cheyenne and flows generally eastward to a merger with the South Platte near Julesburg.

The line of the South Platte across Logan County, therefore, is more than the feebly flowing channels and more than the trees bordering them. It is the central explanation of an excavation in the plains which in some places is more than 20 miles from rim to rim. Not the least of the distinctions of this strip of terrain are the sandhills that rise in folds from the valley floor to the level of the divide on the south and east for all of the river's course through the county. The river gets credit for having washed in the sand which the winds of countless centuries blew into dunes and the patience of other natural forces finally cloaked with grass.

This river, this valley, this giant furrow was the route of moving Indian tribes, of John C. Fremont on two occasions, of trappers, traders and gold seekers. It dictated the course of the Union Pacific tracks from Julesburg to Denver and the subsequent routes of state and federal highways. It beckoned the first cattlemen, the first farmers. Here was a natural corridor along which Logan County's agriculture and commerce concentrated. Seven settlements grew up along the reach of the Union Pacific through the county. The first to attain any size became the county seat, Sterling. Others were Merino, Atwood,

Iliff, Crook, Red Lion and Proctor. The last-named, situated between Iliff and Crook, for almost 18 years was our town, never incorporated and destined never to count as many as a hundred persons in its population. But it was at this pinpoint on the map that I began to sense man's historic relationship with rivers, even the small, unspectacular ones, the ones which sometimes run dry in the summer, as did the South Platte.

# 3. HOW WE GOT THERE

## ... With Notes on W. S. Hadfield, W. J. Powell and Others

James Newton Hamil, my father, arrived in Logan County in 1899. A native of Tennessee, he had worked on farms in Richland County, Illinois, and St. Louis County, Missouri, and was looking for a place to establish himself as an independent farmer in the tradition of his forebears, dating back, some genealogical tracings suggest, to one who had been a captain in George Washington's army.

The valley of the South Platte as he first saw it had been subject to the alterations of settlement for less than 30 years. Agriculture had come in two stages. Big cattle operations, spreading out from the Denver area, had moved down the river immediately following the Civil War. Among the biggest was that of John Wesley Iliff, who had come from Ohio to build an empire marked by the branded hides of cattle that roamed the left side of the river for much of the distance between Greeley and Julesburg. His range included Logan County, and his name eventually was given one of its towns.

Both men and cows were transient in those early days when the only extractable wealth of the country was thought to be its grass. There were some scattered cattle camps along the valley, but no one thought of any of these as a permanent abode.

Permanence in a new land is largely a state of mind, of course, but it was in the mind of William Shaw Hadfield that he had come to stay when, in 1871, he filed on a homestead at the point where Pawnee Creek joins the South Platte. And stay he did. In due time he became one of the larger landowners of the county,

16

*W. S. Hadfield*

but the honor that distinguished him from other graying pioneers of my boyhood was that of having been the first real settler in the county.

A native of Derbyshire, England, Hadfield had come to the United States as a young man and, after spending a couple of years in Wisconsin, he made his way to Denver as driver of a six-mule team with a load of freight from Atchison, Kan. He spent some time at Greeley before heading for his homestead site, and it can be presumed that he took note of what the Union Colony there was doing in the way of irrigation. In any event, he settled on land that was subject to irrigation even though his interest was in the production of cattle and sheep rather than crops. With first a tent and then a sod house, he became a permanent resident and set a pattern that others followed in short order.

Mr. Hadfield, it was said, had looked with displeasure on some who followed him. Among them were men with a mind to dig irrigation ditches, grow crops and thus launch the second phase of the county's agricultural development. Though he had broken from the pattern of the original cattle barons when he

17

chose to live close to his livestock, Hadfield still favored animal agriculture to the tilling of fields.

The new settlers came from varying backgrounds. Some were an overflow from the Greeley area. Some came by train to Julesburg or Sidney and from there by wagon. There was an obvious appeal to families in Mississippi, Alabama and West Tennessee who had been restless ever since the end of the Civil War. Among the Alabamans who came in the 1870's was W. J. Powell. In the 90's, he and Frank H. Blair undertook a ranching venture along the river downstream from Iliff at a place where the Union Pacific had built a siding that was designated as Proctor.

When Jim Hamil arrived at Sterling in 1899, one thing he did not arrange for was a chronological record of jobs he would hold. One of his first places to work, though, was the Powell and Blair ranch. He helped plant trees, build fences and otherwise add to one of the most completely equipped ranches in the county. Little did he dream, one can suspect, that in nine years he would be living on this place as general manager. The record is unclear as to how long he stayed with Powell and Blair. Sometime in the first year or so he started working for W. S. Hadfield.

What all he did for Mr. Hadfield was never recorded. In all likelihood he worked some at the homestead upstream from Sterling about four miles. He probably handled some jobs at the new Hadfield home in town. I recall his telling about Mr. Hadfield's prescription for building a lawn. Whether Father actually helped plant the lawn, I cannot say, but I recall his detailing how Mr. Hadfield, an Englishman with an apprecia-tion of green grass—even though he had seen precious little of it since leaving Derbyshire—insisted on the laying of several loads of river sand under the heavier soils on which the Hadfield lawn on South Second Street in Sterling was planted.

The record is clear enough that in December, 1903, when Father asked for a leave of absence so he could go to Tennessee to marry Ada Gertrude Walker, he had been in the employ of Mr. Hadfield for some time—perhaps two years. His job at that time was to supervise a cattle operation in the northern part of the county, with headquarters on Lewis Creek. While this involved responsibility for several hundred cattle, Father apparently handled the job alone for long periods. A prime concern was that Colorado cattle on unfenced range be kept from straying into Nebraska, where fence and herd laws were such that Colorado owners could be forced to pay for the return of strays. He referred often to having gone for two or three weeks without seeing another human being. But he did save money, and when he took the train for a three-day ride to Tennessee and matrimony, he pinned $1,200 to his underwear and figured he had achieved a degree of independence that many men in their 20's could not match.

That $1,200 seemed to be very important to him in later life; he talked about it often. And it could have been that he had considered how close its availability came to changing the whole course of his career. Ada Gertrude Walker, as the eldest daughter of David Campbell Walker, had taken over the farm household on the death of her mother in 1901. While there were two younger unmarried girls in the family, D. C. Walker could not readily accept the idea of his eldest daughter's going to the untamed West. He wept openly, a fact that his grandchildren would ponder, when Mother told about it in later years. The idea of a man who had gone through the Civil War and marched with Sherman from Atlanta to the sea—the idea of his sitting down to cry! The truth was that David Campbell was a timid man, a cautious man. When things seemed to be going to his satisfaction, he didn't want change. In his heart, I am sure, he resented this neighbor-turned-cowboy who had come home with $1,200 and plans to upset the tranquility of his household. But all of a sudden that $1,200 attained new importance. Word came that a neighbor wanted to sell his farm. A man with $1,200 was in good position to buy. Under some prodding, I am sure,

Father made a deal, and with the wedding over, after one postponement because of a death in the family, it was decided the newlyweds would stay in Tennessee. But the seller of the farm also was a man inclined to be upset by the prospect of change. He became increasingly sick of his deal, and after a round of offers and counter-offers, he took back the farm and Father had his $1,200, plus all it would cost to get him and his bride to Colorado. The newlyweds were soon on their way, a bit apprehensive in the final days, perhaps, lest another neighborhood farm might crop up for sale.

While Father seemed happy to scrape the red mud of an East Tennessee winter from his shoes, he had reason to share Mother's concern about the conditions under which they were to face a new life in Logan County, Colorado. While Father had his $1,200, he was going back to the scene of his recent triumphs with no assurance that he could find a place to work, let alone a place to live. On completing the deal—or so he thought—for the Tennessee farm, he had notified Mr. Hadfield that he could not return to Lewis Creek, and Mr. Hadfield in all likelihood would have found a replacement after these many weeks.

And so this young couple set forth in contrasting moods that cropped up every so often for the 28 years that they would face problems and crises together. Mother, reflecting some of the caution that came with the blood of David Campbell Walker, and Father, covering up any anxieties with a cool front and a belief that there was more to be gained by tackling a problem than worrying about it, came to offset each other in a manner that made for a generally harmonious relationship. There was a testing of temperaments as they made their last train change at Brush. Their train from Kansas City was late, and the one daily train that would take them to Sterling had left a few minutes before their early-morning arrival.

They took a room in a boarding house, where Mother rested and pondered this streak of hard luck, while Father roamed the streets, and probably the pool halls, visiting with merchants, farmers, loiterers—anyone who would talk. But something went wrong with their timing the next morning, and they missed the train again. This was a Sunday, and Mother tested and proved to her satisfaction a dictum she would pass on to her seven children: "You can always find good people at a Presbyterian church." A friendly couple—ex-Tennesseans, in fact— noting the strangers, approached them and took them home to dinner. Colorado looked better to Mother from that day, but always she had reservations about Brush. It was no place to spend 48 hours, she would declare, and never get an argument. While W. S. Hadfield had filled Father's old job, he was not without concern for his former employee, and he was at the Sterling station with an invitation to breakfast and assurances that his home would be the abode of the young couple until they found permanent quarters. And so Mother's introduction to Logan County was as the guest in the home of its first settler for two full weeks. During that period she met many residents of the community, and there was considerable relief in the discovery that several of the women had broken ties of generations with southern farming communities quite similar to her own Big Spring community in Blount County, Tennessee. Mrs. Hadfield herself had come from Mississippi.

Within a few days, Father was on the trail of a job and a place to live. Frank Frost, owner of a farm north of Sterling, was looking for someone to live on the place and manage it. There was a comfortable house, a good garden plot, milk cows for the resident family and some fruit trees. For the next three years this was the Hamil home.

Father received $45 a month in cash, and Mother was paid for boarding any hired men. At the end of the three years their savings were enough that, with some drawdown perhaps on the symbolic $1,200 with which Father had entered the married state, he could buy 40 acres of irrigated land near Atwood—the first of a series of land purchases that would create their largest single investment over their years together.

In January, 1905, Clara Ruth Hamil was born at the Frost place, and in September, 1906, James Harold became the second addition to the family. Within a matter of months, Mother suggested that she might take her two babies to Tennessee for a visit, and in due time the trip was arranged. Beyond the fact that I caught whooping cough from another child on one of the trains and almost died in Tennessee, the trip itself was uneventful. But by the time we arrived back in Sterling, Father had accepted a new job for $100 a month, a house and its complete upkeep, including all food. He was to manage the old Powell and Blair ranch at Proctor. Powell and Blair had sold the place to an investment group at Cedar Rapids, Iowa, and had agreed to help find a manager. Powell or Blair, or both, recommended Jim Hamil, and he seemed to fulfill the requirements of the new owners. And so I was removed from the house of my birth before it became a part of my memories. And the world of which I was first conscious centered at the ranch near Proctor on the South Platte, about 20 miles downstream from Sterling.

# 4. PROCTOR

## . . . By No Means the Fairest Village of the Plain, But There Were Those Who Loved It

Proctor, Colo., was born to share the relative obscurity of thousands of little places that were routinely spotted by the railroads as they pushed their way across middle America. But for those few of us who shared its best years there was no obscurity. Proctor was real and vital. It was the only town we knew with any degree of intimacy. We had to identify with it or go unidentified.

Whether Proctor ever had community ambition, or pride, or hope, is perhaps a moot question. The truth is that it never was incorporated, never established as a legal entity. We who had known no other home address tended to think we would be there indefinitely, and we sensed vaguely that the outlook might be brighter if Proctor could grow a little more and offer some of the amenities and attractions that distinguished Iliff and Crook. These towns, each about eight miles away, had populations of 200 perhaps when Proctor could claim a bare 60. We envied them as they went through the formalities of incorporation and the building of water systems marked by stilted storage tanks that pierced the horizons and seemed almost to look down on their humble neighbor in between.

Not the least of Proctor's handicaps was that it got a late start. Both Crook and Iliff had stores and postoffices before Proctor was more than a siding on the Union Pacific, with livestock loading pens and two large hay barns.

People seemed to know about General George Crook, the Indian fighter, and why his name should have been memorialized by the Union Pacific. But nobody seemed interested in knowing how Proctor got its name. There were vague references to a "General Proctor" and suggestions he was a companion or contemporary of Crook, and this was picked up and written into the first printed history of Logan County. After scanning numerous books on Indian campaigns and checking with the State Historical Society of Colorado and the public relations office of the Union Pacific and finding no positive clues, I have concluded that the place probably was named for Redfield Proctor, secretary of war in the administration of Benjamin Harrison. His name is in the records of Indian wars as the man who overruled General Nelson Miles and dismissed charges of misconduct against the colonel in command of troops involved in the 1890 battle at Wounded Knee, S. D.

The advance of Proctor from rail siding to trading center, postoffice point and a regular stop for passenger trains started shortly after Father and Mother got settled in the big ranch house a mile north of the railroad in the spring of 1907.

Father's new employer, the Logan County Development Company, owned the land on both sides of the Proctor siding. I am sure that Father had taken the job of ranch manager with the understanding that he was expected to make the place pay as a producer of livestock, hay, grain, sugar beets, potatoes and other crops. But he was not long in finding that the new owners dreamed of big profits from selling off land in small parcels. And some of the small parcels would be lots in a new town that Father helped lay out on the north side of the tracks.

J. D. Blue, Jr., secretary of the development company, put pressure on the railroad and the Postoffice Department, and by 1908 there was a modest station house at Proctor and plans were afoot to open a postoffice in the first general store. Father, meanwhile, had laid out and graded three north-south streets and three east-west streets that were duly named for men who had helped in the founding, including Father. Blue Street, nearest the railroad, was the main drag, and all the commercial structures ever erected—with the exception of what passed as a hotel—fronted on it.

Just how the first buildings were financed was never clear to me; my presumption is that the development company, along with the bank that was established in 1909, took the lead. I am sure that the first retail business, the lumber yard, was a project of the development company, as was the so-called hotel, the second building to be finished.

The hotel in many ways seems to have summed up the dreams of J. D. Blue and his associates. It was boldly marked as the "Proctor Hotel" in letters large enough to be read from passing trains. It was an invitation to the transient and curious to stop, investigate and possibly buy a farm or a town lot. In the years of my earliest memory, the invitation to invest in Proctor or its surrounding farm land was proclaimed openly from a solid wooden billboard that was big enough that it served as backstop for the first baseball game I ever witnessed. The sign, on the west edge of town, also faced the railroad. In about 1911, a high wind toppled the structure, and Father salvaged the sturdy pine facing for the building of two heavy rolling gates for a new horse corral at the ranch. So far as I know, the sign never had claimed a sale.

This is not to say that Proctor was an inactive place for a period, say, of four or five years after the railroad station was established. The first store building went up in the 1908-09 period, as did the bank and several residences. By 1913 there was a second store building, a blacksmith shop, an icehouse and a modest horse barn near the hotel. Some chroniclers of Proctor history allude to a livery stable. It could be that someone kept teams for hire in this barn, but if so, the fact is lost in the mists of my memories.

My recollection is that the first store operator was Joseph F. W. Fedder, but some say another person actually stocked the place. In any event, I recall that Mr. Fedder, along with his sizable family, was the first to live in the hotel. Mr. Fedder was the postmaster until he gave way to Lee Lamb in 1913. Meanwhile, E. I. Pashby had come from Overton, Neb., as operator of a second store, and the Pashby and Lamb establishments flourished until the early 1920's, when Pashby sold out and moved to Fort Collins. The first person I can place in the management of the lumber yard is Glenn Ballard, a son-in-law of Joseph F. W. Fedder.

Several residences were built in the 1909-1913 period, along with the schoolhouse, which was situated outside the northwest corner of the townsite on an acre or so of land.

Most of this physical development took place between my third and sixth years, and Father was closely involved with

much of it. Trailing along with him on occasions when he checked on progress of this or that project, I got an impression of Proctor as a place of bare two-by-four studdings and piles of sand and dirt, with the smell of freshly-cut pine hanging over the scene and men with canvas nail bags across their chests presiding over it. A man named Jim Stewart was one of those presiding carpenters, and he probably did more work on early Proctor buildings than any other person. He added an imposing porch to our ranch house.

While the emergence of Proctor as a trading center, town, village, or what have you, meant some management headaches for Father, it contributed immensely to the convenience of

*Street Parking, Proctor*

living on the ranch. For their first two years there, my parents got their mail through Iliff, nine miles away, and they went to Iliff or Sterling, 12 miles beyond, for food and other supplies.

With Proctor's new importance came need for a new road. The old route between the ranch buildings and the railroad had been built for travel to and from the area of the livestock pens, the hay barns and the original beet dump. These were almost a quarter of a mile from the new center of town. With the help of a professional surveyor, Father laid out the new road on a north-south course that lined up with the street forming the east boundary of the new townsite.

Bridges were built over irrigation ditches, a wood culvert was installed at the "alkali spot," as we called one of the low places, and a bridge of some size was placed across the Big Slough, a water course that picked up the water from Skinner Draw and seepage from irrigation ditches and was marked by heavy growth of cattails and coarse grasses. With this new road, the main street of Proctor was just about a mile from the front of our house.

This was a quite ordinary stretch of road by most people's standards, but it was a miracle mile, almost, to youngsters for whom it was the principal outlet from home, the route to Proctor, the first leg of any trip to the outside world. We trudged the length of those two lines of barbed wire fence at least a thousand times on the way to and from school. It was the route of our first horseback ride, our first trip at the wheel of a Model-T.

But it was on foot that we developed familiarity with every detail. We favored the soft, alkali-flecked dirt shoulders in summer when we were barefooted, and we sought out the widest wagon ruts when we walked in clumsy overshoes through the snow and ice of winter.

We made friends of every bridge and culvert, every gate, every misshapen fence post, every break in the wire, every clump of weeds. There was the "big ditch," which wasn't big at all, but considerably bigger than the "little ditch." There was the "pigpen ditch" that we crossed on the outbound trip just as we emerged from the last line of trees that shielded the ranch buildings on the south.

The slough and the alkali spot were major landmarks, and about midway between them was a fence post that had been designated as the half-way point between home and school. (Somebody had counted the steps on the full trip and then stepped off half the total.)

On sunny spring days when the meadowlarks sang from the greening pasture grass and blackbirds fluttered over the slough, the trip home from Proctor seemed short and easy. We threw rocks at an occasional loping jackrabbit and tried to sneak up on nighthawks which tried to camouflage themselves on the tops of weathered fence posts. We peeked under culverts and bridges in the hope of seeing a cottontail, and we scanned the dark and smelly waters of the slough in the hope of spotting a carp or muskrat. On wintry days, though, there was no loitering. We bent into the north wind, walked backwards now and then to allow the sting to subside from our faces and longed for the moment when we would sense that first slight weakening of the blast as we came within the influence of the trees at the "pigpen ditch."

Over a period of a couple of years, Father succeeded in building the Proctor road into a model of what could be done with sand or gravel as a surface for the soft roads up and down the valley. During his first four-year term as county commissioner, 1913-1917, he graveled several miles of the road between Proctor and Iliff and took a lot of abuse from the owners of automobiles who found the fresh gravel hard to get through. The idea, as Father had demonstrated in the Proctor road, was that passing vehicles would force the gravel into a mixture with the dirt surface that was especially soft and viscous after rains. This was true, of course, but it took time, and car owners didn't like being used in this manner. Their cars jerked out of control sometimes when they plunged into fresh gravel, and the going was heavy even when one could avoid steering troubles. The graveling of roads eventually was commonplace throughout the region, but Father pioneered in his community and took the criticism that is so often the fate of those who get a little ahead of the pack. The streets of Proctor eventually absorbed hundreds of wagonloads of sand and gravel. It came, one cubic yard to the load, from the river and from deposits along the edge of the valley.

For two periods in Proctor's history its skyline was marked by one of the gravity beet dumps of the Great Western Sugar Company. These were distinctive and novel architectural creations, looking something like long, high bridges over narrow streams. But they stood on dry land, paralleling the rail sidings wherever sugar beets were grown in sizable quantities.

The beet dump was a practical application of the inclined plane to the elimination of some of the hard work of moving a heavy and bulky crop. The loaded wagons, after being weighed, proceeded up the approach ramp to the level stretch at the top from which the load was dropped over a screen into an open hopper car. The wagons were built with sides that could be lowered, and the dumps were equipped with machinery that permitted a sidewise tipping of the wagons. The down ramp was much shorter and steeper than the up ramp. Once on the ground, an empty wagon passed under a container into which all dirt and trash screened from its load had been collected. This went back into the wagon before it returned to the scale for the tare weight.

The first of the dumps at Proctor was removed after a few years, apparently because there had not been the anticipated interest on the part of the community's farmers in growing beets. In the late years of World War I, after some new land had come under irrigation, a second gravity dump was built. In the interim, a few growers who persisted in producing beets had forked every load into cars from a so-called "shovel dump," a smaller and simpler "bridge" on which the wagons attained a height barely level with the tops of the rail cars. The one at Proctor, as I recall, was long enough that three wagons could be unloaded at the same time. But there was no dropping of sideboards; the hauler transferred his load to the car by hand, one awkward forkful at a time.

The shovel dump would have been more of an insult to the beet producer if it had not been for the fact that even when gravity dumps were available, a lot of beets had to be unloaded by hand. Adjacent to every dump was a spot where beets could be piled on the ground and left for two months or more before shipment. This arrangement enabled the sugar company to regulate the flow of beets to the factory, where the processing season usually extended through the cold days of winter.

I have many memories of the beet harvest, but one of the most pronounced is of the pall of dust that hung over the vicinity of the dump on a dry fall day. Some of the dust came from the dirt-crusted beets as they rolled over the screen into the cars or were forked onto the pile. But much of it came from the movement of heavy wagons behind two- and four-horse teams, every hoof shod in sharp iron to make for sure footing on the hard pulls to the top of the dump. All roads leading to the dump were deep-rutted before the harvest was very far along, including those which were part of the street system of Proctor. But nobody seemed to mind. Beet checks would be coming in; hand laborers and transient haulers would be paid in cash, some of which would ring the simple registers of Proctor's modest mercantile establishments. Beet money made the prospect of a rugged winter easier to face.

The beet dump was a part of what might have been called Proctor's bulk shipping zone. It was near the livestock pens and loading chute and immediately across the road from the two large hay barns, or warehouses, that had been in use since long before the town had started taking shape. There had been a time when Powell and Blair filled the barns with baled hay for eventual loading onto rail cars. By the time Father got the feel of his job as ranch manager he was hauling most of the hay he marketed direct from the fields to the rail cars. In about 1912, he dismantled one of the track-side barns and moved it to the ranch to house work stock. At about the same time, he cut some 30 feet off the other hay barn and used the lumber and sheet-iron roofing for building new hog houses at the ranch.

The tallest structure Proctor ever knew was the grain elevator. It was built in about 1913 or 1914, along the conventional lines of most such buildings before the era of the concrete silo. Within a couple of years it was determined that the capacity was short of the need, and we looked on with some wonder as a contractor jacked up the headhouse and inserted some 12 feet of additional bin space beneath it. Tens of thousands of bushels of wheat moved through this building into rail cars during the war years and immediately thereafter.

Just when Proctor reached its zenith is hard to say. I tend to relate it to two events. One was the decision of the Union Pacific to build a modern station house, with living quarters for the agent and his family. The first station had been a mere shack, and the second had been a converted boxcar. The final building matched in design and size the stations in much larger towns between North Platte and Denver. It went into use, as I recall, during or just after World War I.

Another landmark event about that time was the opening of a third store. This one concentrated mainly on groceries, whereas the two older stores had rather full lines of work clothes, dress goods and the like, along with groceries. While the opening of the new store may have been a high-water mark for Proctor, it was a disaster for the operator. Within a year, possibly a shorter time, he gave up.

Through this period there were growing signs that the internal combustion engine might replace the horses and mules that had powered the economy of the Proctor community for its first few years. During the mid-teen years, on a summer day or a Saturday night, there were about as many automobiles as wagons and buggies in front of the stores. But come winter, the farmers who ventured out were inclined to favor horse-drawn vehicles, and some rode horseback to pick up the mail or buy a few necessities. The cars that did show up in town in cold weather were thoroughly winterized, with side curtains, radiator covers and a handy jack in all Model-T's for raising a rear wheel to make cranking easier when the oil was stiff and the cylinders were slow to fire. Those left standing long had blankets over the hoods.

The arrival of the automobile was heralded in the later teen years with the building of the "garage," a low structure facing south on Blue Street about half way between Lamb's store and the site that was occupied originally by the blacksmith shop and later by the pool hall. For several years the establishment offered general auto repair service and for a time, as I recall, was agent for Ford cars under an arrangement with a dealer at Sterling or some other town.

One day when we were mowing hay in a field across the tracks from Proctor, I heard a sound that suggested somebody might be using dynamite in the neighborhood. On our way through Proctor at noon we saw a big hole in the roof of the garage. Something had gone wrong with the automatic shutoff on the gasoline-driven compressor, and the "free-air" tank had gone through the roof and into the air 25 or 30 feet.

My memories of Proctor at its best merge with memories of World War I. I was growing; Proctor was growing; and both of us were attracted and distracted by what went on in Europe. The sale of war bonds was a matter of serious interest in Proctor, as in thousands of communities, and Proctor was awarded one of the flags that went to all communities meeting their bond quotas in one of the early drives. But where was Proctor to display its flag? Somebody proposed erecting a special pole across the street from the Lamb store, which housed the postoffice. The pole was a couple of lengths of one-inch iron pipe, extending perhaps 35 feet above the ground. Its erection, however, was a study in bad planning that led to one of my more memorable boyhood experiences. Before the pole was raised and set in concrete, the flag of the moment was firmly wired into place.

This first flag flew for several months and was quite tattered and soiled when word came that Proctor was getting a second flag for having gone over the top in another campaign. It was not until then, apparently, that anyone considered the problems of replacement. It was generally agreed that the pole would buckle under the weight of a full-grown man, but would support a boy. The word got out that on several occasions I had climbed to the level of the flag. My weight was about 65 pounds. For the first time in my life I was tagged for high duty of great consequence to my community. But I had grave misgivings.

Getting to the top of the pole unencumbered was not easy. Getting there with a flapping flag in tow and a pair of pliers and some baling wire turned out to be more than I could do. I got a lot of advice from the growing crowd of onlookers, but I had not accomplished much when our old friend and neighbor, Charlie Morton, drove a wagonload of hay onto the site and somebody placed a ladder on top of it. Thus I was rescued from a tense and humiliating situation. My only consolation was in the fact that nobody had come out of the crowd to climb the pole, or even offer to try. I'd been up and down a couple of times.

Some years later I was to know a man whose chief claim to fame seemed to be that he was the first and only person to climb the flagpole in front of the courthouse that once stood at Bloomington, Neb. Every time he launched into a review of that great day in his life, I thought back on my embarrassing encounter with a flagpole and wondered if my memory might have been charged and recharged, as his seemed to have been, if I had succeeded that day in the presence of a friendly and encouraging crowd in front of Lamb's store in Proctor.

Proctor was built on low land where water tended to collect

after heavy rains. And where water tended to collect on the flat grassland along the South Platte there was bound to be alkali. This made, unfortunately, for a sort of sterility about the place that was acutely noticeable after a visit to Sterling with its tree-lined streets and green lawns. Scores of trees were set out in Proctor, but none survived more than a few years until the advent of the Chinese elm. This tree was unheard of in my day, but it became the top favorite of tree planters in the Great Plains during the drouth of the 1930's. On a sentimental inspection of the last survivor of the original business buildings, the Proctor State Bank, I was surprised to find in the 1960's that Chinese elms had sprouted at random around the windowless structure. If in 1910, say, there had been trees with that much determination and immunity to alkali, Proctor might have covered some of its early nakedness.

Those who have grown up since the coming of electric water pumps and the acceptance of indoor plumbing as a necessity of our most isolated communities can only imagine the extent to which the outdoor privy stood out in any panoramic view of a new community on the treeless plains.

For practically every occupied building in Proctor there was one outhouse. For the school there were two, and for the hotel there was a rather pretentious combination of men's and women's accommodations in one structure that was at least double the size of the standard, single-family, two-hole unit. Proctor in some respects resembled a flock of hens, each with at least one chick.

For each house there was a well, and for one, as I recall, there was a windmill to power the pump. All of the wells were relatively shallow, and the water from them was so heavy with alkali that a pump would be in use only a few weeks when white stains would start showing around the spout and wherever water spilled.

Proctor at its peak had at least a dozen single-family residences. Most were one-story bungalows, but at the north edge of the townsite, in a straight line about a block apart, were three two-story houses that had been built by the development company about 1910. The idea had been that these would spread the bounds of the town and encourage building in the spaces between them. But the additional houses never came. In their stark and ugly loneliness these three outriders could have been more discouraging than encouraging to further building. They were taller than they were wide at the base, and their two-bedroom upper stories were little more than over-sized cupolas, with windows that seemed to stare with a cold glint across the open pasture to the north. For all the years I knew Proctor these three houses stood like stern sentinels ready to challenge us as we approached from the ranch.

The center of life in Proctor, if such there was, had to be the general store that housed the postoffice. This was the Fedder store until about 1913, when Lee and Howard Lamb took over, and the former became the postmaster. During the school year we children were willing carriers of the ranch mail from the postoffice. This took us about a quarter of a mile out of our way, but I cannot recall ever having balked at the responsibility. The daily ritual took us where the action was, where there was always a chance of seeing someone we hadn't seen before or hearing first-hand about somebody's illness, somebody's run-away horses, somebody's latest trip to Sterling or Denver.

It was a rare afternoon when there would not be a familiar team or two, an automobile or a saddle horse by which we could anticipate the number and kind of people we would encounter in front of the mail boxes or sitting around the stove near the center of the store. And within 150 feet there would be a horse, a wagon, a buggy or other conveyances in front of the Pashby store to indicate who had chosen to patronize Mr. Pashby that day. When the indications were of someone likely to be interesting, we dropped in at Pashby's before heading for home. A strange automobile at either store made it mandatory that we hang around until the owner was spotted and identified.

While Mr. Pashby operated without the benefit of postoffice traffic and without the drawing power of a farm machinery department such as that in the Lamb operation, he enjoyed substantial patronage. We children followed the lead of our parents in trying to keep in good standing with both proprietors, but in a showdown I suspect I would have voted for Mr. Pashby as the storekeeper I would have preferred to spend a day with. He treated a 10-year-old as an adult equal. The Lamb brothers, Lee particularly, were more inclined to kid and tease and ask questions about matters that we considered strictly the business of our generation. It was Mother's practice to divide her business, including the big orders of groceries that she paid for with eggs and checks on the development company.

The two stores and the Proctor State Bank, which stood between them, would have fit well into western movie sets of the next 50 years if they had been closer together. The Lamb store and the bank had the conventional false front. The Pashby store had a second story reached by an outside stairway. In front of each building was a sturdy porch, and between the bank and the Pashby store was a four-foot plank walk that bridged a stagnant puddle much of the time. In front of this walk was a row of hitching posts tied together with two-by-sixes at about the level of a horse's nose.

The stocks of goods in these stores were, in the composite, a good study in what it took to maintain life with minimum comforts and diversions in a community of homes that ranged from the large and solid to sod houses, dugouts, beet labor shacks and the cook wagons of construction camps. Each store had a sizable stock of piece goods. Each carried rolls of canvas for making movable irrigation dams. There were piles of overalls and work shirts, gloves and work socks. Each store carried shoes—more for men than for women—rubber boots and overshoes. There were no ready-made dresses and few cosmetics. The patent medicine shelves were lined with epsom salt, castor oil, Mentholatum and cough syrups. A big seller was

Castoria, for soothing infants' colic. It was hard for a youngster to know just how much sale there was of Lydia E. Pinkham's heralded comforter of women and the various concoctions for the pain of piles. Adults didn't talk much about the use of these.

Each store kept its food lines at the rear of the building. Each had a big ice-cooled refrigerator, but Lamb's was much the larger. A bunch of bananas hung from the ceiling most of the time, and there was always a big cheese from which pie-shaped pieces were cut on order. Flour was sold mainly in 48-pound bags, and some families, ours included, bought sugar in 100-pound bags. Somewhere around each store was a stock of rock salt for livestock. About the only non-essentials were candy, tobacco, soda pop and near-beer.

Except for Hershey bars, the candies were in bulk form until about 1918, when more 5-cent bars began appearing. It goes without saying that my earliest recollections of the first store were of the dozen or so varieties of candy that were stacked in glass compartments of a case designed to keep most of the merchandise at the eye level of children just my size. My first experience with money was the spending of a nickel at the Fedder (later Lamb) store for a mixture of these candies that I took home in a striped bag that seemed almost as tantalizing as the candy itself.

The apportionment of counter and shelf space for tobacco reflected a very different product mix than would have prevailed 50 years later. The tobacco section was dominated by a guillotine-like device for cutting the plug form of chewing tobacco. At the Proctor stores, I would venture, the sale of chewing tobacco brought close to as much revenue as the sale of smoking tobacco and much more than the sale of cigarettes.

Around Proctor, as elsewhere in the country, the tailor-made cigarette was the target of a criticism that was wholly undocumented, yet valid enough in its premise as to become the basis of national policy in the 1960's. When World War I came along, though, the tobacco companies and various organizations devoted to building soldier morale teamed up to make cigarette smoking much more respectable and acceptable than it had been before the first draftees were called up in 1917.

Those who bought cigarettes in packages had at least three choices of brand in the Proctor stores. They were Camel, Chesterfield and Fatima. Far more in evidence in the two stores were the packaged smoking tobaccos, some for rolling into one's own cigarettes, some for pipes and some that were suitable for both. Bull Durham and Duke's Mixture, in small cotton bags with draw-string openings, were the favorites of the roll-your-own cigarette smokers. Prince Albert, Velvet and Tuxedo led the list of pipe tobacco brands, all three of which were sometimes used in rolling cigarettes. Horseshoe was the best seller among the chewing tobaccos, with Star, Climax and Peachy Plug and various fine cuts and Copenhagen snuff rounding out the offerings to patrons of the weed who preferred oral application.

For those who liked the taste of raw tobacco along with smoke, there were several brands of cigars in display cases at both stores. Each case contained a clay-like object that was explained as being capable of keeping the cigars soft and moist, provided someone took the thing out of the case every so often and soaked it in water. There were frequent complaints that these gadgets either didn't work or were not properly cared for. Smokers generally bathed a Proctor cigar in saliva before lighting it—even when it came from a box indicating it was made for high-altitude or dry-climate smoking. Cigars and countless other products made their way to the consumer in those days without the benefit of a moisture-preserving sheath of cellophane.

The drip from vinegar barrels, the hanging bananas, the exposed boxes of dried and fresh fruits, the cheese, and the chewing tobacco made for an aggregation of smells that pervaded the rear sections of the two stores with about equal intensity. Toward the front, each store seemed to smell of the ginghams, calicos and other piece goods, the cotton socks, leather gloves, overalls, shoes and other items with which the shelves were stuffed. Both stores in early morning smelled strongly of the cedar-scented compounds with which the floors were swept, and near the postoffice corner at the Lamb store one often caught a whiff of ink from the newspapers in the arriving mail and the pads used in the cancelling of stamps. In the center of either store, on a cold winter afternoon, all odors from the merchandise or other sources were lost in the fumes from the red-hot stove, the pipes and cigars of loiterers and the wooden match ends that sputtered in spittoons and on the tin pads that shielded the floors from occasional hot coals that popped out of the ash boxes.

The Proctor State Bank occupied the smallest business building in town and from the standpoint of my generation that was quite in order. Very little ever happened at the bank. It was a one-man operation, with no suggestion that a person should wait around unless invited to come behind the varnished-oak and frosted-glass partition for a private conversation with the banker. These conversations always broke off when someone came to the window to make a deposit or cash a check. Thus the in-and-out patrons could only speculate over whether the fellow behind the partition was there to ask for a loan or take a scolding for having overdrawn his account.

During the tenure of O. W. Knapp, the bank was entered one night by persons intent on opening the safe door with a charge of dynamite. The blast woke the whole town and brought Mr. Knapp to his front porch—about 100 yards away—clad in a nightshirt and carrying his shotgun. The story was that he fired one shot and then heeded the advice of a voice from the darkness to get back in the house. For several years the warped doors of the safe and other mementos of that occasion lay in a rusting heap at the back of the bank. (This was a commentary, I must concede, on the indifference of Proctor folk to community housekeeping.) While they wrecked the safe, the robbers failed to get to the inner space where most of the money was.

Mr. Knapp's successor was P. R. LaCalli, and my most vivid recollection of him has him at the wheel of a large and impressive Kissell automobile. When he left, the bank board turned to the man who was in his third term as teacher of our one-room school. He was W. L. Strickland, and he remained at the bank through its best years and then presided over its liquidation in the late 1920's.

Father sat in for Mr. Strickland now and then when the latter wanted to be away for a day or two. On these occasions we could hardly wait for the end of the school day so we could rush to the bank and observe Father in action. It turned out most of the time that he would be sitting in a chair with his feet on the table. He was inclined to treat himself to cigars on his banking days, and this seemed entirely proper. Mr. Strickland smoked cigars, and we had seen bankers in Sterling with cigars in their mouths. As a matter of fact, I grew up with a feeling that when there was cigar smoke in the air, there had to be money somewhere around.

We children were encouraged to start savings accounts in the Proctor bank, and after I started drawing pay for my summer work on the ranch—at the age of nine or ten—I established a checking account.

The lumber yard has received short mention, but it was very important to the welfare of Proctor as a trade center. It supplied materials for scores of houses and barns and untold miles of fencing. It brought in coal by the carload and offered several grades from bins along the track. Along with lumber and other materials, the lumber company handled hammers, saws, shovels, forks, other basic tools and rope. Its manager was also the manager of the grain elevator.

Proctor's first pool hall was opened early in the war period in a building opposite the bank. Later this recreation center for men only was transferred to a new building. The owner-operator in this location was Jim Heth, who had come to the community with a brother, Ed, to live on a sandhill place south of the river. The Heths later operated a store in Crook.

The blacksmith shop was in the hands of several persons before it was abandoned in the 1920's, but the smithy I remember best was John Zvetzig, whose brother, Jacob, had worked in the shop on the ranch in our early years there.

Among Proctor's shortcomings as a community center was the absence of any service for the ill or injured. Our family doctor for all our years at the ranch lived at Iliff, and his prescriptions were filled at Iliff's one drug store. It was to this store that we went to sit around iron tables and learn the tastes and names of the great variety of sundaes, shakes and malts that were a part of a wonderful world that excluded Proctor.

The prospects of Proctor's having its own doctor developed one spring with the arrival of a man from some state to the east who said he was a physician in search of a new place to locate. He and his wife put up at the hotel and spent several days getting acquainted. The two came into Lamb's store one day with someone who had taken them on a long drive through the countryside. The woman said she liked what she had seen. It reminded her of Iowa. I had seen a little of Iowa one August day from the window of a train, and I wondered if she and I had seen the same Iowa. The couple left in a few days, and for several weeks adults talked among themselves about this middle-aged man with a young wife who had thought of opening an office in Proctor. Some said if he had come, a drug store would have followed.

For a lack of a doctor, a drug store and many other services and institutions, Proctor never attained the level of a complete and integrated community. But Proctor was there, the center of all that passed as community life by the standards of our experience.

In and around Proctor we observed people in their reactions to situations we would see repeated in different surroundings and under different conditions many thousands of times for more than half a century. It was a benchmark from which we would measure later moves, later experiences and associations. It was the starting point of our involvement with people outside the family. Some of the people and some of the involvements will be treated in subsequent chapters.

By no stretch of the imagination could one borrow from Oliver Goldsmith and refer to Proctor as the fairest village of the plain. But for those of us who grew up there and knew no other place, there was, at the proper stages of our lives, some of the feeling that Daniel Webster expressed when he said of Dartmouth College that while it was small, there were those who loved it.

# 5. Spring Valley Ranch

## ... A Good Place with a Good Name
## That Nobody Used

Early settlers along the South Platte in Logan County were quick to spot the desirability of land on the left edge of the valley near the mouth of a draw. In some of the larger draws there was reliable running water, but also important was the fact that the flash floods of many centuries had left fine layers of alluvial soil over the valley floor at these points. Thus most draws opened onto a sort of dryland delta that was fertile, well-drained and adaptable to the first crude irrigation systems.

The home buildings of the ranch at Proctor were situated at just such a spot. It was at the point where Skinner Draw merged into the main valley, about a mile from the Union Pacific tracks and a mile and a half from the river.

The buildings, corrals, orchards, garden plots and various enclosures for livestock and poultry covered at least 50 acres. The main house, of gray sandstone, had nine rooms. Eight of them were in a square, two-story section with a roof that sloped to a peak from all four sides. Heavy stone chimneys pierced three of the slopes and a large attic dormer dominated the fourth. The ninth room, a mammoth kitchen with a walk-in pantry and washroom (later to be a bathroom) was a one-story attachment on the north, its stone walls blending into those of the two-story section.

The house faced south, but much of the character of its quite imposing front was lost in the belt of trees that shut off any but a close-up view from that direction. As a matter of fact, most visitors were admitted through the kitchen.

44

The road from Proctor angled through the trees from the southeast, went past the east side of the house and terminated in a sort of quadrangle from which one reached the barns, the granary, the chicken houses and the blacksmith shop. This was the action center, the place from which teams sometimes ran away while only partly hitched to a wagon; the place where saddle horses were tested on a cold morning and sometimes found in a mood for bucking. At the age of three or thereabouts, I saw a weaving hay wagon go by the back door, pulled by a single horse that was hitched by a single tug that somebody had forgotten to unhook. At about the same time, a fractious riding horse trampled a kitten as I looked on from the sloping cellar door. I sensed no particular danger, as I recall, but Mother did, and when I was about five years old, and there were two children younger than I, Father moved the road about 50 feet to the east and placed a fence between it and the house.

This change did not isolate the east side of the house. It remained the point of entrance and departure. In some respects this was the side that gave the house personality. Its five windows, two upstairs and three down, seemed to shift in boyish imagination into the features of a human face that looked out in a friendly and watchful manner on the hedges, the fences, the changing fields and pastures and the parallel lines of the railroad, the river and the sandhills, all angling from southwest to northeast and coming to a vanishing point in the vicinity of Crook, about eight miles away.

The house alone, in its time and place, was impressive. Set in one of the largest plantings of trees between North Platte and Denver and supported by an array of outbuildings and corrals, it drew the attention of travelers on Union Pacific trains and those who ventured into Colorado on the dirt and gravel highway that paralleled the rails.

The attic dormer was the only part of the house visible from Proctor when the trees were in full leaf. But enough of the total layout was visible that travelers looking for an overnight room, and hungry hoboes, kicked off a sidetracked train, often showed up at the ranch, sometimes under direction from someone in Proctor and sometimes on the hunch that a place with a big house, surrounded by trees and barns, might offer more than could be found in a treeless little town.

For travelers from the east, the ranch was in view for most of the way from Crook, with the house dominating the layout. Anyone approaching Proctor from the west could not help being impressed by the tree plantings, but few buildings were visible from that direction.

The land had been known to cattlemen since the herds of J. W. Iliff had grazed there in the 1870's. Most of it had been included in the Box-J Ranch (named for a cattle brand that was the letter J enclosed in a box). Powell and Blair acquired some 5,000 acres of Box-J holdings in 1896, and they managed, in a matter of five years or so, to develop one of the most completely equipped ranches on the South Platte.

They brought stone masons from Cheyenne to build the house, the blacksmith shop, the chicken house, the stone portion of the bunkhouse-coal house-ice house and the founda-

*Oxen digging the drainage ditch*

tion of the water tank. The stone was blasted from an outcropping about two miles to the northeast. It was used in the foundations of several frame buildings around the place, including the hay barns on the rail siding.

We took for granted that the first residence on the site was what we called the "old bunkhouse." It was a one-room structure, with outside walls of 12-inch vertical planks and two-inch battens. There was an inner wall of wooden wainscoting that extended across the ceiling. Mr. and Mrs. Powell had lived there at one time, and the bunkhouse designation seemed to denote that Father had lived there when he worked on the ranch shortly after his arrival in the county.

For some reason the full significance of the building was never clearly established in our family. Its history was reviewed for me in 1974 by Colonel William Powell Blair with considerable pride in what the women among his ancestors had contributed to the success of his father and grandfather in their ranching enterprises.

This was once the dwelling of Mrs. Christina Elizabeth Flemming. Building it and living in it had enabled her to meet the homestead requirements and become the first holder of patent on that quarter-section.

Mrs. Flemming, mother of Mrs. W. J. Powell, was a native of Germany. Five years after she and her husband migrated to Alabama, he died, and it was in her widowed state that she had the courage to face the lonely vigil on the edge of the South Platte Valley and establish more or less the desirability of this spot as headquarters of the Powell and Blair ranch.

Col. Blair, great grandson of Mrs. Flemming, was warm in his praise of her contribution to the ranch's ultimate development, even though she had returned to Mobile when Powell and Blair augmented their holdings with the 5,000 acres purchased from Box-J interests.

The old building, during our years on the ranch, hardly got the respect it deserved. It was used temporarily as a residence for hired help. A young married couple was in it for one summer, and two men, fresh from Mexico, lived in it through the season they tended some sugar beets. A beekeeper used it for a while to store supplies, and Mother found it a good place for setting hens when other quarters were crowded.

The convincing evidence of the place's having been established as a cattle ranch was in what we called the "lower corral," situated southeast of the house, beyond the trees and in direct line with the shipping pens at the east end of the Proctor siding. This was a complex of sheds, barns and pens that covered several acres, the outer boundaries of which were a solid board fence that was at least eight feet high. There was one large barn that must have been close to 100 feet long and 50 feet wide. A long, low barn was apparently built for housing calves, but in our time it was mainly occupied by hogs.

There was a chute through which larger animals were moved to a squeezer and stanchion for branding, dehorning and vaccinating. All such treatment of calves involved their being roped and wrestled to the ground, and one of the pens was reserved for that use throughout our years on the ranch.

At about the time of my first recollections, Father abandoned the dipping vat. It was made of wood, and some of the planks had rotted beyond repair. In the years I helped with cattle we drove ours to the neighboring Dillon ranch at dipping time.

I pondered on these occasions the great loss that had been ours with the decision not to maintain our own dipping vat. Nothing that took place in the routine of caring for cattle had more appeal to me between the ages of, say, nine and twelve, than dipping. I used every excuse imaginable to promote my being kept out of school to help drive cattle to the Dillon ranch on our day for dipping.

In a little house alongside the long, narrow concrete pit was a coal-fired boiler for keeping the contents of the pit at a reasonably warm temperature. (We always dipped during cold weather.) That boiler, presided over by a man we saw each summer and fall on the steam engine of a threshing outfit, never lost its mystery and charm.

But after the chill of the two-or three-hour ride had yielded to the heat from the firebox, one was bound to turn from the boilerhouse to the center of action. The Dillon dipping vat must have been 30 feet long, four feet wide and eight feet deep. The mixture of water and Blackleaf 40, plus what other ingredients were used, was kept at a depth of five to six feet.

From a pen of dry cattle at one end, the animals were crowded, one at a time, into a sloping chute where the slippery floor pretty well established a point of no return. The first splashing plunge meant complete immersion for even the largest of cows and steers. Men with long poles and hooks helped guide the partly-blinded animals through the narrow channel and onto the cleated ramp that led into a pen where all were held until most of the dip had drained from legs and bellies and had been blown from nostrils. The floor of the dripping pen sloped into a channel that carried drippings back into the vat.

When all our cattle had been dipped and we were working the tight-haired and forlorn-looking creatures down the road toward home, I was inclined to ponder how much better it would be if we could have this mid-winter festival in our home corral. Among other things, it would have meant a lot less time in the cold winds that seemed always to characterize our day at the Dillon dipping vat.

The truth was that the cattle operations during our years on the farm never matched what they had been during the Powell and Blair era. In the spring of 1896, Mr. Powell and a crew of riders had brought a herd of 1,500 all the way from eastern Oregon to winter on the ranch. As a boy I heard only casual comment on this event, but as the years have passed, I have come to believe it was an extraordinary feat. Surely it involved as many problems, as many risks almost, as the storied cattle drives from Texas to rail points in Kansas and Nebraska. For one thing, the Powell crew had to contend with mountainous terrain. There were no Indians, perhaps, but there were wild streams to ford and some long stretches where the shortage of water could have been disastrous. There is no written record of the trip, but it is taken for granted that for much of the journey the herd was moved along trails that had been followed 50 years earlier by wagon trains on the way to California and Oregon. Mr. Powell and his men went west by train, taking their saddles and sleeping gear and apparently counting on the availability of horses and wagons at the place where the cattle came from.

At almost the center of the lower corral complex was a windmill that pumped into a circular tank made of upright two-inch cypress planking and held together by a couple of iron rods that served in the manner of hoops on a barrel. The windmill ran almost constantly, providing water for any cattle in confinement and for the hogs with which Father started populating part of the corrals quite early in his career as ranch manager. Overflow water ran in a channel along one of the partitioning fences within the corral and into a ditch outside that emptied into the Big Slough, some 300 yards to the south.

Almost as far to the north of the house as the lower corral was to the southeast was the potato cellar. Father gave up on potatoes as a cash crop about 1911. I can recall at least one season when the cellar was full and oil stoves were kept burning during cold weather. I remember there was a manually-operated sorting machine and that the interior of the cellar was an eerie place, with very little light and strange combinations of smells, including on one occasion the scent of a skunk.

Architecturally, the cellar was a hole in the ground with a roof over it. The hole was perhaps 40 by 50 feet and seven or eight feet deep. Stone walls had been laid from the floor to a point about two feet above ground level. Over this was a wooden superstructure, with a corrugated iron roof. Ventilators projected from the roof, and there were, as I recall, a few small windows in the narrow space below the eaves.

The only entrance was a ramp about 10 feet wide that sloped

from ground level to the floor level, where heavy double doors swung to the inside. Potatoes were stored in bins around three sides of the big room, with the central area left open to accommodate a team and wagon. Powell and Blair toured potato farms around Greeley before building their own cellar.

The decision to quit growing potatoes for anything but home use was followed by quick action on Father's part to utilize the lumber and roofing of the potato cellar. As he did eventually with several original structures, he converted this to hog pens and sheds. For many years the potato cellar was an open hole that collected water and debris and more skunks. Eventually, it was filled in, but for several years it was a convenient place to pick up rocks for repairing a ditch bank or for other use.

The primary source of irrigation water for that part of the ranch which lay in the valley was a ditch that Powell and Blair had constructed with teams and scrapers. Its diversion from the river was about three miles upstream from Proctor. Cutting through land of F. H. Blair, J. P. Dillon and Jesse Stewart, it attained the valley's edge for its course across the ranch.

A second direct-flow ditch served the ranch to a limited extent. This was the Iliff and Platte Valley, which came out of the river several miles upstream from Iliff. While the Iliff ditch looped into the draws and cut through low hills across the ranch for several miles, most of the ranch's rights to Iliff water were exercised by releasing water from it into the Powell and Blair ditch for final distribution.

A third source of water became available during the World War I period, with the construction of ditches that brought water from the North Sterling system, the main stem of which flowed in a northeasterly direction some five or six miles from the ranch.

A sizable acreage of ranch land, all lying above the Iliff and the Powell and Blair ditches, had been "bonded" for service from the North Sterling system, but Father did not get around to bringing water to it until after he had taken a series of bumper wheat crops from it without benefit of irrigation.

While irrigation has been the lifeblood of agriculture in the South Platte Valley since the days of the first settlements, it has been damaging at times as well as constructive. Seepage from ditches and watered fields collected in low spots, making the land unworkable and encouraging alkali. One of Father's first attacks on this problem was the digging of a network of drainage ditches in some of the low pastures and hay lands south and west of the ranch buildings. The work was contracted to an itinerant operator whose equipment included a giant plow and some 40 head of oxen. The plow threw up twin banks that stood at least two feet above the level of the ground for several years. Some of the ditches picked up surface water and carried it off quite well. Others apparently didn't have enough fall to drain, and they became stagnant pools where mosquitoes seemed to breed by the millions.

A dozen or so years later, the ranch cooperated with other land owners in the digging of a drainage ditch with a dragline. This ditch was about eight feet deep, compared to the two or three feet of the oxen-dug ditches, and its greater effectiveness was about in proportion to its greater depth. It drained land west and south of Proctor.

Something about oxen power caught Father's eye, and before that early contractor had moved on, the ranch had acquired two yokes of steers that served to pull plows during a couple of years of breaking sod for the development of new cropland. One of the steers was named Mike. Little else do I recall about them.

Powell and Blair had been prodigious tree planters. A few of the largest cottonwoods probably pre-dated their arrival, but there were literally thousands of trees and shrubs that they had set out in the late 90's.

The trees nearest the house were mostly cottonwoods and American elms. There were two orchards, one immediately west of the house and another above the Powell and Blair ditch not far from the potato cellar. There were about 40 cherry and plum trees in the so-called upper orchard, and a variety of apples, mainly crabs, along with cherries and plums in the plot near the house. Along the west edge of each orchard was a mulberry hedge that eventually stood 20 or more feet high and served as an effective windbreak. A row of wild plum bushes paralleled the mulberries at the lower orchard. In this lower orchard there were three rows of black and yellow currant bushes. There were currant hedges along one edge of each of two garden plots, each about an acre in size. I once estimated that if all these wild currant bushes had been planted in a single hedge, it would have been nearly half a mile in length. At several spots there were random plantings of gooseberries and chokecherries. There were two large lilac bushes on the east side of the house.

South of the house was a tract on which American elms and black locust had been planted in rows about four feet apart. Father said Powell and Blair looked upon the locusts as material for fence posts, but no such use ever was made of them. By 1912 they had grown to a height of 20 to 30 feet and their tops had come together to provide complete shade for hogs that roamed the area with seeming immunity to the sharp thorns that protruded from every trunk. Here and there were ash and box elder, willows and Russian olives that seemed not to have been basic to the original planting plan. There were no evergreens, a fact we lamented each Christmas season.

Nearest building to the house was a two-story structure broadly designated as the bunkhouse. But only half of it was bunkhouse—the second-story half. The lower half was a rectangle of solid stone, divided into two parts. One part extended about four feet below ground. This was the icehouse, one of the most distinctive facilities on the whole ranch and the envy of residents for miles around. The remaining portion of the space under the bunkhouse was the coalhouse, where, along with the coal, there was a 50-gallon kerosene tank and a sort of crib that was the sleeping place of all resident dogs and some occasional strays.

The bunkhouse area was reached by an outdoor stairway that was equipped with a marvelous handrail, well-rounded, splinter-free and practically friction-free against the blue denim seats of our overalls.

The bunkhouse was divided into two large rooms, each with a separate door. In the one on the east there was a heating stove. The west room was reserved for overflow men in summer and, except for a year when a man and wife lived there, it was not used in winter.

Beyond the bunkhouse was the windmill, and immediately beyond it was the water storage tank. The tank rested on a circular stone foundation that extended about 10 feet above the ground. The wooden staves of the tank proper extended another eight to ten feet and were held together by a half-dozen or more encircling iron rods.

An underground system of pipes carried water from the tank to outlets in the house, the cow corral, the horse corral, the chicken yard and two points where hogs were watered. The bunkhouse was above the level of the tank, so there was no running water there. The tank was rebuilt once during our years on the ranch, but Father never seemed to be able to stop its leaking. In summer, when usage was high, and the water low, the upper portions would get dry and shrink. As the windmill started catching up, after one of those periods, the seams would leak profusely until the wood had time to soak up and swell. In winter there were thick veils of ice around the tank, hanging sometimes from points near the top all the way to the ground.

Immediately east of the tank was the engine house, and the two were connected in an odd way by an angling length of three-inch pipe that came out of the engine house about three feet above the ground and ended in a section that curved into a hole in the top of the tank.

To a small boy the ranch at times seemed to harbor ghosts of things past, and one of these was the rusting centrifugal pump that could be spotted in a dungeon-like space beneath the floor of the engine house. There was a well there, and Powell and Blair had installed the gasoline-powered pump as a primary source of water. Thus the angling pipe to the top of the tank.

This gasoline-driven pump typified the extent to which Powell and Blair had mechanized the place. And its non-use and neglect during the Hamil period of occupancy typified to some extent Father's reluctance to accept responsibility for keeping complicated gadgets in operation when he could get along without them. He did, finally, back up the windmill with a small gasoline engine, but both served the same pump.

The heart of the engine house was a sleek, one-cylinder stationary International of about 1900 vintage, with a pair of flywheels weighing several hundred pounds. Its accessories included a cooling tank that must have held 200 gallons of water, a box of wet batteries that sat on the floor and a 50-gallon gasoline tank covered by a sort of lean-to outside the building.

A heavy rubber belt tied the engine to a pulley shaft extending the full length of the building. To whatever extent the centrifugal pump had been operated, it had been by means of a belt extending through a hole in the floor to the pump shaft about six feet below. It drew no water in our day.

In the years of my earliest recollections, the gasoline engine was used for running a grindstone, a feed grinder and a power saw. The saw was a fascinating contrivance. Its basic elements were a crosscut blade of the kind and size foresters once used in two-man teams, a wooden wheel about two feet in diameter and a frame on which railroad crossties were slid into position for cutting into stovewood lengths. The wheel, linked to the main power shaft by a pulley on the outside of the engine house, was connected to the saw blade by an off-center arm, or journal, on its open side. One turn of the wheel produced a full back-and-forth thrust of the saw. In operation, the arrangement required that one man guide and apply pressure to the saw from its unconnected end while another moved the tie into position for each new cut.

Powell and Blair had been under contract with the Union Pacific for the plowing and maintenance of fireguards along the track through their grasslands. The pay for this service was access to all discarded crossties along that stretch of track. Father had continued the relationship for track-bordering land under the new ownership, and with the development of new sidetracks at Proctor this meant there were piles of old railroad ties on the ranch most of the time. Many were used for stovewood, but when the power saw started giving trouble, Father abandoned it. The wooden wheel was moved from junk pile to junk pile for several years before it finally disappeared.

Among bits of discarded machinery on an open spot north of the barn there sat for many years a simple wooden chassis on four flanged wheels. This and some battered lengths of light steel rail were all I ever saw of another arrangement that attested to the readiness of Powell and Blair to experiment with things mechanical.

To what extent they were used and to what extent they were practical, Father never really expressed himself, but he explained that the flanged wheels and the bits of rail were the last traces of an attempt to simplify the loading of baled hay from the Proctor storage barns onto rail cars. The conventional procedure was to load hay onto horse-drawn wagons and, after a trip of less than a thousand feet, transfer it to cars. The Powell and Blair idea had been that a lightweight railroad between the barns and the siding would enable men to move hay with less effort than was required to manipulate the teams and heavy wagons in and out of the barns and along the siding. As already mentioned, there was no clear-cut record of how well this had worked. The circumstantial evidence seemed to be against it.

Frank H. Blair, a native of Elk Point, S. D., had come to Sterling in 1891 immediately after graduation from the University of South Dakota at Vermillion. His first job was that of assistant principal of the new high school. He later advanced to principal, but after marrying one of the graduates of his school, he chose to leave the field of education and go into ranching with his new father-in-law, W. J. Powell, who had come from Alabama in 1874 and was well established as a cattleman.

The young man from the classroom and the older man with his years of experience in the saddle and the hayfield made an unusual combination. The bold and innovative spirit of the older man seemed to combine with the quiet, methodical approach of the younger in all sorts of developments around the ranch. They were in many respects far ahead of their time, each possessing characteristics that invite thoughts of Leonardo da Vinci and Thomas Jefferson.

The engine house alone, with its provisions for grinding grain, sharpening sickles, sawing wood and pumping water with a single gasoline engine probably was not duplicated on one in ten-thousand working farms or ranches in the United States at the turn of the century.

While Mr. Blair generally gets credit for having been the idea man, the mechanical designer, and in many cases the mechanic, Mr. Powell was not without an inventive streak. He was fascinated by the possibilities of a machine for perpetual motion, and during Father's stay on the ranch as a hand, Mr. Powell had worked with a large wheel to which he had attached an arrangement of weights that were supposed to shift position at the right moment and thus keep the wheel turning. One of his especially designed weights was still around in our day, serving as part of a motley collection of iron castings that were heated in an outdoor wood fire and then placed in a barrel of water for scalding hogs at butchering time. And what we always presumed was Mr. Powell's basic wheel—a rather strange-looking object—lay for all our years on the ranch across two overhead beams in the buggy shed.

Father recalled that Mr. Powell had experimented also with

a machine to kill grasshoppers. The central element of this was a wooden shaft about six feet long, from which several hundred wires extended about 18 inches to form a sort of giant brush. The wheels and cutter gears of a mowing machine had been utilized to support the brush and transmit power to the shaft. The idea was that the whirling wires would strike and kill the grasshoppers as they rose up ahead of the moving machine. Father recalled that while the machine did perform, it tended to be about as damaging to growing alfalfa or small grain as to grasshoppers. In any event, the octagonal wooden shaft, with steel journals still attached to the ends and many wires still in place, lay with other junk at the side of the blacksmith shop for several years after I was old enough to notice such things.

As Frank Blair advanced in years and was repeatedly cited as one of the outstanding men of the county, newspaper accounts of his career invariably recalled that he created quite a stir in the 1890's with the high-wheeled bicycle that he rode to and from his work at the high school in Sterling. Whether it was the same bicycle or another one, the record doesn't say, but when he quit the ranch in 1907, he left behind a high-wheeled bicycle that was still usable and a source of much entertainment for hired men of the earliest years of my memory. Eventually it was run over by a wagon and never repaired. As I viewed bits of the solid rubber tires and other parts of the wrecked bicycle that lay around for a while, I wondered as I did many times, why so many of the mechanical marvels of another day were wearing out or disappearing before I was big enough to use them.

An inventory of all mechanical devices and memorabilia that Powell and Blair left for us is almost beyond belief when one considers that their years on the ranch were no more than 10 and that major building, tree planting, and land preparation had been a heavy drain on their time and attention. Their legacy to the boys of the Hamil family was a place of infinite variety in things to see and do. When other boys came to play we could take them into the engine room, lift the trap door and show them the sophisticated pump and explain its non-use as we saw fit. We could hold hands in a circle around the gasoline engine while we sent shocks from palm to palm by placing a pair of pliers at the right spot on the magneto. If no adults were around, we could start the engine and watch the old grindstone whirl. We could adjourn to the blacksmith shop, start a fire in the forge, heat a piece of iron and pound it into various shapes. We could drill a hole in a rusty iron hinge or put threads on the end of a bolt. Or we could go behind the blacksmith shop, into the chicken yard, and show them the circular excavation that Powell and Blair had used as a pond for ducks and geese. It was fun to speculate on what it would have looked like filled with water.

Suspended from a couple of hooks in a shed at the lower corral was an ox yoke to which I could point and recall a dim past when four big-kneed steers had been a part of the work stock. Against one end of the stone chicken house was a warped and weathered cupboard with a one-inch plank door that was hinged at the bottom. Mother used it to store utensils, medicines and other essentials to the care of poultry, but it had known a more romantic use. This was, in fact, the business end of a chuck wagon. The door had opened into a table, and the various compartments in all probability had held the salt, the flour, the sugar, the bacon and the rattling pans that had traveled with Mr. Powell and his men on the long drive from Oregon in 1896.

In summertime, of course, there were trees to climb, cherries, gooseberries, plums, currants and crabapples to eat, rhubarb stalks to chew on, and mulberries to smear on each other's faces. There were horses to ride, a goat or a buck sheep to tease, machinery to climb over and barns and granaries to hide in. It was an interesting place, thanks to its inventive and innovative builders.

The pale-blue sheets on which Mother wrote all of Father's

business letters in a neat, flowing hand said that the Logan County Development Company was the operator of Spring Valley Ranch at Proctor, Colo. For some reason, though, nobody ever said "Spring Valley" in conversation about the place. It was "the ranch" in all our talk. Around the neighborhood it was generally referred to as the "Blue Ranch," for the secretary of the development company. We of the younger generation were flattered when some of our contemporaries insisted it was the "Hamil ranch." They believed in honoring the name of those they knew and associated with the place.

The "Spring Valley" name undoubtedly came from the fact that water oozed from the edge of Skinner Draw at a point a half-mile or so from the house. Powell and Blair had built some boxes there for cattle watering, but in our day the area was covered by a pond that had been created when the Iliff ditch was built across the draw.

The movement of water down the draw was measurably increased when land upstream came under irrigation from the North Sterling system. As a matter of fact, North Sterling irrigation changed the character of all the draws along the South Platte in that area. Some that had been completely dry and without a marked water course developed large wet areas and had to be ditched. There was a well-defined water course in Skinner Draw that entered the valley west of the ranch house and extended into the Big Slough, which wound to the southeast and reached the river several miles away.

In retrospect, I can't understand why I didn't encourage the use of the Spring Valley name. I can't understand, either, why Mother didn't choose to popularize it. She had a definite inclination to the poetic designation wherever it might apply. It could have been that she so disliked the isolation and rawness of the place in her first years there that her normal tendencies were lost in her longings for the tall pines, the temperate winds and the mature neighborliness of her home community in Tennessee.

In retrospect, again, one must say that the ranch by any name was a great place for growing boys. It seemed at times to offer too many opportunities for work, and Father seemed especially adept at spotting such opportunities. But when the work was done, or to be avoided, there were countless opportunites for diversion, for exploration, for testing of physical skills of all kinds and for just plain messing around, as a later generation might have explained it.

# 6. THE HIRED HELP

## . . . Of Blood and Muscle and a
## Potpourri of Personalities

The hired man of American agriculture has become an elusive legend. He is not around in his old form, but even in his old form, he was not the stereotype some sentimentalists have tried to make him. He fit no mold.

The aura of stability—of nobility, almost—that some have tried to build around him can be explained in part, I believe, by the fact that he was vital to American farmers and ranchers during some of the most prosperous years they have known.

He was a source of low-cost energy at a time when agriculture was producing for strong markets. His relatively low wages were a part of the equation that made the years from 1910 to 1914 so good that they became the base years for computing the so-called farm parity that farmers have striven for and only rarely achieved in all the years since.

The hired man peaked out, it might be said, at some point during those parity-making years and the boom years of World War I that followed. His gradual recession coincides with the coming of the internal combustion engine, central electric power and a long list of other improvements over the blood and muscle that had been the basic inputs of agricultural production from the beginning.

There were no tractors or trucks on the ranch at Proctor for most of our 18 years there. But there was a constant coming and going of men. Some worked a day, some a week, some a month, some a year or longer. They came in all shapes and sizes, and they ranged in age from mere boys of 15 to men of 50 or older. For Father they were the management problem that transcended all others. He took for granted that many were basically incompetent and issued careful instructions. He managed to be on hand for every new man's hitching of a team to a wagon or implement. In times of need he hired any man who came along, but once he was convinced that the person couldn't or wouldn't do the work assigned, he got out his checkbook, paid the fellow and wished him well in his next experience.

Some who tried out were simply without qualifications. One of these was a young priest just arrived from Russia. One was a wealthy young man from Denver who came with one of the biggest automobiles ever seen in the community. The day of his arrival, he put it on blocks to save his tires from the deterioration of standing on bare ground all summer. Two days later he removed the blocks and headed back to the city.

For us boys there was only casual interest in a new man's skills with a shovel, pitchfork or a team of horses, except as we tended to appreciate excellence in the occupations we knew best. We were interested in the new face, and we never ceased to hope that behind it would be a warm and responsive personality. The number of new people we saw in a typical month could be counted on the fingers of one hand. Every new hired man, therefore, came as a fresh and welcome envoy from the outside world, and we never tired of hearing about things as they were in Nebraska, Kansas, Iowa, Missouri and other far-away places.

Some, of course, were silent and furtive. Every now and then, one would confess that he was running away from angry parents or an impossible wife. Some were suspected of hiding from the law, and a young Mexican, unable to show that he had registered for the draft during World War I, finally conceded that he had come into the country without benefit of clearance by immigration authorities.

Some who came along were provincial and ignorant to the point they could not win the attention or confidence of an equally provincial 10-year-old. Some got attention through their sheer crudity and vulgarity and their boasting reviews of recent brushes with things risky, irreverent or erotic. Some were reserved and gentle. Some were gay and friendly and especially capable of easy rapport with youngsters. Men showed up with banjos, mandolins, accordions, mouth harps and guitars, but relatively few could produce appreciable music. A few had their own horses and saddles and some had buggies. There were at least three who had motorcycles. And toward the end of our stay on the ranch there were men with cars.

A few came direct from Russia, Holland, Mexico, Sweden or some other country and could speak little if any English. A majority, I am confident, had lived or worked in Nebraska or Kansas.

Most of the help slept in the bunkhouse and ate in the kitchen, but almost always there was at least one full-time man who lived with his wife in a field shack, a house in Proctor, a converted granary or some other makeshift residence. In the summer, of course, there were families or groups of single men on hand as "beet labor." The latter included at least one group

*Interlude at the horse corral*

of Japanese in our years on the ranch, several German-Russian families, a Mexican family or two and several groups of Mexican men who came without wives. These workers lived in field shacks, generally, with a minimum of comforts and conveniences. As a general rule, they packed their meager belongings at the end of the beet harvest and sought more comfortable quarters in Sterling or elsewhere. Some of them, I am sure, would have been about as well off in the shacks as they were in the limited housing available to them in town. It was a truth of the times that beet laboring families were accorded a sort of second-class citizenship. And it is a tribute to countless men and women who came to work in the beets that they lived to see sons and daughters take their places among the leaders of business and community affairs throughout the beet-growing areas of Colorado and Nebraska. Theirs is a story to give heart and hope to all who ponder the plight of minorities in our free and fluid society. They worked, they listened, they learned. And they overcame. Some of these will get attention in a subsequent chapter.

One man who slept in the bunkhouse and ate in the kitchen paid cash for his keep while working through a harvest season as weighmaster at the Proctor beet dump. In his spare time he did oil painting, and he gave Mother a picture of the ranch buildings as seen from the scale house about a mile away and one of the "Lone Tree of the South Platte," a battered cottonwood referred to in an earlier chapter.

### Hadley Dillard, Bill Bailey, "Slims," "Shorties," Etc.

Of all the names of hired men that I recall there was none that had more of a ring of distinction than that of Hadley Dillard. He was a tall, thin man, and he became something of a hero to the family for the gentle attention accorded Sister Edna after she fell from the windmill and suffered fractures of a wrist and thigh when she was about three years old. Hadley heard her whimpering as she lay helpless at the base of the windmill and carried her into the house.

65

Another man with a distinctive name was Charles Von Brecht. Born in St. Louis and orphaned at the age of four, he had come to Colorado to be with a sister. I was to learn many years later of the Von in his name and of the fact that for a time Father had acted as his legal guardian. At the ranch he was plain Charlie Brecht. He figured in the first adult conversations and speculations I was to overhear about a young man's courting of a young woman. The young woman was Marion Flock, one of several sisters living with their grandparents some three miles away. The two were married in 1912, and in 1972 they were honored as the couple with the longest residence in the Crook community.

No man, regardless of the fine sound of his name or any shows of sensitivity or compassion, could rise above Father's tendency to settle on the descriptive nickname that seemed to suit. Hadley Dillard was an inescapable "Slim." There were more "Slims" than "Shorties," but not many more. There were "Fats" and "Heavies." A man named Gunard Hultquist was known as "The Swede." A young fellow who mentioned that he was part-Indian became "The Indian." An itinerant trapper named Napoleon Bouteau lived on the ranch one winter and was quickly dubbed "The Frenchman."

There was Billy Bailey, whom I remember for more than a name made popular in song. He was hauling beets one fall when I was perhaps 12 years old. On a couple of Saturdays he arranged for a second team and wagon and put me in charge of it, with Brother Dave as my helper. While Bill was forking beets into his wagon, Dave and I strained away at our forks and managed to have about a third of a load when he had finished filling his wagon. He would then help fill ours, and we would go driving off together to the dump. He was paid by the ton, of course, and he picked up a pretty good bonus from the eight to ten additional tons he could deliver with the second wagon. I don't recall whether Dave and I got paid by the day or the ton, but there was never any feeling that Bill took advantage of us.

As a matter of fact, there was a reward for us in the privilege of going back to school on Monday to boast a little about having hauled beets. That was man's work of the highest order, and I am confident we talked about it as though we had forked almost every pound that had gone to the dump in our wagon.

Bill was proud of the fact that his name was in a popular song, but the song was not about a man who wouldn't come home; it was about "Old Bill Bailey (who) Played the Ukulele Down in Honolulu Town."

### The Kohlers from Nebraska

Among those who stayed the longest—about three years—was Roy Kohler, and probably no single person among the hundreds who occupied the bunkhouse between 1907 and 1924 became closer to the family. He suffered a broken leg while at work, and for about three weeks he lay on his back in a bed in the parlor—a bed made from the davenport. We children enjoyed waiting on him and he, in turn, regaled us with stories of his boyhood in Nebraska.

Shortly after his leg had healed, he went into Sterling to work in a creamery. But he had been in his new job only a few months when the United States entered the war with Germany, and Roy Kohler was one of the first from the county to be called into service. He came back at the close of the war, still weak from a wound that left him with several ribs missing, and during a tour of the ranch he remarked that the best-looking wheat he had ever seen was in the battle area of France where he was wounded. He got back into the dairy industry, and for many years he was in charge of milk inspection for the City of Lincoln, Neb. He fell to his death from an upper-story window of the Nebraska State Capitol.

I last saw Roy about 1944, and he recalled how his hard work on the ranch had helped condition him physically for the ordeal he was to go through in France. Hit by a shell fragment, he had lost much blood when he was picked up by stretcher bearers. Then came a long ride in an ambulance and a longer one in a

French rail car before his wound got anything but cursory attention.

Roy was preceded by an older brother, George, who worked some as a hand, but had the courage one spring to devote a season to the growing of vegetables. He rented 20 acres of some of the richest irrigated land on the ranch and laid out plots for onions, cabbage and celery. He produced reasonable crops of all three, but he had trouble, as I recall, finding markets. Many of his onions were lopsided for not having been adequately thinned, and his system of bleaching celery in earth trenches seemed not to have worked as well as expected. From George's point of view, the venture was discouraging, but from mine it was a milestone of economic advancement. When the time came to set out the cabbage plants, George proposed that I go into his employ at a dollar a day. His first check for $5 or thereabouts almost doubled a savings account that I had been trying to build up for a couple of years from my penny bank. I remember George Kohler in several situations, but the one that stands out above all others is that of the man who first wrote my name as payee on a bank check. He was one of the men who owned a motorcycle. That, too, was something to remember as exciting in 1913 or 1914.

### Ernest Was Earnest and also Frank

One of the truly unforgettable men came for the wheat harvest in 1917, or 1918, and for at least one additional summer. His name was Ernest and he had worked at various jobs in Denver and other cities. He made it clear from the beginning that he was on the ranch for the summer only. No outdoor work for him in the winter.

Ernest had marked idiosyncracies. He chewed a carefully measured mixture of tobacco and snuff, and one filling lasted a full half-day. He never went to the field without tying a bandana snugly around his neck. He washed his own clothes with care and precision. He was good with horses. He talked with and about his team—a nervous stallion and a steady gelding—as though they were two men with whom he went forth each day to mow alfalfa.

He was a philosopher of sorts, I guess, and a raconteur, but nobody applied such terms to anyone around the ranch. Father always referred to him as "well read," and he (Father) took special delight in those occasions when Ernest would move into the conversation with a polite put-down for some windy guest. On at least one occasion Ernest took exception to a statement by one of the visiting owners of the ranch. That was a bold move, but it was one that Father chuckled over when the visitor had gone.

One morning in early July, Ernest and I were hoeing potatoes at the edge of the creek in Skinner Draw. A quarter of a mile away, beyond a patch of green alfalfa, was the edge of a field of the wheat he had come to help harvest. Leaning on his hoe, he studied the greenish-yellow waves that curled their way up the slope and into the horizon. Without seeming conscious of my presence, he spoke words that burned their way into my memory: "Third prettiest thing in the world. First is woman. Second is a full-rigged ship at sea. And third is a turning field of grain."

His soliloquy completed, he went back to hoeing. I have wondered down through the years if those were Ernest's own evaluations or if they came from something he had found in his considerable reading. I wanted to ask at the time what might have ranked fourth or fifth, but there was a certain magic in the moment, a solemnity, even, in the tone of his reveries. I kept my thoughts to myself and moved to the next hill of potatoes.

One warm night as we sat in darkness at the door of the engine house, he mused about women and expressed some curiosity about the wife and mother in a family that was tending beets on the ranch that summer. Would she be interested in an extra-marital adventure? If not, where was there a woman who might respond to his advances? The raw language in which he summed up his longings was not new. It was what I had heard since about the age of six from a whole parade of bunkhouse occupants. But I was startled, in a vague sort of way, to hear it from the man who had seemed to reach the heights of romanticism that day in the potato patch. I was yet to learn that the lives of poets do not always square with their couplets.

Most of what I had been told about either the sexual activities or the ambitions of hired men generally related to times, places and people far from the vicinity of the telling. And parties of the second part almost always went unnamed and unidentified. But there was Ernest talking about that Mother Hubbard of the beet fields who couldn't even speak English. And while he surprised me, he probably contributed to the solidarity of the image he was building in my consciousness. In due time I would learn that men who speak forthrightly—men who are frank in discussing their own lusts and weaknesses—almost always turn out to be interesting.

### And There Were Women

It should be said in defense of those hired men who liked to talk about women that there were very few women in the neighborhood toward whom they might have directed any legitimate attention. Four single women came to teach for one year each during the eight years I was in our one-room school. With few exceptions, the only other unattached females in the neigborhood were farm girls too young to leave home. There was, of course, an occasional hired girl on the ranch in whom the men in the bunkhouse would show interest. Some of these—most of them, in fact—were mere girls of 14 or 15, and Mother kept them under her wing. Some were widows, including a high percentage who could have been classified as neurotic. One of these was just a few months out of Austria and had come to be near relatives. She brought a collection of her own feather-stuffed bed clothing. But the downy ticks and other reminders of old-country customs were not enough to stave off homesickness, and after putting up with her crying spells for a couple of weeks, Mother arranged for one of the woman's relatives to come get her and her belongings.

One woman who worked for a short time had some cause for a nervous condition that seemed to reduce her effectiveness. She had been cleared only a few weeks earlier as a suspect in a murder case.

If Mother had a sentimental favorite, it was Lena Otzenberger who, as a mere girl, had helped her at the Frost place and who came and helped for a short time at the Proctor ranch. Some of the hired men showed interest in a buxom Italian girl, who was with us several months, but she quickly made up her mind that the only man in the neighborhood for whom she had any time was the Union Pacific station agent, whose office was a reconditioned boxcar. It could have been the difference between a fellow who worked in a necktie and could tell you what the wires were saying about when the next train was due and those in the bunkhouse who wore denim overalls and could talk mainly about the condition of the hay or the level of the irrigation ditch.

One widow, a Mrs. Thomas, who came out from Denver brought a 14-year-old son with her and he proved to be a lively addition to the scene for the two or three months they were around. He was perhaps five years older than I and, for a time at least, the object of some envy. Among other things, he was authorized to ride Old Tom, Father's aging saddle horse, while I was still stuck with Buster, smaller, slower and more determined against any involvement in youthful pranks. But young Thomas rode Old Tom at full gallop into an eroded ravine one day and came up limping after Tom had turned a complete somersault. Tom himself developed a limp, and the incident had to be explained. I got some satisfaction from some of the limitations Father then put on horseback excursions and felt a little better as I bounced along on Buster while the Thomas boy continued to savor the comfortable cow-pony gait of Old Tom.

Another widow, Mrs. Ella Walker, brought her daughter for

71

a summer on the ranch, and that was quite a different matter. The daughter's name was Lucille, and she was preparing to enter high school at Sterling in the fall. She was a cheerful, intelligent person who knew how to fill a day with interesting activities that she seemed always ready to share with Ruth, David and me. Lucille could draw and paint pictures and, with this talent, she spent most of her adult years as a staff artist on the Denver *Post*. For me, at the age of about eight, she had feminine charm that I was sure would never show up in another person. When I think back on the intensity of that infatuation, I can only speculate that if I had been 13 when Lucille was 13, she might not have died a spinster.

### Fred and Mr. Erickson

One summer in the early 20's started off with me as the substitute for a hired girl. Mother, with twin babies on her hands, had come close to a nervous breakdown, and Sister Edna looked after her and the twins while I manned the kitchen. No cows to milk, no horses to harness, no exposure to the hot sun. For a week or so, this was the life! Then the situation began to pall. I took to saddling a horse each afternoon and riding out to the hayfield or wherever else any of the men might be working.

This went on until early July, when Father came home from Sterling with a woman he had hired to take over the kitchen. She was a divorcee in her 20's, and that is about all I recall of her beyond the fact that she stirred the interests of at least two hired men.

One of these was a bachelor of perhaps 60 years of age. He had stopped in one day and explained to Father that he had just sold out after a dozen or more years on a homestead in Weld County and was heading for his old home in Nebraska. He came in a spring wagon behind a team that included one gray and one dark-brown horse, and after Father had indicated the need for some help with the unusually heavy wild hay crop, he turned his horses into our pasture and went to work.

This man, whom we shall call Mr. Erickson, explained that

he had been active in the little church of the community he had just left, and when we were seated for one of his first meals at the ranch, he asked Father if he might say grace. From then on, through the month or more he was with us, we all waited a bit impatiently for Father's signal and Mr. Erickson's set prayer. Until then, there had been no invocations at the kitchen table, except on the rare occasion when a visiting clergyman happened in on too short notice for Mother to organize a second table for the family in the dining room.

The presence of three or more able-bodied persons was all that younger members of the family needed to organize some kind of running game for the final half hour or so of summer daylight. The new hired girl entered into these with enthusiasm and, to the great surprise of all of us, so did Mr. Erickson, gray mustache and all. Some noted, with unwarranted cynicism, perhaps, that he was especially aggressive at those times when the game required catching or tagging the young divorcee.

A second man who also came along just in time to help with the wild hay harvest that year was in his early 30's. His name was Fred, and he had come west at the suggestion of his doctor, he said, after working for several years as a refrigeration technician in the packing houses of South Omaha. He avoided the hide-and-seek games, but he didn't ignore the young divorcee. They went on walks after dark, and one weekend he arranged to borrow the company-owned Model T to take her to Sterling. The explanation was that she wanted to visit friends or relatives and that our man from Omaha was willing to drive if he could borrow a car. On the way to the hayfield the morning after their return, he told me in some detail of how they had stayed at a hotel and really hadn't seen anybody's friends or relatives.

In what might be called a gesture of classic magnanimity, he offered to make an arrangement with the divorcee on my behalf. It could be that Fred anticipated my declination and was merely trying to consolidate his position as a man of the world as it had unfolded for him in South Omaha. In any event, his proposition was something I mulled over at some length as we drove our mowing machines through the lush wild grasses of the Box-J pasture that day. Fred was an interesting fellow to have around. At about the time of the sojourn in Sterling, Mr. Erickson took his horses out of the pasture, hitched them to his wagon and headed for Nebraska.

## Beachhead for Tennesseans

The fact that extra help could be used at the ranch at almost any time was a boon to a steady stream of young men who came west from Blount County, Tennessee. Father had left there in the late 1890's in company with a cousin, Will Logan. They stopped in Illinois, where they had relatives, and eventually arrived in Logan County in 1899. Four years later, Father returned to Tennessee, married the girl who had waited all those years and returned to Colorado. A young Tennessee friend and neighbor, Will Lane, came with them and worked for Father at the Frost place near Sterling. In the winter of 1906-07, Mother took my older sister and me on her first trip back to visit her family. When we returned in March, three more young Tennesseans accompanied us. They included Father's brother, Robert Hamil, Dave Ledford and John Phelps, and all three came to the ranch and filled in as hands for a time. Robert Hamil was the only one of the three who settled permanently in Logan County, but they set the pattern of a story within the story of the hired men at the Proctor ranch. For the next 18 years there were few times when not at least one man from Blount County was working as a hand or farming ranch land on his own on a rental basis.

These Tennesseans represent a sort of microcosm of a western movement that has gone largely unchronicled. It was a movement as distinct and real as the coming of the trappers, the traders, the wagon trains and the homesteaders. The participants were not the founders of new towns or states. They settled in communities that had been staked out by persons arriving a few years earlier. Their starting points were in a thousand counties in states from Georgia to New England and extending westward through Ohio, Michigan, Indiana, Kentucky, Tennessee and the Gulf South. Our story deals with those who started from Blount County, Tennessee, at the edge of the Great Smokies, and landed in Logan County, Colorado.

Richly timbered and well watered, Blount County was an attractive place to those who looked westward after the American Revolution. After 100 years, though, the area lacked this kind of appeal to young men of Father's generation who knew no ambition but to be farmers in the tradition of their forebears. Most of the pines, oaks, chestnuts, hickories and other great trees that had greeted the original settlers were gone, and with them the protective undercover that had held the red soil against some of the heaviest rainfall of any part of the United States. The land was occupied beyond its agricultural capacity, as was the case throughout many eastern and southeastern states. Change was coming in the form of new industries and new approaches to the control of erosion and restoration of soils. But Father and his contemporaries were in no mood to wait. Word kept coming about an abundance of new and fertile land in the states to the west. Father's first move was to Olney, Ill., where relatives had settled before the Civil War and where his father had gone at the age of 15 to sit out that conflict rather than be conscripted by the Confederate Army.

In a matter of time Father decided he had not gone far enough west. The land he worked on in southern Illinois was as badly worn, almost, as that of East Tennessee and, besides that, there was the same reluctance on the part of settled farmers to sell land at prices a beginner could afford to pay. Others in that Illinois community had gone westward and settled at a place called Sterling, in Colorado. They were sending back good reports of the country and its prospects. A touch of malaria that Father had picked up while working in the strawberry harvest near St. Louis was enough to convince him that there might be something besides farming opportunities to recommend that high, dry country the ex-Illinoisans had been writing about. And thus he became a part of the migration from Richland County, Illinois, that led in the end to a larger migration to Colorado from Blount County, Tennessee. His cousin, Will Logan, went to Sterling with him, and four years later, Will Lane came from Tennessee to work under him at the Frost place. Thus the trickle of Tennesseans started. For more than 20 years it continued, with the remote station of Proctor being the destination and the first stopping place of most of the migrants.

There was always a bed in the bunkhouse and a plate at the kitchen table. And for a surprisingly large number of those who came unannounced there was a place on the payroll—long enough to let a fellow get his bearings and decide whether this part of the country was to his liking. Father can be credited, therefore, with having established a friendly beachhead, a place where young men venturing from Blount County for the first time would be among people with common backgrounds and usually some common acquaintances. I can't recall his ever having mentioned the similarity between the situations of these new arrivals from Tennessee and his own situations on two separate occasions, but it was there. His choice of Olney, Ill., for his first stop after leaving home was based solely on his knowledge that he would be among relatives. His choice a few years later of Sterling, Colo., as his next stop was made because Illinoisans he knew, including some distant relatives, were there.

This is the pattern of western movement of literally millions of Americans that came in the wake of the pioneers. One or two ventured first into a new community in a new state. They liked what they found or, in their pride, they were too stubborn to write home in any but favorable tones. The word spread among old neighbors. The restless and ambitious took note, and when the chance came to make their break, they bought rail tickets that would land them among people they knew or had heard about. The unfolding of that story was a part of life at Proctor for all of our 18 years there. At Father's funeral in 1931, three men in the list of pallbearers were ex-Tennesseans, and a fourth was one of those who preceded him in going to Sterling from Olney, Ill.

### Cook, Cowboy and Ranch-Style Baby Sitter

When Charlie Morton was past the age of 80 and laid up by the illness that finally took him in 1971, it dawned on me that I had known him longer than I had known any living person, except perhaps for my younger brother. The world of my first memories included the walls and windows of the ranch house and several persons moving about. One of those persons was Charlie.

He was in the kitchen most of the time, baking great quantities of bread every few days, setting the long oil-cloth-covered table, dishing up meat and gravy, potatoes, beans and cabbage, and then pulling vigorously on the rope that rang the old school bell on the roof. His impatient tugs sometimes caused the bell to stop on dead center and go mute. On those occasions we youngsters were fascinated as he went to the kitchen door and shouted in the direction of the bunkhouse the time-worn ultimatum: "Come and get it, or I'll throw it out!"

Charlie had grown up in Tennessee and had spent some of his boyhood with Father's parents. He arrived at the ranch with full intention that he would work in the fields, but the big shortage of help was in the kitchen. And so my first conscious-ness of someone named Charlie was of the ruler of the kitchen, a person who went intently about his business and brooked a minimum of interference. It is almost unbelievable in these permissive times that he kept a freshly-cut currant switch on top of the pots-and-pans cupboard and never hesitated to reach for it when young tormentors seemed out of hand. He threat-ened with the switch more often then he swung, but there were occasions when I ducked into the living room with a stinging

77

sensation about the calves and ankles.

He was little more than 20 years old at the time, and it can be taken for granted that he yearned for release from the coal range, the cold-water sink, the mop and pail and those inevitable trips to the hog pen with the day's garbage. (We called it slop.) His very youth, of course, enabled him to rush through his mid-day duties and take a little time in the afternoon for a relaxing ride on one of the saddle horses. He visited crews in the hayfields, and sometimes he took them lunch.

Every now and then he was relieved from the kitchen to meet an emergency in the fields. And once he was chosen to take a load of potatoes behind four horses all the way to Sterling, some 20 miles away.

He took advantage of his free time to become something of a master of the lariat. He was one of the few men I ever saw around the ranch who could twirl a looped rope in the manner of rodeo entertainers. And he raised some eyebrows once when he came in with a young coyote he had roped from a running horse. Some said it couldn't be done.

Once Brother David walked too far into the soft mud bordering the nearby slough. He was stuck tight, and I bogged down when I tried to rescue him. When I reported the situation at home, Charlie saddled Old Tom and was back in a matter of minutes with a mud-spattered boy in the saddle in front of him. He rescued youngsters from tops of buildings and from the probing noses of rugged greyhounds. He led them through corrals filled with curious cattle. He killed snakes and rats as occasion demanded, and wrung the necks of chickens.

I never knew just why he tried to carry three of us on one horse, but he did once, and Old Tom made a quick sideward shift when a hog emerged from the roadside brush. Sister Ruth hit the ground, and I found myself looking at it from the level of the horse's knees while Charlie held me by one foot. How he managed to control the horse while holding Brother Dave, the youngest of the three of us, in the saddle with him, I never quite understood.

In due time Charlie brought a bride from Tennessee and was ready to strike out for himself. He was especially ready to get out of the kitchen. His first farming was as renter of some irrigated land at the far end of the ranch. His crops were mainly alfalfa, oats, barley and sugar beets.

While he was not the only one in the neighborhood, he stands out in my memory as what was known as a hard worker. Up at 4 a.m., always moving at a near trot, finishing chores at dusk, even in the long days of summer. Recollections of Charlie and his operations provide a good picture of a young man trying to get ahead in farming when the measure of accomplishment was in large part the amount of energy that could be regenerated, day after day, week after week, in human bodies. Fortunately for him, his body seemed never to run down.

For all farmers in the sugar beet country harvest demanded a particularly hard pace. Men forked the beets into specially-built wagons with sides that could be dropped for dumping. Teams strained to move the loads of three and four tons out of soft fields and over narrow roads where the steel-tired wheels cut deep ruts as the harvest progressed. Men and horses raced with the clock and the schedules of the sugar company crews that manned the scales and dumps.

Some growers were satisfied to put two horses to a wagon, but Charlie Morton was a four-horse man. He pushed his teams, and the dust rose in heavier clouds around his wagons than around those powered with fewer animals and going at a slower pace. As a matter of fact, he attained some recognition as one who got a lot out of horses and mules as well as himself.

He remained in the neighborhood as long as I did, and through exchange of work and other experiences, our friendship that had started in the kitchen went from that of man-to-child, man-to-boy and man-to-man. Ultimately he gave up farming and worked winters in the sugar factory and summers as "ditch rider" for an irrigation district. Only near the end did Charlie's tough physique start showing the wear of his years. What seemed to hurt him most at our last visit was his difficulty in hearing. It hurt me, too.

## Death on Sunday Morning

Among occupants of the bunkhouse in the summer of 1910 were the two Armstrong brothers from Tennessee. One of them, Guy, was the victim of the only fatal accident to befall anyone working on the ranch during our 18 years there.

It occurred on a Sunday morning in August, a little more than a month before my fourth birthday, but major details fixed themselves in my memory.

We children had assembled on the front porch, where Father had chosen a cool spot to attack a several days' growth of whiskers. He was moving his pitcher of hot water, mirror and razor strap into place, when a young man from Proctor came to the front of the house to explain that, unless there was some objection, he would be hunting rabbits in fields north of the house. Father issued some cautions and sent him on his way. We didn't know that he would stop at the bunkhouse and that Guy Armstrong would join him.

Father still had lather on his face when the young hunter came around the corner of the house, tears streaming down his face and explaining with every step almost what had happened. "Guy is dead. Guy is dead. I shot him." He was still repeating the message when Father took him by the arm and insisted that they head for the scene.

Though under instructions to stay where I was, I tagged along until I witnessed an outpouring of men from the bunkhouse, one of them holding Guy's weeping brother by the arm as they came down the stairs.

The explanation that seemed acceptable to all was that Guy didn't know that the young hunter's shotgun was a repeater. The first shot had sent a rabbit rolling. But the animal regained its feet, and Guy ran out to catch it. He stepped into the path of a second blast and was almost decapitated.

The undertaker-coroner came out from Sterling, and after an exchange of telegrams with relatives in Tennessee, it was decided that burial would be at the Sterling cemetery. It was decided also that the body would remain at the ranch and simple services would be held in the living room.

Our dining room was turned over to the undertaker, and I was placed under a strict order not to enter the room, even after the undertaker had left. I forgot once and opened the door. I found myself staring at what seemed to me the biggest pair of shoe soles I had ever seen. There was no viewing of the body in the casket, as I recall, and that one glimpse from which I backed away as quickly as possible provided my last clear recollection of the tragic end of 19-year-old Guy Armstrong.

One young man from Tennessee, Lloyd Sterling, often broke away from the other hired men following meals to spend 15 or 20 minutes at the parlor piano. He returned to Tennessee shortly before the United States entered the war with Germany and was among Blount County's first casualties in France.

Charlie and Jim Talbott arrived at the ranch about the time of declaration of war in 1917. They had come from Blount County by way of Guymon, Okla., where they had worked on a ranch for a Mr. Hitch, also an ex-Tennessean. Each of them came with a battered and sweat-stained gray Stetson with brim creased and curled in the manner preferred by working cowmen of the day. Charlie eventually settled down in Tennessee, but Jim married Mabel Stewart of Proctor and established himself as a stockman and farmer.

During the late teen years word came that Emerson Logan, brother of Will and cousin of Father, had developed chronic lung trouble in Tennessee and wanted to come to Colorado to see if the climate would help him. Father arranged for him and his wife, Clara, to live at the ranch, and he immediately assigned Emerson to various duties. For Emerson, as he had done earlier for Rudolph Wiltein, who had come from Wisconsin with lung trouble, Father worked out a rigorous schedule of activities, including much exposure, on horseback, to the coldest of winter weather. Whether or not he had any medical support for his belief in the restorative powers of the icy blasts into which he led these men in turn, Father's method seemed to work for them. They both outlived him by many years.

## Some By-Passed the Ranch

There were some Tennesseans who came to Logan County and did not tarry at the ranch, if they stopped at all. There were a few who came, stayed with us a few days, looked things over and were settled into farming on their own in a matter of months. Some of these went back to Tennessee to gather up families and belongings before making the final move. Some didn't like what they saw in Colorado and never returned.

J. B. (Bert) Montgomery, to the best of my recollection, was at the ranch briefly before going to Tennessee to be married. His return with a bride was followed by the arrival of his cousin, Cass Montgomery, and Ralph Kiser, whose wives were sisters of Mrs. Bert Montgomery. Bert Montgomery farmed in the county for about 20 years, then went into the trucking business, with headquarters in Denver. Cass Montgomery returned to Tennessee after a few years; Ralph Kiser farmed J. P. Dillon land west of the Powell beet dump for several years, then went to a farm south of Sterling. He returned to Tennessee in the 20's.

Robert Montgomery, brother of Cass, and a cousin of Bert, farmed for many years in the Atwood-Merino area. Homer Kostner, brother-in-law of Cass and Robert, farmed immediately south of Sterling several years and was killed in an accident with a team of horses. Floyd Anderson, a distant cousin of Father, farmed the Congressman Charles B. Timberlake land near Atwood for several years.

Mr. and Mrs. Edgar Goddard stayed at the ranch for a few weeks after their arrival from Tennessee. He managed the Proctor lumber yard for a time and then went into similar work at Venango, Neb.

Some who came with full intention to go into farming shipped their belongings in a special freight car. I recall the arrival of Ralph Kiser's car at Proctor. His coming was of special interest to us because he and Mother were first cousins, and he was the first blood relative of hers who had been induced to try living in this new country.

We visited frequently in the Kiser home. Their daughter, Catherine, was about the age of Sister Edna. One Sunday we discovered they had a phonograph record of a timely song, "When the Lusitania Went Down."

### Billy Blair Camped Out

It was no minor event for us children when word came one spring that young William Blair would come out from Sterling to work on the ranch for the summer. He was just finishing high school and would enter the University of Colorado in the fall. Billy, as our parents called him, was one of two boys (the other was his brother, Harrison) who had lived in the old stone house ahead of us. His father and grandfather had been builders and developers of the place, and Father had known the family since his arrival in Logan County. Somewhere in the discussion of Billy's coming it had been agreed that he would not live in the bunkhouse, but rather would pitch a tent under an elm tree in the front yard.

I am a bit hazy as to what the ground rules were, but we children probably were under orders to stay out of the tent when Billy was not around. Whatever the arrangement, it permitted enough visits with Billy that I think of that tent on the front lawn every time I smell new canvas.

William Blair eventually won an appointment to West Point. He served in the artillery through World War II and then came back to Logan County with the rank of colonel. We renewed our acquaintance in the late 1960's, and from several pleasant visits with him and Isabel, his history-minded wife, I refreshed my memories of the Proctor ranch and gained inspiration when my interest in completing this book seemed to lag.

The day Bill went back to Sterling at the end of the summer is very clear in my memory. He was going to ride his bicycle the full 20 miles. It happened that one of the men who had been working on the haystacks was going to Sterling the same day and would be riding a motorcycle. One of the hired men suggested that Bill tie his bicycle to the motorcycle. Somebody produced a rope, and my recollection was of the two cycles going off in tandem. Interestingly enough, Colonel Blair had no recollection of that day when I reminded him of it. My guess is that the towing arrangement didn't work on the rutted and dusty roads and that he pedaled most of his way to Sterling.

One of the several ways we preserved the memory of his summer at the ranch was in the form of a gray tweed jacket that he chose to leave behind when he packed his belongings that Sunday morning. Mother had an eye for good fabrics, and she recognized in the discarded garment the material for putting a winter coat on her oldest boy. With a minimum of alteration, mainly a big cut out of the middle of the back and a shortening of the sleeves, she came up with what turned out to be a very wearable overcoat that served me, and, in turn, Brother Dave, through several winters. It was known as the Billy Blair coat until the day it finally went into the rag bag.

## Rates of Pay

The rate of a farm hand's pay varied during our 18 years on the ranch. Before the outbreak of war in Europe, $30 and $35 a month seemed to be going wages, varying with the length of time a man had been around and his reliability. Pay was usually higher for summer work than for winter work. The monthly figure went up to $45 and sometimes higher during the late teens, with some special rates for working in the wheat harvest and as haystackers. Men working in header barges during harvest earned $4 a day and more. The stackers of headed grain got as much as $9 and $10 during the harvests of 1918 and 1919, as I recall. These rates, of course, were based on the presumption that farm help also got bed and board.

## For Special Jobs

It was necessary from time to time to bring in someone with special skills. I recall at least one occasion when a surveyor occupied an upstairs bedroom. A plumber and his helper came from Sterling and stayed several days while they installed the pipes and fixtures which made a bathtub and running hot water available for the first time. On two or three occasions Mother arranged for Edgar Foy, who lived on a homestead north of Iliff, to come and put new paper on the walls of some of her rooms. These jobs usually lasted several days, and he was assigned to an upstairs bedroom.

## A Thin, Scrutable Line

I was five years old perhaps, and I had been allowed to go out among the men as they sat in the shade of their wagons waiting for repairs to the threshing machine. Someone had given me a small hammer, and I had discovered that I could pound dents into a flattened tin can. I was demonstrating. I hit the tin at one corner and it bounded away. It seemed the proper moment to repeat what I had heard men say at a moment of exasperation, and I said it: "You sonofabitch!" Somebody may have laughed, but not one young fellow in the audience. He proceeded to tell me that such words offended him, especially when spoken by one of my age. It was quite a putdown for one who had seemed just moments before to be winning admiration. This was a reversal. Most hired men had encouraged me in the broadening of my vocabulary. This nameless transient gets credit for a lesson better remembered than were the several times when Mother washed out my mouth with soap.

I was about 10 years old the time Carl Kimmel saw me catch the handrail and take a short ride on the steps of a coach as the morning passenger train pulled out of the Proctor station. We boys had just learned this trick and were getting quite a thrill from it. Carl didn't hesitate to call me aside and lecture me seriously on the dangers of jumping on and off moving railroad trains. I could lose a leg, he said, and that would be a high price to pay for a few moments of fun.

There were other occasions when hired men lectured me, but these two stand out.

The relationships between a boy on a ranch in those days and the men who did the work were unavoidably intimate. All the men—and some were boys, in level of maturity as well as years—were interesting. They were at the center of the only action that seemed to count. A fellow might seem tongue-tied as he sat silently through meals in the kitchen, but if he could stack 80-pound hay bales to the sixth tier, he was a high man in the bunkhouse and equally high with a 10-year-old observer.

Granting the intimacy of the relationship, I have to look back thankfully on the variety of men—and women—who passed our way. Some were sober and serious; some were lazy; some were ambitious. Some had considerable knowledge; some only thought they had it. Some were rude; some were gracious. Some had tact; some didn't.

Passing, as they did, in a thin and scrutable line, they exposed their individuality, their fluctuating moods, their strengths and weaknesses. Their impressions on me were a combination of what I saw and heard on my own plus what I heard by way of Father's and Mother's ready assessments of each person's good and bad characteristics.

The sum total of these impressions certainly was a wonderful preparation for future involvement with people in greater mass and a faster parade. For this I am most grateful as well as for the countless favors that hired men could and did bestow on boys who followed them around and were sometimes in the way.

# 7 A PARADE OF NEIGHBORS

## ... Including Latter-day as Well as
## Early-day Homesteaders

In 1888, twenty years before the laying out of the Proctor townsite, there were enough people in the vicinity to justify organization of a school district. The records show that 24 adults attended the organization meeting and that 17 children of school age were listed as living within what was designated as District 50.

Of the families mentioned in the 1888 records only two were still in the community when I began taking note of my surroundings. Others were still in the county, but they had left the Proctor community. It is safe to speculate that there were about as many people in the vicinity in 1888 as when we arrived in 1907. Many of the first settlers put down very shallow roots. They were there to prove up on homestead land, and with that completed, some sold out. Some who retained title to their land chose to live elsewhere. Some, of course, didn't stay long enough to establish title.

Through the early homesteading period and well into the years of my memory those who lived on the land included about as many families with temporary or transient status as of those with substantial holdings. There was a steady trickle of in-migration, but there was an out-migration, too, and when I think of neighbors and friends of my grade school years, I see more of a passing parade than an established populace.

The fluidity of what was a sparse population at best made problems for the school district, especially in its earlier years. The first school building that I recall was one that had been moved at least once, maybe twice. When I knew it, the location was on a gravel knoll at the edge of the valley about two miles northeast of the ranch buildings. It was called the Colburn School then, because most of those attending were grandchildren living with Mr. and Mrs. C. W. Colburn, about a mile and a half to the northeast of the school. The teacher of the last term at that school lived with us, and for years the room she occupied was referred to as Miss Miller's room.

There was a time when school was conducted at the ranch in the original homestead dwelling of Mrs. Christina Flemming. The teacher was Mrs. Flemming's granddaughter, Mrs. F. H. Blair.

It was not until 1910 that a decision was reached to place a school in Proctor. Sister Ruth was ready for school, and Father, in all likelihood, used his influence to locate a school nearer our home than was the Colburn School. With the completion of the North Sterling irrigation project a few years later, the district would have several one-room schools. Eventually, there was a replacement for the Colburn School and, ironically, it went to a site within a stone's throw almost of the old Colburn place, from which children had walked a mile and a half to the former location.

Mother always said she could count on the fingers of one hand all the women with whom she had any contact for the first three or four years she was on the ranch. One was Mrs. Phil Dolan, living between Proctor and Iliff and thus on the route to Sterling. The others were Mrs. J. W. Ramsey and Mrs. C. W. "Grandma" Colburn, both of whom had attended that first school meeting in 1888 and were the only women who could offer much assurance that the community was one Mother eventually would get used to.

J. W. Ramsey had been a part of the early movement of people from the Greeley vicinity to Logan County. He worked for one of the large cattle outfits for a time and then took a homestead along the South Platte about three miles downstream from the site of Proctor. His wife had come to the Greeley vicinity with her parents in the early days of the Union Colony. The tall cottonwoods around their home were visible from the second story windows of our house and the place was something of a landmark.

The Ramsey home was spacious and comfortably furnished. It included, among other refinements, a piano, and one of the Ramsey daughters was Sister Ruth's first piano teacher. Mother had arranged for me to take lessons also, but when Father declared there would be no relief from whatever duties I was then responsible for in the barns and fields, I begged off.

My first recollection of formal observance of the Fourth of July was a picnic under the trees east of the Ramsey house. Mr. and Mrs. Ramsey sponsored these neighborhood affairs for several years, and through them our family got acquainted with several families from Crook and vicinity. There were probably not more than 50 persons in attendance on any occasion, but for the time and place that was quite a crowd.

The Colburns had taken up their homestead in about 1875 and were the real pioneers of the community. Mr. Colburn, a Union Army veteran, had used stone from an outcropping on the place to build the two-story house, a low barn and a large corral. In summer there were always flowers around Mrs. Colburn's front door, but what fascinated us children as much as anything was the fact that the family burial ground was within view at the back of the house.

Mr. and Mrs. Colburn had taken over the rearing of five grandchildren following the death of their daughter, Mrs. George Flock. From the youngest of these, Margaret, I learned about firecrackers. I was with Mother on a visit to Mrs. Colburn a short time after July Fourth, and Margaret got out her leftover fireworks and introduced me to what seemed one of the real wonders of the world.

My most vivid memory of the Colburn place—and Brother Dave seems to have been equally affected—relates to the death of Mr. Colburn. When it came time to go to the funeral, which was held in the home, a wet snow was falling, and Father hitched one of the heavy work teams to the surrey for what he expected to be a rather rough trip.

The open casket in the small, crowded room, the medals and ribbons on the blue G.A.R. uniform, the face in repose—these I can see as clearly as if the event had been yesterday. This was one of my first encounters with death, of course, and I think it would have left less of an impression if it had not been for the dreary weather outside and my recurring speculation as to final movement of this kindly old neighbor to a hole in the ground that was probably half full of snow. If there was a graveside service, I was not allowed to observe it.

One of the Flock girls, Marion, married Charles Von Brecht, who had come to Colorado as a teen-aged orphan and for whom Father acted as guardian. Another, Saloam, married Bill Pigeon, and I recall distinctly the day Mother read us the report of the wedding in either the Iliff or the Sterling newspaper. The reporter had made the inevitable reference to a "Flock of Pigeons" and Mother wanted all of us to enjoy the humor.

The Pigeon family lived on a homestead near the head of Skinner Draw. Only one other member left a definite impression on my memory, and that was Bill's brother, known as Shorty. I recall seeing him not more than once, but his occupation as a clown with the Sells Floto circus gave him the status, more or less, of a celebrity. Father seemed to time his stops at the Pigeon place just right to catch Shorty on visits there. He told once of seeing a trained pig that was part of Shorty's act and, on another occasion, of a rooster that had replaced the pig.

Among events marking the emergence of Proctor as a trading center was the building of bridges across the channels of the South Platte immediately south of the townsite. Upstream about three miles from the bridge on the opposite side of the river was the headquarters of the Sam Rice ranch, and downstream from the bridge a couple of miles or more were some improvements on another large tract of Rice land. While Rice cattle, roaming the sandhills to the south, had come to the river to water at a point near where the bridge was built, some of the land in this vicinity had remained open to homesteading or acquisition by other means. The presumption was that Sam Rice, following a general practice of early ranchers, had acquired title to valuable haylands and lands essential to maintaining access to the river, but had not bothered to seek title to land nobody seemed to want. It turned out that Rice and others had overlooked many tracts that would be filed on by latter-day homesteaders. Most of these bits of land were too small and unproductive to sustain a family, but there were those who saw enough potential value to justify fencing and the erection of modest dwellings. Whether justified or not, the reputation for being antagonistic toward homesteaders or squatters was pinned on Sam Rice.

Among the early settlers on land immediately opposite the site of Proctor and pretty much in the middle of the rather vast sweep that had been considered the Rice cattle range was the Elmer Sheaffer family. The head of the family was a man of mechanical bent, and one of his accomplishments was the development of what he called a "steam bucket." He had been in railroad construction before coming to Proctor, as I recall, and with his steam bucket he was later involved in a project for the Burlington in the vicinity of Guernsey, Wyo.

The "bucket" was actually a steel scoop designed for excavating narrow cuts or tunnels. In operation, the bucket was tied to a cable that extended through a pulley near the face of the excavation and back to a steel drum on a steam traction engine of the type used for operating threshing machines. The Sheaffers called their engine "Old Betsy," and there was much talk of her around the Proctor school the first year or two of my attendance. Among other feats, she pulled herself across the bed of the South Platte, at low water, with a combination of wheel power and the power of the drum winding a cable attached to "dead men" set at the necessary intervals. Old Betsy was too heavy and cumbersome for the river bridges.

The crossing of the river was the first leg of the journey to Guernsey. It was quite a day at the Proctor siding when Elmer Sheaffer guided the big engine up a ramp and onto a flatcar. As the front of the engine started up the ramp, it cut off the driver's view, and my recollection is mainly of Mr. Sheaffer standing on the seat and turning the big iron steering wheel as the puffing monster made its ascent.

One morning during my first or second year of school, the Sheaffer children came with a story of violence at a point near the southernmost of the Proctor bridges. What they said, in effect, and what was corroborated later in the reports of adults, was that some men had accosted Elmer Sheaffer and beaten him severely. There was widespread acceptance of the charge that the attackers were employees or associates of Sam Rice.

Sam Rice had come to the county from Texas, and he seems in retrospect to have been almost a stereotype of the isolated, independent cattleman of many western movies. Now and then, two or three of Rice's men would show up at our ranch, in search of lost cattle or horses or for some other reason. Invariably, some of them would be wearing big hats, woolly chaps, high-heeled boots and jangling spurs. Sam's son Ray was a member of some of these parties. Sam Rice sold out to the Cunningham family in the early teens and moved to Denver. He came as close to being a legend as any resident of the vicinity that I can recall.

Historians have pointed out that the federal homestead laws worked in a variety of ways that probably were not anticipated by their drafters. Early cattlemen were quick to seize upon the homestead process to control strategic sites along the South Platte. J. W. Iliff was following a common practice when he arranged for employees to homestead land along the river upstream a mile or so from the Proctor crossing.

When this land was transferred by Powell and Blair to the Logan County Development Company (and later taken back by them), it included a full section which touched the river at its southeast corner. There was another contact with the river in an 80-acre tract that lay south of the section across its west half. There were on this land, therefore, two points of access to the river. But because the river flows from southwest to northeast, and section lines run with the compass, there were two triangles of solid land which lay unclaimed between ranch land and the river. As a result, it was possible for a surveyor or promoter, or somebody, to point out the availability of 160 acres in an L-shaped tract that included enough land outside the river for the kind of improvements homestead laws required. I recall a Mrs. McMurray living in a sod house on this land at the edge of the river, but the patent records show that the first private owner was Martz (or Hans) Lutzman, who lived on it for many years and harvested his little patches of hay in much the manner he had harvested hay in his native Finland.

It was a matter of record that the fence between one of his patches and one of the ranch's large wild hay fields was two or three feet out of line. His choice, rather than move the fence, was to cut the hay on that narrow strip with a scythe and rake it under the fence with an enormous wooden hand rake that was one of his favorite implements.

Another homestead, a mile long and a quarter of a mile in width, extended through the river immediately south of the Lutzman place. Its little corner of solid ground was on the south side of the river, and I recall when Louis Wiscamb, who eventually acquired title, built a tarpaper-covered dwelling on the bank of the river. I knew little about Wiscamb, but I recall that he had a son named Dewey and that Mother calculated Dewey's age after presuming that he was born while the nation was still celebrating Admiral George Dewey's victory over the Spanish at Manila Bay in 1898. Many families, Mother recalled, latched onto the name of Dewey for a year or so after Manila Bay, and her climactic comment was that one of the most offensive dogs in her home neighborhood in Tennessee had been named Dewey.

Elmer Hawkins, who had worked in the railroad switch yards in Denver, laid claim to some land that adjoined the Harmony Ditch at the point it veered away from the river directly south of the Proctor beet dump. He and a son, Edgar, lived there for intervals over a period of two or three years, and records show that he acquired title. Edgar, somewhat older than most of us, attended the Proctor school and, because of his age and his recounting of experiences in Denver, was held in some awe. Among his other accomplishments, he could drive his father's towering Rambler touring car. (It was probably a 1911 or 1912 model.) He boasted of having hit 40 miles an hour, an incredible speed, or so it seemed.

For several years there were two homes on the river east of Proctor, occupied by a father and son, John and Harvey Whitacre. The latter was a full-time beekeeper, and I recall his having been on the scene ahead of his father. The father had discovered at some stage, though, that a sizable chunk of river land that had been considered a part of the J. W. Ramsey pasture was still actually part of the public domain. He built a house and barn, both modest, on a sliver of land that jutted out from the river, and for several years rented his river tract to our neighbor, Jesse Stewart, as a summer cattle pasture. This was quite upsetting to the Ramseys.

It was my impression that Harvey Whitacre had purchased his land from a private owner. In any event, he had enough for his house and outbuildings and a sizable bee yard, plus some that extended into the river and was an addition to his father's rentable pasture. During his years in the community he cared for bees at several locations up and down the valley, including the 40 or 50 stands that occupied space within the shelter of the trees south of our house.

Mrs. John Whitacre was an accomplished pianist, and she soon found some pupils in the scattered homes that could claim a piano. She traveled behind a slow-paced black mare in a spring wagon that seemed to have an unnecessarily high and exposed seat for a woman of her age and gentility. Through heat and dust and sometimes the chill of early spring or late fall, she traveled the crude roads around Proctor, and she always was dressed as though going to tea back home in Terre Haute.

Just why Mrs. Mabel Vinacke ever subjected herself to the punishment of the two or three years she spent developing a home on a quarter-section of raw land was a question that had not been answered to the satisfaction of the community when she packed up and went back to urban living. I have presumed that the land she settled on had become available through some quirk in the homestead laws. Her attitude always was that she had to live on it to acquire title. It lay about four miles northwest of Proctor, and while within the area served by the North Sterling irrigation district, it had no water rights.

She was a widow, between the ages of 35 and 45, to the best of my recollection, and her son Billy was about the same age as Brother Dave. So far as I can recall, she hired neighbors to plow and till her land, possibly on a share basis.

She had lived at Eagle Rock, Calif., and had relatives in Denver, where she may have resided at some time. She gave every evidence of having more financial resources than most homesteaders, but she was essentially frugal and cautious in money matters. She came to Mother with many of her problems, and when they related to land or livestock, they ended up with Father. Somebody's cattle would break through her fence. A cow would become ill. She had no telephone, but she had a buggy and a reliable brown mare to pull it. Late one summer afternoon she drove across our pasture, carefully dressed, as always, with a list of emergencies on which she wanted to consult. She was wearing a hat over which she had tied a veil in

95

a rather modish arrangement.

She was on the back porch as George Trumbley, a somewhat garrulous hired man, arrived from the cowbarn with the evening's milk. Noting her headgear, he asked, "Are you a member of the Sisters of Charity?" "I'm not, but I could use the Sisters of Charity with some of my problems," she quickly replied, and then continued to unload her worries on Mother or Father, or both.

Mrs. Vinacke's brown mare gave birth to a colt shortly after she started traveling the roads between her home and Proctor, and I can hardly recall seeing her in her buggy when the colt was not tagging along. As a lively yearling he would race back and forth as his mother plodded along ahead of Mrs. Vinacke in her buggy. He explored every puddle and washout along the way, it seemed, and almost always he would walk through or jump the ditches rather than cross bridges and culverts on the grade.

By the time Mrs. Vinacke decided to leave the farm, the colt was as big as its mother, but it was still accompanying her on her buggy-pulling expeditions. I hadn't thought much about the colt's future until Father said he was buying him and that someday he might make a good saddle horse for me. By this time he was two years old and his coat had turned from brown to a brownish roan. He had a dark brown mane and a splash of white on his face. Jim Talbott, working on the ranch at the time, named him Chigger, rode him a few times and then left for Tennessee. Father instructed me to finish the breaking, which I did, and it was the beginning of my finest relationship with a horse.

Chigger was considerably more spirited and quick of foot than his mother. Word was that his sire was a quite outstanding animal, but I had never seen him. By the time he was four years old, Chigger was as steady and reliable a horse as I have ever ridden. He was not as fast as Old Bird, Father's favorite horse at the time, and some who rode him insisted his walk was rough.

He had one characteristic, though, that was unmatched among our saddle stock; he was sure of foot. This very well could have come from his impatient capers up and down the roads and through and over ditches and mudholes while accompanying his mother and Mrs. Vinacke and their buggy. A professional trainer once told me that breeders of fine riding horses often make the mistake of keeping them confined to smooth pasture land where they never get the feel of soft or rough ground or develop an eye for ditches, rocks, logs and other obstacles. In any event, it soon was apparent that Chigger could jump irrigation ditches and other obstacles without losing a stride, and he learned to move quickly to head off an animal that might try to break from a herd we were driving or holding. And he always seemed to perform for me with a bit more verve and determination than for anyone else.

One Sunday morning in the spring, about 1920, we observed a man on horseback among our cows in the pasture northwest of the barn. It turned out to be District Judge H. E. (Hal) Munson, who spent many weekends and vacations on his farm about three miles north of the ranch.

He had come in search of his red Shorthorn bull, which we had recognized among our cows a day or two before. The bull, however, was happy where he was, and Judge Munson, a man of some weight, and the light horse he was riding were no match for the bull's evasive tactics. The judge asked if I might be able to help him get the bull through the gate of our pasture, and I welcomed the challenge. The judge lent me a length of buggy whip, as I recall, and Chigger and I started working the bull from among his new-found friends. He broke away two or three times perhaps, but finally we got him on a line for the gate and never gave him a chance to turn. Once in the road, with fences on both sides, it seemed the bull could be handled by the judge alone, but for good measure, I hurried the animal over a hill and out of sight of our cattle. At that point the bull was foaming a little at the mouth and amazingly tractable, and the judge insisted he could handle him for the rest of the trip. Before dismissing me, though, he took a $5 bill from his pocket. I don't recall how much I protested accepting so large a fee, but ultimately I took it, and it was probably the most I was to receive for an hour's work until I was approaching middle age. There was the chance the judge came up with the only bit of money he was carrying. But I always liked to think that he recognized some virtuosity in Chigger's ability to cut a bull from a herd of friendly cows and make him like it.

It seemed entirely proper in 1924, when I had gone to college and Father was preparing to leave the ranch, that Chigger should be sold to Jim Talbott, the first man to ride him and the only person who seemed to share my affection for him. Jim was then living on a farm near Iliff, and Chigger was his until he and other horses strayed onto the Union Pacific right of way one night and were hit by a train. Death in this manner seemed quite out of character for a horse that always had seemed to know just when to jump.

This is supposed to be a chapter dealing with people rather than horses, but horses figured prominently in our relationship with people. Consider the day of the Ramsey sale. That was a big event; the livestock, the machinery, certain household items and all the "articles too numerous to mention"—as the sale bills always related—were to go at auction. The Ramseys were moving to Denver. There was the usual free lunch at noon, so just about everybody would be there. Brother Dave and I had our parents' consent to leave school at noon. Al Stewart, my classmate through most of the grades and all of high school, had the same privilege, and we were to have our horses in the school barn and be ready to ride to the Ramsey place and perhaps get there while the free lunch was still available.

For reasons I can't recall I got permission to leave school about 15 minutes before noon to run an errand. Again for reasons I don't recall I mounted Rex, Dave's horse, instead of Chigger. The younger children, excused earlier, were at the front of the school and there was the usual impulse to stage a fast getaway. Before even putting my feet in the stirrups, I kicked Rex in the ribs and dashed around the schoolhouse. Rex was a no-nonsense animal that had thrown Dave and left him with a bad wrist. I soon found myself grabbing for the saddle horn and reins, but it was too late. I quit rolling when I hit the base of a hitching post. Rex, meanwhile, galloped down the road toward home.

I nursed my aches till Dave and Al came out, and after a quick conference, we decided to leave it to some hired man to admit Rex to the barn. We would double up on one of the two horses remaining and head for the free lunch. I soon discovered it was more comfortable to ride behind Dave or Al and hang both feet over one side of the horse than to ride in the saddle. I was hurting everywhere, it seemed, but there was some relief in sitting sideways, even on the gallop. I could have ridden home from the sale in the car with Father and Mother, but I didn't want to admit having been thrown in the school yard in the presence of children whose parents had complained to Mother that Al Stewart and I were inclined to be bullies and show-offs when riding our horses to and from school. Because of my misadventure with Old Rex I can look back on the Ramseys' last day at their ranch as one of my longest and most miserable. Luckily my injuries were mainly superficial and I was back in full action in a couple of days.

Al Stewart was the youngest of six children in the Jesse Stewart family, whose land lay along the edge of the valley immediately west of our ranch. The Stewarts came into the community a few years after we did, and I don't recall that Al and I had anything in common until I started to school. He was ahead of me that first year, but when the next year started, the teacher, W. L. Strickland, found it convenient to let me skip the second grade and move into the third with Al and one or two others. We were together through the eighth grade and four years in high school at Sterling.

Other boys of our age bracket came and went through the Proctor school years, but Al and I were the only pupils in the graduating class of 1920. We were different in many ways, but we managed an amazingly functional camaraderie. His was a Catholic family; mine was Presbyterian. He was older, larger and stronger, and I may have been more tactful and resourceful because of the futility of any thought I could dominate him physically. He could lift things I couldn't touch, and he was trusted with holding down one end of a calf at branding time long before I was. He was a good horseman, in a strictly conventional sense, but I was the undisputed champion when it came to such things as standing behind the saddle or emulating some of the other stunts of the trick riders at the county fair. He made the football team in high school. I finally managed to earn a letter in track. And so we offset and complemented each other through a dozen or more years. Al didn't take college preparatory work in high school, but after three years at home he decided to study civil engineering. He spent a semester in the preparatory division at Hastings College the year I was a senior there, and then went on to get his engineering at the University of Wyoming. He had taught a rural school and raised a couple of good beet crops, and he brought a new Model-T Ford coupe to Hastings that was available to me on a couple of occasions when I needed transportation for a new girl friend. Some Hastings contemporaries wondered how I could exercise such influence on the newcomer. They didn't know we had been influencing each other since the third grade, and we were still telling each other what we thought and planned. It was Al's observation during one conversation about borrowing his car that the girl who presided over his table at the college dining hall was more to his liking than the one I was dating, and he wondered about my judgment in not having carried further a brief freshman-year romance with her. His opinion may have had some weight, because in the end his choice was the one I married. This came up in one of the few reminiscing sessions we had after college, just a year or two before his death in early middle age.

Since Al Stewart came into this narrative on horseback, more or less, I can perhaps justify another story that involved him and a horse. Our final years in grade school were the post-war years when the prices of many things, including horse hides, were high. We had skinned a horse or two and the returns were such that we were looking for more horses to die and the permission of their owners to skin them.

Word came that a horse belonging to Basil Fox, a newcomer to the neighborhood, was sick and "down" in a field immediately south of the Stewart place—a field that was rented at the time by my Uncle Bob Hamil.

Al brought daily reports of the animal's condition, and we agreed that almost surely it would die before the next Saturday. (We needed a Saturday for the job we had in mind, because the evenings were short and we both had chores at home.) Al brought word that somebody was carrying water to the horse, but that there were no signs it was eating. But one Saturday passed, and the horse was still alive. We couldn't believe that any horse in such condition would live beyond another Saturday. That day came, and at about 10 a.m., Al rode to our house and, somewhat disgustedly, informed me the horse was still alive. What should we do? We decided to take matters into our own hands. I would get Father's .32 caliber revolver, and we would shoot the horse and skin him that day. After all, a horse that had been on his side for almost three weeks should be put out of his misery. I got the gun and a couple of cartridges, and we set forth. We decided en route to stop at the Stewart home for the noon meal. Our story was that we were going into the field to see if the horse was dead, and if it was, we might skin it and settle with Mr. Fox later. But just about the time we sat down for lunch heavy snowflakes started falling. The snow persisted, and Al's parents vetoed our suggestion that we go on with our plan to visit the horse. What was bothering me all this time was the growing weight of that revolver in my overalls pocket and a suspicion that somebody surely had spotted the bulge and the sag. It seemed to make noises when I walked and when it bumped the seats or arms of chairs. I suggested going home, but Al's parents insisted I wait out the storm. Finally, I got away, and over Sunday I concluded that if there could be as much worry and anxiety over our ill-fated plot, when nothing had happened, what horrible consequences there might have been if the weather had been clear and we had gone through with the plan. When we got our heads together on Monday, we were in full agreement that the whole idea was wrong and that we'd wait for the horse to die. Strange thing, though, the brute lived, and every time I saw it switching flies in the corner of the Fox pasture during the next summer I had queer feelings—a mixture of compassion, I suppose, along with some guilt and a kind of resentment against the animal for having contributed to a situation in which I seemed to look worse in retrospect with each passing day.

From Basil Fox's horse to Basil Fox himself: He had come from the Chicago area. His home was a tiny house on a quarter section immediately to the east of Mrs. Vinacke's. The logic of his being there seemed no better than hers. His farming activity was limited, and he seemed all the while to be filling time rather than launching a career. A bachelor when he arrived, he returned to Illinois or Indiana to get married, but within two or three years, to the best of my recollection, he and his wife had moved on. I remember him as an interesting conversationalist. He had attended college, possibly Notre Dame. In any event, he seemed knowledgeable of football and such things as an over-supply of civil engineers he had noted on a visit to Arizona.

In 1916 the Development Company sold 160 acres of land to John Barney of Monticello, Iowa. This was against Father's wishes, I am confident, because it meant cutting about 100 acres out of a vast alfalfa field he had spent nine years developing. As part of the deal, the company built a modest house and a barn for the buyer.

The Harmony ditch angled through the Barney land, and the 50 or more acres below it were wet and alkaline and usable only for pasture. Within a year or two after Barney took over, his better land below the mouth of a small draw was showing seepage from North Sterling irrigation, and a drainage ditch had to be cut through his land and ranch land above it.

John Barney rode out in the railroad car that carried household goods, some implements, three horses and a large long-haired dog. The dog got tired of waiting for the rest of the family to arrive and disappeared. Mrs. Barney, I faintly recall, insisted she and the children spotted the dog on the railroad right of way somewhere in Nebraska as they were coming out by passenger train. In any event, it showed up back at Monticello several months later.

Among the three horses the Barneys brought was a blind mare named Molly that was amazing in her willingness to strike out at a fast trot with nothing but the driver's messages through the lines to tell her about curves in the road, rough spots or obstacles. Within a matter of weeks, that mare had memorized the road between the Barney place and Proctor, and Mrs. Barney, a thin, restless woman, averaged almost a trip a day. There was no buggy horse in the community that could approach the mare's speed, and there was speculation she could have run with the best in the harness races at the county fair.

The cards were stacked against John Barney almost from the beginning. Behind a jovial demeanor were the worries about the debt on a farm that was uneconomical to start with, the demands of a growing family and, after 1920, the postwar agricultural depression. He started looking for ways to augment his income and made the mistake of going into the manufacture and sale of alcohol when prohibition was at its height.

In this new sideline he took full advantage of what had happened to his land at the point water had started flowing across it from North Sterling seepage. The growth of sweet clover and weeds provided a cover for a still. And the steady flow of cold water was ideal for condensing the alcoholic vapors. We boys quietly cased the operation after hearing reports that Father also knew about it and was pondering his next move. Through a mass of weeds that stood perhaps seven feet high, somebody had trampled paths and open spaces that gave the area a very business-like appearance. There were several barrels of mash, with dead grasshoppers and crickets very much in evidence on the surface. The still was fueled from a pressurized gasoline tank, and the condensing coils ran perhaps 50 feet through the flowing water to a point far enough downstream that they could drain into a jug that was set in a hole at one side. What bothered Father, quite obviously, was the fact that while John approached his operation through the high weeds on his own property, the major equipment was beyond his fence, on ranch land. Father was tight-lipped about matters of this kind, but in due time the still and mash barrels had been removed from the original site. How much longer John engaged in any phase of the liquor business is lost to my memory, but eventually he was arrested, convicted and sent to prison. The story was that he had developed a rather select clientele in Sterling and that his deliveries were disguised as eggs. There would be a layer of eggs over a cluster of quart jars.

The family, including five or six children, broke up and left the farm, and I heard very little about any Barneys until the late 1940's when I renewed acquaintance with Andrew, the oldest son. We were living within a mile of each other in St. Louis. He had spent some time as a professional boxer, then got into the service station business. Later he operated a wood-working shop and appeared to be quite successful. The father, he informed me, had remarried, returned to farming in Iowa and had known comfortable prosperity in his final years.

During World War I the Postoffice Department established a rural delivery route out of Proctor. This embraced a roughly rectangular area on the left side of the river, extending about five miles east and west and 10 miles or more north and south. Some patrons were in the normal trade zones of Iliff, Crook, Peetz and Sidney, Neb., and for them the postoffice address was about their only link with Proctor.

Shortly after the route was laid out, Roy Mason became the carrier, and he continued in that service until his retirement in 1959. While I have no confirming statistics, I can say with considerable confidence that he and Lee Lamb, the long-time postmaster, were the two men with longest terms of service to any of the institutions of Proctor. They saw it through some of its rise and most of its decline.

The oldest of the four Mason children, Hubert, was younger than Brother Dave, but this did not deter him from joining the two of us in countless work or play situations. For him there was generally more happening at the ranch than in Proctor. He showed up unannounced on countless Saturday mornings during the school year. If we were working, we were quick to utilize whatever effort he could contribute. We taught him to ride and took him with us on many cattle driving assignments. He went home with us often after school, helped with the chores and then walked the mile back to Proctor for supper with his family.

Dave and I took full advantage, I am sure, of Hubert's desire to please. One of his many concessions was to let me practice on him while learning to cut hair. What he got, of course, was hardly reflective of any special skill, because it was a close clip, all around.

Other families with boys lived for short times in and around Proctor and, invariably, they found the ranch, with its trees, corrals, livestock, machinery, barns and sheds, the most interesting spot in the whole community. But Hubert Mason was the outside boy most seen around the ranch from the time he was no more than seven until he was ready for high school.

The Proctor postoffice was closed in December, 1963, and its records were transferred to the Iliff office. Through the courtesy of the Iliff postmaster, Cecil Hofmann, I obtained a copy of the names of all persons who received registered mail at Proctor through the years 1909 to 1918, inclusive.

I found many familiar names in the list of 286. But in some respects this struck me as a sort of rollcall of the forgotten. On subsequent readings and after checking some names with Brother Dave and others, I began to link more names with faces, events, places and situations. Without that list I probably would not have undertaken the writing of this chapter.

First name on the 1909 list is Forrest G. Salisbury. I went with Mother once to visit a Salisbury family at a modest home on the side of a hill that was referred to as a "dugout."

Ludwig Harrach got mail in 1911. He was the head of a large family and lived in a stark, two-story house at the top of a hill overlooking a big bend in the North Sterling ditch where it crossed Skinner Draw. The oldest of the Harrach sons, Ed, farmed in the Proctor vicinity for several years and then went to Grant, Neb. Another, Henry, raised the first wheat crop on a quarter section of land that Father acquired on his own, for $14 an acre in about 1914. When the wheat was ready to harvest, World War I was on and Henry was in uniform. He got a special furlough to come home and cut his wheat. Edna Harrach helped Mother with housework for a season, and another daughter, Helen, married Peter Ottosen and lived for many years on a farm that adjoined two sections of pasture land where ranch cattle grazed each summer.

Peter Sturbaum lived south of the river, east of the Elmer Sheaffer place. During the war the family spent a year or more at Bremerton, Wash., where Mr. Sturbaum worked in the shipyards. There were four Sturbaum children, Lawrence, George, Izetta and Myrtle. All four attended the Proctor school at least one year, and George, who was near my age, probably was there more than one year. We saw quite a bit of Mr. Sturbaum and the two boys one summer when he contracted to handle the stacking of a considerable portion of our hay crop under a contract arrangement of some kind. A brother of Mr. Sturbaum ran the meat market in Iliff for many years.

William (Bill) McBride is on the 1912 list. He had come west as a boy and worked for several years for big cattle operators in the Nebraska Panhandle. It was said that in his prime he could ride bucking horses with the best. I recall the summer when he lived in the bunkhouse at Uncle Bob's place and was faced with the problem of getting Jack Sheaffer, one of his fellow workers, up in the morning to help with the chores. He ended up with a regular ritual of going outside and picking up a quart whiskey bottle that had lain all night in the wet grass. This he would place between the bare legs of the sleepyhead and then duck out the door.

Lee Koontz got registered mail in 1912. He was another ex-cowboy about whom there were many stories as to prowess with bucking horses. He lived for a time on the Drag-X ranch near Crook. His wife was a daughter of Mrs. Ella Walker, who managed our kitchen one summer.

Pete Korwelt, on the 1911 list, worked some on the ranch but struck out as a farmer in his own right and was for many years the operator of the farm near Sterling where W. S. Hadfield had pitched his tent and established himself as the first permanent settler in the county.

Peter's brother, John, was the only hired man on our ranch ever to be bitten by a rattlesnake. He was irrigating at the time, and the snake's fang penetrated a heavy rubber boot. I was awakened from a nap on the living room couch by Father's rather anxious tones in a telephone call to the doctor at Iliff. I followed him as he cut a length of binder twine from a ball in the engine house and joined John at the horse watering tank where the latter had been cooling his aching foot, apparently. I observed a spot of blood on the big toe as Father tied the twine around it and helped John into the buggy to which somebody had hitched Old Nugget, our most reliable horse for this kind of trip.

Acting on the doctor's advice, Father had obtained a bottle of whiskey from Mother's medicine closet, and John took a heavy swig before the buggy started. There was speculation later as to just how long it took Old Nugget to cover the nine miles to Iliff, but the details of the trip on which Father seemed to dwell most had to do with his having to drive while at the same time holding John in the seat. The man was manageable, as Father put it, but quite indifferent toward the possibility of falling between the wheels. In any event, the emergency treatment, plus what the doctor could do, saved John from any serious consequences, but he remained in Iliff under the doctor's care for several days.

Tom McGinley lived on the western edge of the mail route, and the McGinleys tended to look more to Iliff than to Proctor as a community center. They were friends of Mrs. Ella Walker, and the summer she was at the ranch she arranged for their son, Dan, to visit for a day or two. He was about my age and the thing I remember about him is that he could stand on his head. That was enough to start me practicing, and some 60 years later it was one of the few remaining skills of my boyhood that could elicit admiring words from a couple of grandsons.

There was a second Dan McGinley, brother of Tom and uncle of the Dan I knew. He and his family lived north of Iliff. I saw little of the Dan McGinleys, but there were reports that their daughter, Phyllis, a bookish type, was a bit beyond the general run of farm girls of the county.

I wish I could say I really knew Phyllis McGinley when, at the age of 12, following her father's death, she and her mother moved to Utah. But I can't. I'm not sure I ever saw her. I remembered the name, though, when it began to show up in the *New Yorker* and other magazines to which she became a regular contributor. In 1965, after she had been at the White House as one of President and Mrs. Johnson's special guests for a festival of the arts, *Time* magazine ran her picture on its cover. I couldn't refrain from chiding her a bit in an article I wrote for a company publication. It seemed to me that if she had lived at Proctor, as I had, she could not have been as disparaging as she was in her comments to *Time's* reporter about Iliff. For us a trip to Iliff was a great experience—a trip to the outer world almost. I sent her a copy of my article, and she came back with a gracious letter.

Among those who got registered mail in 1912 was Frank W. Waterfield. I associate him with a big string of horses and several wagonloads of dirt-moving equipment. He made his headquarters at Proctor while working on some project nearby. He could have been building roads. More than likely, he had a contract to build ditches that were part of the North Sterling irrigation development.

Frank Waterfield probably never knew it, but his name lived at Proctor for some time after he had gone to the sites of other contracts. He was a tall man of more than ample girth, and he seemed to come to mind whenever any of the grade-school set (and some adults) wanted to make a point of somebody's size or protruding stomach.

Outfits such as his were quite common during the years of North Sterling construction. While there was at least one steam shovel operator among the contractors, most of the ditch work was done with horses and mules and scrapers and wagons.

The horse-and-mule outfits were big buyers of hay and grain at a time when Father usually had these to sell. As a matter of fact, he took long excursions on horseback to call at the various construction camps, sometimes to collect on earlier sales. The crews lived in tents or in shacks on wagon wheels, with one such shack usually called the cook house. Father came back from one of his visits with a rather hairy story about a midday meal at one of these camps that seemed to be a contest between the men and the flies as to who got to the food first. I recall his describing how the fellow next to him skimmed flies off his coffee.

One of these contractors, with some time between jobs, was allowed to line up his gear in a corner of a small pasture about 300 yards from our house. The couple living in the cook wagon continued to occupy it, and in due time I became acquainted with their daughter, who was perhaps a year or so older than I.

One day she led me on an excursion that ended up with our concealing ourselves in an empty enclosed water tank that was part of the load on one of the several wagons. There, in the dark, this young miss of five or six years was on the way to teaching me some things I had never known about girls when her mother yanked the lid off the tank and ordered us to get elsewhere.

Frank A. Miller is shown as a recipient of mail in 1915. He and Mrs. Miller had come from Fullerton, Neb., and their farm northeast of Proctor was distinguished by one of the larger barns of the area. Whether they planned to do so from the start, I cannot say, but in a short time they had converted the loft of that barn into one of the more popular dance halls of the county. Dances were held regularly, and patrons drove from as far away as Sterling. Their success with a dance hall as a sideline to farming was a factor, I am sure, in the decision of the Frank Clevengers to build on their farm, about three miles northwest of the Millers', a one-story structure that was used for little else but dancing.

The 1915 registered mail list includes the names of R. R. Dollarhide and Charles J. Gordon. The former, I am certain, was a Union Pacific agent. There was an agent named Gordon, also, but I am not sure about his first name. Both operated from a converted boxcar, painted yellow. With the opening of a rather ornate station building, with built-in living quarters, the agent was Glenn Davis, whose sister-in-law, Norah McGuire, came from Hoxie, Kan., to be our teacher in my final year at the Proctor school.

The name of Reynolds shows up frequently in the list. The head of the family lived for a time on Skinner Draw, and one of the daughters, Lucille, who had grown up at Shelton, Neb., was our teacher in 1917-18. A son came from Shelton to operate the Proctor garage and another daughter, Mrs. Will Francis, and her husband and five children occupied the hotel for several years.

The Correll family was another with several adult members. The patriarch of the clan, so to speak, developed a neat farmstead on the edge of what we had known as Simpson Draw. Mr. Correll, with an interesting mixture of good word sense and family pride, proclaimed Simpson Draw to be Coral Creek, and the name stuck to the point that a new school was officially called Coral Creek School. On land immediately adjacent to the Colburn homestead, it was, in effect, a direct descendant of the school which once bore the Colburn name, but it was a mile and a half away.

The Gentry family came into the community at about the same time as the Corrells, and one of the Gentry boys married Cecil Correll, who with her brother, Forrest, had attended school at Proctor the first year after their arrival. Forrest played the violin, and this inspired me to invest $7 in the cheapest violin then offered through the Montgomery Ward catalog. Forrest gave me a lesson or two, and I practiced some, but my flimsy fiddle found its way into the more adept hands of a hired man and he, in turn, left it lying on a bed in the bunkhouse where one of his fellow residents sat on it and crushed it beyond repair.

The C. W. Colburns had come to Colorado from Weeping Water, Neb. A young Englishman they had known came out later from Weeping Water and took up a homestead not far from the Colburn place. His name was Fred Gothorp, and one story was that he was a rival for the hand of the Colburn daughter, Dolly. It turned out, though, that Dolly married George Flock, and Fred Gothorp married a girl in Nebraska and continued to live at Weeping Water after proving up on his homestead.

Eventually, the Gothorps settled permanently on the home-

111

stead and developed it under North Sterling irrigation. Fred Jr., several years older than Sister Ruth and I, attended school at Proctor with us for at least one term.

The Gothorps occupied their land for many years, as did some of the other early families. Many others may have had such intentions, but with the first adversity they became discouraged and started looking for more attractive opportunities elsewhere. The latter-day homesteaders were for the most part transient by intent. Some who came with limited means and failed to make it as dryland farmers had records of failure behind them, in Nebraska, Kansas, or some other state to the east. Students of demographics would probably find that Proctor was among countless other communities in the Great Plains that were way stations on the routes of tens of thousands who originated in central states and ended up in California or the Pacific Northwest.

The opening of new land to irrigation under the North Sterling system contributed much to the in-movement between 1910 and 1920. The growing of sugar beets, in fact, made for a sizable transient population.

Several Japanese families came to the vicinity to do field work or to grow beets. The 1913 mail list includes the names of Yuku Ono, W. Yasuda and H. Tomita. The last named rented land from the ranch, and was referred to as "Mr. Tomato." One Sunday afternoon he rode up on one of his field horses for a conference with Father. When he got ready to leave, his horse started bucking just as he got himself firmly seated in the saddle. For a work horse the animal put on quite a show, and "Mr. Tomato" soon was rolling in the dust. He got up, gave us a forced smile, which somebody said was really a demonstration of the fact that he had lost none of his several gold teeth, and headed off to catch his horse. It was Father's contention that some of the men from the bunkhouse, itching for some break in the Sabbath monotony, had placed a cockle burr under Mr. Tomato's saddle. If that was the case, this was one time a burr under a saddle meant more to me than a figure of speech.

There were others who came to tend and grow beets, but they are saved for a special chapter. Some others who might have been mentioned here as being in the passing parade through Proctor get attention elsewhere, also.

Beet Dump

# 8. THE ROOSHINS CAME

## . . . And They Also Overcame

In June of 1972 I attended the third annual meeting of the American Historical Society of Germans from Russia at Boulder, Colo. I was there to learn more about the ethnic minority I knew best while growing up in Logan County. What I witnessed at Boulder was the stirring of interest in a people's heritage after two full generations when the idea had seemed to be that the less one knew or told about his ancestors, the better.

The picture came into easy focus for me, because I could recall when German-Russians in Colorado were subjected to a sort of second-class citizenship. I knew them as the butts of neighborhood jokes and as people somewhat derisively referred to as "Rooshins."

The bright side of the story is that they did not stay down long. Still, they seemed to deprive themselves of their rightful place in history and literature by being so preoccupied with throwing off a stigma of their heritage that they almost forgot the heritage itself. And so the American Historical Society of Germans from Russian was formed in the late 1960's to help amend some attitudes and dig up facts that would make German-Russians proud of their history and accomplishments.

The story of these people has strong agricultural overtones. Their ancestors went to Russia from Germany in the eighteenth century on invitation of Catherine the Great. She was looking for able and thrifty farmers to develop raw land along the lower Volga and around the Black Sea. The czarina's offer included freedom from military service, freedom from taxes and an amazing freedom to live as Germans in the depths of Russia.

In less than a century these people had made the steppes bloom, so to speak. But in 1871, the Russian government withdrew the special privileges they had enjoyed, and the movement to America was on. Some of the first landed in Kansas. They included Mennonites, who brought Turkey Red wheat and helped start that state toward becoming the greatest winter wheat growing area in the world. In the long run, the Mennonites from Russia were far outnumbered by Catholics, Lutherans and others who were also reacting to the czar's new rules. Some went to Canada, some to South America, but the largest number chose the United States. As descendants of men and women who had braved the wind-blown Russian steppes, they were not awed by the prospect of settling in open, treeless areas. And it was in such areas that U. S. railroads were promoting settlement.

One of the first groups from the Volga region went to Hays, Kan. Others from the Volga landed in east-central Nebraska. Those coming from the Black Sea region tended to favor the Dakotas. Many who came after the turn of the century went farther west, and for the early years of the sugar beet industry in Colorado, the Nebraska Panhandle and elsewhere, they provided the principal supply of hand labor for thinning, hoeing and topping.

These agriculturally-oriented people headed, naturally, for rural areas, and they were content to do hand work in the fields until something better came along. Relatives and neighbors who left Russia in the 1870's and 1880's had arrived in the United States in time to find cheap government or railroad land and had become farmers in their own rights, without having to go through the apprenticeship of migrant labor. The Great Western Sugar Company was a factor, of course, in guiding many of the late arrivals to the South Platte Valley, where it was helping farmers get started in the production of beets.

There was a movement of German-Russians in and out of the Proctor community for most of our years there. Some who came just prior to the outbreak of war in Europe, in 1914, were just a few weeks from their landing in New York or some other port. They wore old-country clothes and could speak little if any English. Others had been in the U.S. for a few years.

My first recollection of a boy of my own age with whom I played frequently is of George Zvetzig, whose family lived in a small white house near the center of a vast stretch of alfalfa and tilled fields, including some that were devoted to beets. The father, Jacob, had learned the blacksmith trade in Russia, and my recollections have him, in leather apron, at the forge and anvil of the ranch blacksmith shop or out front with a horse to shoe.

But their home was one of the ranch's "beet shacks." These were to be found on every farm or ranch where beets were grown. On some places there were two or three of them—most with a single room. Jacob Zvetzig, with two older sons to help him, went into farming on his own near Merino before George and I were ready for school. Jacob's brother, John Zvetzig, came to Proctor shortly thereafter and operated the town blacksmith shop for at least a half-dozen years.

While the non-English-speaking children in school created special problems for the teachers, the rest of us seemed to take them for granted, and, in our own way, we helped them learn to express themselves in their new environment. I recall noting with some glee one fall that Mr. Strickland was so busy teaching new words to new pupils that he seemed to give the rest of us little time for recitation. This suited me just fine, because it meant more time for reading The Book of Knowledge and other materials in the rather skimpy case at the front of the room.

One day during my first year in school some of us smaller boys, including one of our newcomers named Mike, were tricked into entering the door of the school barn where two older boys, stationed on the beams above, greeted us with a shower of urine. I escaped damage, but Mike got it in the face and went

116

crying to his seat in the schoolhouse. We all presumed he had told the teacher what had happened, but she made no mention of the incident after we had taken our seats for the final session of the day.

It turned out that Mike, with his limited English, hadn't made it clear just what had happened. When four o'clock came and we were marching in single file past Miss Mathinson at the door, she pulled me out of line and held me till the room was empty and she could close the door. I imagined myself to be in some kind of trouble, and I am sure my eyes reflected a plea for mercy as I looked up and heard her question: "What did Jack do to Mike at recess?" I must have pondered briefly the fact that Jack was a big fellow and kind of rough and ready to get even with any tattletale. But I came through in what must have been a painfully timid tone. "He pee-ed on him," I blurted, and then broke Miss Mathinson's grip on my arm and backed out the door.

I can't remember whether Jack was punished or if there was any reason for his ever knowing that I had told on him. But I worried about what he might do if he ever found out, and I went through all sorts of agonies over having had to speak in such earthy terms to Miss Mathinson.

It was obvious, of course, that boys and girls striving to be understood in this new community were sometimes confused by the difference between expressions heard on the playground or behind the barn and what was expected of them in the schoolroom. When I was about nine, there was a new boy named Joe who had arrived in the fall with practically no knowledge of English. As were most of the youngsters in his predicament, he was extremely shy and very self-conscious in his efforts to communicate. While almost every word had to be pried out of him in the presence of the teacher, W. L. Strickland, he was beginning to talk some when with us boys of his age. We were more conscious than the teacher was of his growing vocabulary, and I am certain I was not the only one

117

who more or less anticipated an event which at the time seemed like high drama for the Proctor school.

We knew Joe had never once raised his hand to ask the standard euphemistic question: "May I leave the room?" But there he sat one morning, a bit restless in his seat, with his hand high enough that Mr. Strickland saw it. I was watching and listening, and I am certain other boys were, too.

Mr. Strickland, in his usual formal tone, asked, "What do you want, Joe?"

"Can I go by da shithouse?" came the plaintive response.

By no means a timid or retiring person in most situations, Mr. Strickland seemed for a moment to be without words. He hesitated. His face reddened. Then, in all of his typical composure, he spoke almost impatiently, "Oh, sure, Joe, go right ahead."

Then he swept the room with a glare that was an unmistakable warning against the slightest titter or smile. It is my best recollection that the whole room got the message. The incident struck me as very humorous at the time, but as I looked back on it in later years it seemed to illustrate that not the least of the obstacles we place in the paths of newcomers to our country is a sort of multiple language—some words for the barnyard, some for the drawing room, some for the all-male audience, some for the all-female, some for the pool hall, some for the Rotary Club.

The striving of the German-Russians for acceptance and a foothold in the sugar beet economy of the irrigated valleys of Colorado and neighboring states—and the ability of the beet growers to take full advantage of this striving—is illustrated by a story told by R. L. Thompson, in whose home the older Hamils lived while attending high school in Sterling.

Mr. Thompson was the manager of the cemetery, and he reviewed in detail on several occasions the burial of a young mother. At the conclusion of the grave-side service he had waited a respectable time before moving in to lower the casket and "close" the grave. He was surprised to discover that the husband of the deceased held back and was staring at the casket and groping for a final comment. The words, when they came, were quoted by Mr. Thompson about as follows: "She sure vas a goot beet vorker."

Those were strange words for a man's final tribute to his wife. Or so it seemed to Mr. Thompson, and it must have seemed that way to me, or I would have forgotten the story. We could take for granted that the man and his deceased wife were typical of thousands in the sugar beet country. We knew Mr. Thompson was talking about a "Rooshin."

Most had known no English on their arrival. But any who had spent a single season in the beet fields knew the importance of a single English word—"work"—and it didn't make much difference whether it was used as a noun or verb or in some variation on either.

When a man and his family were being evaluated as prospective contractors to handle the hoeing, thinning and topping for a season, the employing farmer made a careful count of the number of "beet workers" who would be a part of the deal. There were questions as to whether the wife and mother would go to the fields and how many children were capable of crawling on their knees at thinning time and how many could wield a knife at topping time in the fall.

Each good beet worker in a man's family was, therefore, a prime asset. When one's wife could hoe and top, and when she was willing to bring a nursing baby to the field and feed it during short breaks at the end of the rows, the family's effectiveness was greatly enhanced. Thus the young widower at the cemetery was merely striving for terminology that carried weight in the society of which he was trying to be a part.

It is ironic but entirely just, in my opinion, that the "work" for which these people drew about the only praise to come from many of the beet growers they served hastened the day when countless families that had started as stoop laborers became renters and owners of the land on which beets were grown.

Not until the 1960's was there much of an effort by their descendants to review the pain and hardship of growing up in a family that had entered the mainstreams of American life by way of the beet fields. It came out in more than one discussion at Boulder in 1972 that the hard work and the secondary status to which some felt they were temporarily assigned had the effect of making many German-Russians want to forget their origins.

One young woman from Fresno, Calif., was obviously there to fill gaps in her family history. Her mother and grandmother, she said, had refused to talk about their backgrounds, except to say that theirs had been lives of hard work.

On the other hand, some men and women—generally beyond 60 years of age—pointed with pride to the fact that they had crawled scores of miles during several seasons, thinning the seedling beets until there was only one at each select interval.

Timothy Kloberdanz, a bright young man from Sterling, was quick to remind everyone that in the annals of the beet workers of his and my home county there were cases of both adults and children who collapsed and sometimes died from overwork and exposure to the sun. Later, he made this observation in a letter:

"Though we prospered in this country, it was primarily through the efforts of parents who had died before their time and sun-blackened children who crawled through innumerable acres of sugar beets. The story of the Russian-German immigrant whose confidence in the American dream was callously exploited, and whose cultural heritage was deemed inferior by Anglo educators, will be lost in the belated applause that greets our accomplishments."

Men and women enjoying senior citizenship could recall at Boulder that there was high excitement in the spring of the year when time came to return to the beet fields. It was the custom of most families to spend the winter in town, where the husband usually could pick up work. Many beet-working families were based several hundred miles from the growing areas; some wintered in the same communities where they worked the rest of the year.

Jack Lofink of Lincoln, Neb., recalled the stir that went through the German-Russian neighborhood in Lincoln when the Burlington started assembling cars for the special train-loads that would head for the beet country each May. It was a big disappointment to him that his mother was one who chose to take in washing rather than move to the beet fields.

There was some excitement at Proctor on a spring day in 1917 when a special train let off several families that had been assigned to farms in the area. The Jacob Lebsacks and a family of Trupps had come from Hastings, Neb., and were assigned to our ranch. The Lebsacks had come from Russia just before the outbreak of war in 1914. Mr. Lebsack had worked for the Burlington in Hastings, but when he came to Colorado it was with the intention of staying, and he did. After one year he was renting a farm. Eventually he owned one. His sons and daughters grew up and launched careers of their own, some in agriculture, some in other pursuits. One son, Clarence, became owner of a feed store in Sterling. Another, John, became one of the state's most prominent cattle feeders and for seven years was president of a Sterling bank.

The Trupps went back to Hastings after one season, but an incident on the day of their arrival has stayed with me in some detail. While the Lebsacks were assigned to the "shack" nearest the ranch house, the Trupps were to work beets on what we called the "lower place," managed on a share-rental basis by Charlie Morton. Mrs. Trupp was obviously dismayed at the general state of the building that would be her abode for the summer. She spoke in German, mostly, but once she pointed to a spot that had been overlooked in Charlie's cleaning of the interior. "Chickee," she said, and what she pointed to was obviously the stain of chicken droppings. To live in a former chicken house was not to her liking, and while I was only 10, I recall a distinct embarrassment.

121

When the Amen families came to Proctor in 1914, it was not just to work beets. They came as purchasers of J. J. Skinner's sheep ranch. They planned to develop the land under North Sterling irrigation and raise beets, grain and other crops. What we had known as Skinner Draw, in due time became better known as Amen Draw.

Conrad Amen, Sr., had come from Russia in 1901, inspired in part by the advice of Conrad, Jr., who had been drafted into the Russian army. There were five other sons, and Conrad Jr. advised his father that his experience convinced him it would be good to get out of the country before any more young Amens were called.

The Amens stopped briefly at McCook, Neb., after arriving in this country. Then they went to Loveland, Colo., and in 1908 to Fruita, Colo. The need for more land than was available at Fruita prompted the deal for the Proctor sheep ranch and the establishment of several separate farming units on it. During the 1914-15 school year, the 10 Amens in our one-room school at Proctor constituted almost half the enrollment. Later they had a school almost to themselves.

The Amen and Lebsack stories illustrate, I think, the speed with which families passed through the strictly beet-worker phase. But even in their cases, the children were not emancipated immediately from the beet work when their fathers became farm owners or renters. Being able to handle field work with one's own family contributed a great deal toward a profitable crop.

It is a little hard for some people to accept hard work as an avenue of escape from poverty or deprivation. It is a little hard for me, because I fear the pitfalls of over-simplification. It does seem important, though, that we review from time to time our attitude toward the so-called work ethic. Hard work can mean pain and suffering. But it does open doors—the doors to better education sometimes. It helps keep young people away from temptation. It contributes to the habits of punctuality and responsibility. And despite hypocrisies in many situations, it brings acceptance by others and contributes to harmony in community living.

But the word "work" is subject to far broader interpretations in our time than in the days of the forlorn young husband in the cemetery. Our technical society's first need is for working people of a different type than those once required to make the sugar beet fields glisten in the August sun. It rewards those with special knowledge and special skills. But some of the reward is still reserved for those who, with all their knowledge and skill, can offer some special measures of diligence, patience and reliability.

It is a cliché of some of our social reformers that the establishment won't give up its positions of power. But the truth is that establishmentarian families and cliques and leaders in business and government are constantly looking outside for new talent with which they will share power in return for know-how and work. It was that way, really, in the beet country 50 and 60 years ago. And the German-Russians made the most of it.

\* \* \*

### Epilogue

The registration records of the German-Russian meeting at Boulder in 1972 showed 10 individuals or couples with the name of Amen, Amend, Ament or Amendt. There were four Lebsacks. There were two Amens who had lived at Proctor.

Each registrant indicated the town from which his or her family traced its Russian origin. Two towns that showed up on more than 50 registrations were Frank and Norka. I hadn't heard of these places for 30 years, but seeing them in the records brought back memories of my days on the *Daily Tribune* in Hastings, Neb. I had written Frank or Norka dozens of times in reporting the deaths of men and women born at one or the other place who had lived out their lives in a land where few people knew about things on the Volga, or cared. It so happened that

123

Hastings, where I spent 16 years, counted its German-Russians as its largest ethnic minority.

At Hays, Kan., Eureka, Ipswich, Leola, Parkston, Aberdeen, Roscoe, S. D., and other places I came in contact with German-Russians during my years with Farmland Industries. The Dakotans were proud to claim Lawrence Welk, native of Strasburg, N. D., as one whose ancestors were Germans who came to the United States by way of the Black Sea region of Russia.

# 9. MOSTLY ABOUT HAY

## . . . And Its Care and Feeding

When I think of work on the ranch, the vision is mainly of hay fields. I worked some in sugar beets, to be sure, and in wheat and barley and oats. I spent many hours on horseback. I milked cows. I fixed fence and spent long days trudging in rubber boots through muddy fields with an irrigation shovel.

But putting up hay was the activity that threaded through the whole summer. The first cutting of alfalfa came in June. Between that and the second cutting we headed the wheat. With the second crop of alfalfa in the stack, we turned to some 300 acres of wild hay. We mowed and then raked. Then we went into the field with a Dane "over-shot" stacker and buckrakes. In a matter of seven to ten days, a 100-acre field of alfalfa would be transformed from a sea of waving purple to an expanse of raw, greenish-brown stubble out of which ten to a dozen stacks would reach up to form a whole new skyline.

For the young there was a clear-cut line of advancement as a member of the haying crew. One served his apprenticeship, more or less, as stacker boy. This involved handling the team or a single horse, as the case might be, that lifted each buckrake load of hay and dumped it on the top of the rising pile. Each load was carefully spread with a pitchfork to assure a generally rectangular structure and one that would stand up against strong winds. The last few loads on each stack were piled toward the middle to bring about a sloping top that would help turn rain.

While smaller boys dreamed of the day when they could advance from handling the horse, or horses, at the stacker to the operation of a rake or mower or buckrake, there was little ambition to work on the stack. That was real man's work and nobody envied the stackers anything except the premium pay they got for long hours of tearing at tough rolls of hay, while standing knee-deep in the stuff.

There were men who seemed to enjoy this heaviest of all work in the hay fields, and memories of two of them persist in vivid detail. During one of the first summers that I worked steadily as stacker boy, the prairie hay was light, and we did most of the stacking with a one-buckrake crew. I was in charge of Old Bill, an aging gelding that was slightly underweight for a stacker horse, but a safe horse for a boy, in the sense he preferred inaction to action even in emergency situations. And the man on the stack (the rule was one man for one buckrake) was George Trumbley, a short, heavily muscled bachelor, whose permanent residence was a homestead "shack" about five miles from the ranch.

George was an individualist. He wore a full beard. He was one of the few men on the ranch who ever subscribed to his own daily paper. It was the Denver *Post*, and his devotion to it was only a whit less than his belief that California was the greatest state in the Union.

It was something of a joke around the bunkhouse that George never finished reading a single issue of the *Post*. He would drop off to sleep, with the paper draped over him. One bold fellow-occupant of the place set fire to the paper one night, and this became a sore issue with George. He could have lost his beard. He could have burned to death. The bunkhouse could have burned. Reverberations from that incident went on for months.

It soon came through to me that George was a talkative man on a haystack as well as at the kitchen table. He never seemed quite satisfied with the way Old Bill and I delivered a load of hay. We dropped it too near the front of the stack most of the time, I am sure, because Old Bill tended to let up the moment

126

he felt the load had passed dead center.

George was especially grumpy on the morning in question. We weren't "hitting it hard enough," he kept saying. He was having to drag too much hay from the front to the back of the stack. He reported the situation after each load was dumped, and his tones became increasingly provocative.

This couldn't go on indefinitely, I concluded. I'm a little uncertain as to what methods I used. Probably I excited Old Bill with a whip before we started with the next load. At the end of the run—the end of the cable, to be exact—I was out in front with my lead rope, going as fast as I could and urging Old Bill to follow.

For a few fleeting seconds Old Bill had seemed to catch the spirit of the occasion. He started in the short lunges he had developed when on a hard pull with a wagon. And he was going full tilt when we came to the end of the cable and the load was thrown across the stack.

It was always part of my story that I warned George that the supreme effort was coming up. But he apparently had given up

Hay Stacker

127

on me and hadn't bothered to stand to one side. I saw the hay rolling across the stack, and there was a moment of satisfaction. Then I saw George's fork fly into the air and caught a faint glimpse of him tumbling off the back of the stack, almost completely enveloped in hay.

He got up limping and mumbling and called a halt to the activities of the morning. The extent to which he blamed me for his accident and injury is a little vague in my memory. In any event, he pleaded a bad back and asked Father to relieve him of further work on the stack. We finished the season with George on the buckrake.

A few summers later I was operating a buckrake and pretty well in charge of the haying. The man on the stack was John Wiltein, a colorful, interesting person in ways far different from those that distinguished George Trumbley. John, a native of Finland, was some 50 years old and powerfully built. He was proud of his strength and demonstrated it now and then with such stunts as lifting the front end of a horse. John had worked in several European countries before coming to the United States. He had acquired some knowledge of German, Russian and other languages. He had bogged down, though, when it came to English, and it was a rare occasion when he put together a complete English sentence. He could rattle off the Russian, German, Finnish and Swedish counterparts of many common nouns. He mixed several languages into some of his pet phrases.

He would see a team and wagon and would ask, "Homestead man?" A "homestead man" to him was somebody who was getting by on a poor or completely unproductive piece of land—as many homesteaders had done in the neighborhood. When a man appeared with skinny horses, skimpy harness and a lightweight wagon with narrow tires, John asked no questions. He labeled the fellow a "homestead man," because with that kind of outfit he couldn't do much in the more prosperous irrigated areas of the community. John had a few aphorisms that we heard frequently. One of them was, "Poor man no goot; rich man besser." His frequent use of this statement had caused one of the hired men to name him "Besser."

John and I developed an amazing rapport. We understood each other, even though we had to coin some new words. I had heard one of his sons advise him in Finnish that it was time to top out a stack. The key word sounded like "cuckoo." The son explained later that I was pretty far off, but after I had used it on John a time or two and had illustrated with my hands, he liked the word. And for a couple of seasons he and I knew exactly what "cuckoo" meant. Nobody else did, but that didn't bother John.

He regaled me with stories about his experiences as a young man in Europe. Much seemed to have happened in Bessarabia. He would start out, "You know Bessarabia?" I would say, "Yes, I know where Bessarabia is." (Which was a bit of an exaggeration.) Then John would launch into a narrative that would include enough English words to establish the subject matter and enough foreign words to keep me in suspense. One thing about those conversations was that they required close attention on the part of both participants. The hay field was a place to learn many things, including the art of two-way communication.

In the hayfields, as in many places around the ranch, there was time to think, time to analyze one's surroundings, time to worry about matters beyond one's control. When I was eight, nine, ten and eleven and was drawing modest pay, I spent a lot of time thinking about the weather. Mine was a sort of inverse concern. It was not that I feared the damage that might result from high winds or rain. I kept looking for clouds and other signs of a break in the weather that would stop the haying for a while. I yearned for a few hours, a half day—maybe a full one—without work.

Our rains came from the west. But clouds that started gathering in that direction shortly after noon often were deceptive. They would provide a dark splotch above the horizon that I would watch intently. Then the light would show beneath them, and they would dissipate without ever having met the descending sun.

I learned in due time that clouds in the west were completely undependable if the wind was in the west. What we needed for making rain was an east wind, and when going to the field after the noon meal and seeing clouds on the western horizon, I always checked the wind direction. If the combination of clouds and wind was there, I could look forward hopefully to a break by four o'clock, maybe earlier. The mere anticipation of weather that might act up was an antidote to the normal boredom. An afternoon with clouds and shifting winds—even when there was no rain—seemed to pass much faster than one when the sky was blue, the winds were steady and the sun was hot.

Once there was rain in the air, there was always a question as to just when to break off work and head for shelter. On at least one occasion I forecast a shower that didn't develop. I was working close to home and decided to make for cover before the drops started to fall. I was admitting my rake team to the corral just as the sun came back out. Unfortunately, Father had observed my premature break, and he was waiting for me with some rather withering comments about being afraid of a few "dry clouds."

Between the ages of eight and fourteen I advanced through all the haying jobs except for working on the stack. I moved to a dump rake when Brother Dave was old enough to take the stacker horse. As I look back on those days on a rattling, jerky rake, with the rumps of two horses just beyond kicking distance, I am confident that they helped sprout the seeds of decision that ranching was not my lifetime ambition.

My graduation to the mowing machine and the buckrake, coming more or less simultaneously, was still the occasion of some rebirth of enthusiasm for putting up hay. The day Father entrusted me with a mower is much clearer in memory than the first time I risked driving two widely separated horses from the seat of a buckrake, or sweep, as we often called it. Both experiences probably came during the summer of my eleventh year.

If I left the dump rake with any regrets, the only reason was that I was giving up my aging team, Bill and Nugget. Bill had been my stacker horse for two or three summers, and Nugget had been Mother's driving horse during our first years on the ranch. Both had been on the job since the Powell and Blair era. The story was that Nugget had been a cab horse in Omaha and was sold because of defective hearing. In any event, he was inclined to interpret any loud sound as being the "whoa" of his driver. Bill had all the marks of having been the colt of a bronco mare by a Percheron stallion. Neither of the horses weighed more than 1,400 pounds when in the best of condition. They were both at least 15 years old when I started working them as a team. While they were absolutely unexcitable, they were amazingly responsive when I used them to help me learn to ride two horses at the same time. One of the stores at Proctor got in a stock of low-cut tennis shoes one spring, and I used my own money to buy a pair—for about a dollar. With these on my feet, I discovered I could stand on a moving horse and engage in all sorts of maneuvers that were impossible with leather-soled shoes. After some practice on a single saddle horse, I started standing with one foot on Bill and one on Nugget as we went from barn to field and vice versa. As my confidence grew, I began looking for situations when I could whip them into a brisk trot. We even galloped a time or two, but that was risky business. There was always the possibility one of them might stumble, but even more disastrous, I knew, would be Father's happening onto such an escapade. For one reason or another—lack of nerve as much as anything—I never reached the point of volunteering to ride in the so-called Roman races at the county fair. But I did prove that I could ride two galloping horses—old

131

ones, in harness.

There was no such thing as a safety manual around the ranch, no printed rules for this job or that. But Father had rules, and his insistence on everybody's sticking to them could very well explain the fact that I grew to manhood with all my fingers and toes and full use of my legs and arms. The very lives of all three of his sons were marvelously protected by his elementary, but stern, insistence on doing certain things according to his instructions.

One of the three or four mowing machines that were operable in 1916 was one Father would never have purchased. It was a Platner, made in Denver, and one of the prizes he won in 1914 at the National Western Stock Show with a carload of fat hogs. It had a five-foot sickle bar, rather than the six-foot bar of the heavier McCormick machines. It was light enough that my aging rake team could handle it without serious strain.

One morning Father announced I was to start mowing alfalfa in the hog pasture. It was a solo performance, with Father walking along in the rear after he had laid out the land and gone through the litany of precautions:

"Throw it out of gear every time you stop.

"Don't stand in front of the sickle bar.

"If a bunch of alfalfa sticks to the guards, stop.

"But throw it out of gear.

"Throw it out of gear. If you don't, you'll get a hand cut off, or a finger or a foot."

Once that morning, after Father had left me to myself, I forgot to kick the gear lever before starting to clean a gob of hay from the sickle bar. But Father had returned to the field without my knowing it, and the tongue lashing I got was lasting.

Another of Father's rules was that no one rode the stacker fork to the top of a stack. This dated from an event of my earliest recollections. It stayed with me probably because it involved considerable distress and excitement over two men with a lot of blood dripping over their faces. On the return of the crew to a stacking site following dinner, the two had taken positions on the stacker fork to be lifted to where they could jump into the hay. The fork was about half way to the dumping point when the cable broke, and the men were dropped to the ground. Both were laid up for a while, and their experience was enough to prompt a rule that was never broken if Father was anywhere around. I must concede that I took a ride or two to the top of a haystack and that I yielded to the pleas of a hired man on one or two occasions and gave him a ride when I was handling the stacker horse.

Of all of Father's safety rules, though, none got the repetitious drumming reserved for his instructions as to how to hitch a team to any implement or wagon that had a tongue. For unhitching the word was: "Drop the tugs first. Don't drop the neckyoke till you know the tugs are unhooked."

For hitching the instructions were reversed: "Put up the neckyoke first. Don't hook tugs when the neckyoke's down."

From his days in Tennessee and Illinois as well as from his years on the ranch, both as employee of Powell and Blair and as manager, he could recite instances of a team's running away and doing a lot of damage when frightened by the discovery that a tug was hooked and that the slightest pull sent the tongue weaving and striking one or both animals in the legs.

By the standards of the 1970's, our methods of harvesting hay were extremely costly in terms of both time and money. We put the hay into the stack on the third or fourth day after mowing. We left it there till it had gone through the "sweat" and winter had brought relief from other pressures and time could be taken for the slow process of baling.

The first baler of my acquaintance was powered by two horses. They moved in a circle at the end of a beam which was geared to a drive shaft over which they stepped on every turn. Very shortly, though, all balers on the scene were powered by a one-cylinder gasoline engine with two large flywheels as its most dominant feature and a big and bulging cast-iron water container that filled most of the space between these wheels.

Men with pitchforks pried the hay from the well-packed stacks and pitched it onto a platform from which it was fed in uniform bunches into the mow of the baler. The man on the feeding platform had to time his moves to be sure his fork was clear when the wood-and-metal "horsehead" came down to push the hay into the chamber where it was compressed, shaped and tied in a continuous series of operations.

Baled hay was hauled by wagon to railroad cars or to a storage barn. When I consider that most of the baling and shipping took place during school months, I wonder if my memory is faulty as to the amount of time I spent hauling baled hay. It seemed like an awful lot.

The extent to which a growing boy could handle a bale of hay was an accepted measure of his progress toward manhood. The bales, weighing generally from 60 to 80 pounds, were handled with hooks. One's ability to stack bales three layers high was dependent on the right use of leverage as well as sheer strength. I rather enjoyed wrestling with the bales while loading or unloading a wagon. but I hated every moment I was in charge of a team pulling a swaying load of hay out of the fields and maneuvering the wagon into position alongside a boxcar at the rail siding.

A wagon equipped for hay was called a hayrack. It was a conventional set of wheels under a wooden platform about 14 feet long and eight feet wide, with a sturdy frame about five feet high at each end. This meant that the load extended beyond the wheels, at front and back and on both sides. It meant much swaying and creaking in rough terrain and always the chance of an upset when crossing the many partly covered ditches in the hayfields. At the age of 11, 12 or 13, I was always under strain when guiding a team on the way to the barn or boxcar.

There were anxious moments always as we approached a car on the rail siding. One had to get in close or leave a gap through which somebody might thrust a leg while dragging bales into the car. For some reason I held the Union Pacific in great awe and worried much about the trouble I might face if I should get the wagon too close and rip off the door of the car or wreak some other damage on railroad property.

But my greatest anxiety when in charge of a team at the rail siding always had to do with the possibility a train might come along, scare the horses or mules and cause a real disaster. Fortunately, my teams usually were among the more docile, and by a little attention to timing we could avoid being hemmed in between the siding and the main line when the faster (and noisier) trains went through. It was, nevertheless, my practice to glance up and down the track every few minutes when responsible for a team that might be even slightly disturbed by a passing train. For me, therefore, the loading of hay into rail cars was the kind of experience that could have brought ulcers.

With the same hayracks, of course, we hauled a lot of loose hay. We stacked wild hay in the horse barn and alfalfa along long racks at several locations, for cows that calved in winter, for the steers we fattened and for the milk cows. Here again the hay had to be moved, a forkful at a time, from the field stack to the wagon and from the wagon to the stacks, or ricks, that ran for hundreds of feet along some of the feeding racks.

In the stack from which we fed the milk cows the hay was always third-cutting alfalfa, a little greener than the other cuttings, a little finer and a little firmer in the stack. As custodians of the milking operations for several years, Brother Dave and I took turns throwing down hay for the cows after we milked them. One winter I agreed to do this every evening, and I immediately undertook to lower the stack at one end by taking all my hay from this spot rather than follow the usual practice of taking off a thin layer from the full length each day. In a couple of weeks the west end of the stack was about a foot lower than the rest, and I had just what I wanted as a place to practice handsprings and flips. In due time I was running down the stack and making my flips off the ledge I had created, even with my coat and overshoes on. A year or two later I would find myself one of the two in my high school gym class who could do a flip without a springboard. The difference between the other fellow and me was that he had learned on mats in junior high gym classes, while I had learned on third-cutting hay, with overshoes on.

For Father this whole operation was an annoyance. He didn't like the idea of an uneven top on that long haystack from which the milk cows were fed. I am not sure, but I believe we never told him just why there was an especially low place on the west end of the stack that winter. He was never much for mixing work and play.

# 10. GRAIN HARVEST

## . . . Some Romance . . . Much Drudgery

The bringing in of the grain has been one of the traditional high points of the annual agricultural cycle since the earliest records of civilized man.

That it should affect people's emotions is quite natural. It is the culmination of a period marked by the whole range of human feelings—hope, fear, anxiety, suspicion, despair—each taking over at some stage in the unfolding of a typical crop year. Mix the emotional strain with the physical strain of the harvest itself, and we have a fair explanation of why memories of past harvests seem to run brighter than do those of some other events.

A farm editor-friend who wrote now and then of his recollections of life in a rural community used to argue that most people tend to overweight their recollections of such things with the cheerful and the pleasant to the point, sometimes, of rank misrepresentation. Funny thing, but there was some of this exaggeration in advance of the harvest-time experiences of my boyhood. The expectation was much more exciting than the realization.

Some of the excitement was in the prospect of a break in the monotony. In our case it was the prospect of a new man or two in the bunkhouse, the coming in of certain neighbors. And when it was time to thresh the "bundle grain"—that which was cut with a binder and shocked in the field—it was hard to believe that anything could be more dramatic than the plodding arrival of the steam-powered "outfit" that threshed for everybody in the neighborhood.

It was fun to stand at a safe distance and watch the engineer turn valves, shift the throttle and open the firebox now and then to toss in a few shovelfuls of coal. It was fun to watch the skittish teams as their drivers coaxed them into the vicinity of this puffing and hissing monster.

And there were high hopes that the day might come when we could join a threshing outfit as the driver of the rickety little tankwagon with which water for the engine was transported from some previously designated watering tank, pond or irrigation ditch. It was the ultimate of ambition, almost, to think of oneself furiously pumping water into the tank and then pushing the horses on a dead run, with the engineer frantically signalling with his whistle that there had to be water in a matter of minutes or his boiler would blow.

But the reality never quite turned out that way. My first role as a participant in the harvest was in shocking oats. It was fun the first 20 minutes perhaps. Then the twine started cutting grooves into my gloves. Sore hands were followed by sore arms and sore legs, and countless spots of itch and irritation. By the end of the day the fatigue was overwhelming.

It was the same when we had our first try at handling headed grain. The job was mainly to clean up around the stack after each wagon had been unloaded by men with forks. There were blisters and sore arms again, but one of the keenest memories of working in headed grain is of the hunger pains that struck about 10:30 a.m. and again at about 4:00 p.m.

My biggest frustration, and ultimate disappointment, came when Father decided that the place for one who was quite light of frame and short of muscle might be as driver of the header. And so I was pushed into a trial run.

Of all the machines ever designed for movement with horses there could have been none more clumsy than a header. It was a rather simple thing, in some respects. The business end included the cutter bar, the platform and the elevator from which the cut grain spouted into the accompanying wagon. The whole

138

apparatus centered on a steel-lugged bullwheel—the transmitter of horsepower to sickle, elevator and other moving parts.

The horses, six in all, were hitched in threes on each side of a long steel pipe, or boom. The rear end of the boom, to which the horses were hitched, rested on a tiller wheel that was controlled by the driver's shifting of his body as he stood astride a combination seat and rudder. When the header was to turn right, the driver twisted the tiller left, held the horses of the right side in tight against the boom and sent his left team swinging out at right angles. And so it was to come to me with shocking clarity that this was an exercise in geometry as well as horsemanship. After I got the bullwheel lodged tight in a hole that had been hidden by the uncut wheat, I was pulled off the header and put back to scratching up around the stack.

Somewhere in my youth I came to distrust a mixture of horses and mules in any work arrangement. It could have been from that brief experience as driver of a header. Some of my six animals had been less than cooperative.

A year or two later, that header was leased to Bob Wiltein, who was farming the ranch's wheat land. He was a believer in

Binding Oats

the superiority of gasoline over oats and hay, and when the wheat was about ready to cut, he offered me the job of steering the header as he pulled it with his new Fordson tractor. This time the laws of physics had to be reckoned with, because the tractor had to run on the stubble in front and to one side of the header. My job was to stand on the driver's platform and hold the tiller wheel at a slight angle to offset the side-draft of our awkward hitch.

Bob's next move was to buy a small separator with which to thresh, and my dream of being part of a threshing outfit came true. But there was none of the excitement of hauling water to a steam engine. I just sat on that Fordson—operating without a governor—and moved the Model-T-type throttle up and down in a rather unsatisfactory effort to keep the separator running at a constant speed.

The appearance of a green or weedy bundle on the feeder was the signal for about two more notches on the throttle. When the man on the bundle fork broke rhythm for a few seconds, I would cut down the gas.

No reminiscing about harvest would be complete without some mention of the way harvesters ate. Here is where my farm editor-friend and I most certainly agreed that some people are inclined to over-romanticize.

The noon repast provided a scene that was not exactly in the style or manner of a Rotary luncheon. It was no time for conversation; it was in some respects a competitive event. Somebody usually went to the table under a strong impression that there might not be enough of everything to go around. And so there were less than friendly glances at the fellow who seemed to overdip the gravy or mashed potatoes or to manage the spearing of two pieces of meat in a single thrust.

These harvest meals must have been a nightmare to the women. Their talents and resources were put to the extreme test. When the action was at a home with a reputation for better-than-average fare, there were surprising errors in the final table count. Somebody outside the regular crew always managed to show up just in time for dinner.

Here and there in any neighborhood there was bound to be a place where the eating was below par. The hired man of one of our neighbors was conscious of this to the point he took a saddle horse with him on days there was threshing at one particular place, and he would gallop all the way home at noon—under some pretense or other. But everyone knew the one reason.

Harvesters could be rough on many things besides the food. Some of them never quite got the chaff off their sweaty shirts or the grease off their overalls. While the washing up was a splashy and sputtering process—maybe at a bench in the shade of a tree—it was by no means as finally effective as a shower and a dash of deodorant might have been.

Some places were always short of towels, and my friend, in our session on the subject, recalled seeing some fellow, late in line, wander with dripping face and hands until he found an old grain sack as an improvement over the wringing-wet wads of towel that remained.

Anyhow, as he put it, the harvest of grain was not a fairy-tale experience. It was an occasion with people where they were and as they were, and with hard work.

# 11. DAMMING THE RIVER

## . . . An Ordeal for Man and Beast

It was generally agreed among those who had worked through at least one summer on the ranch that no job took more from man or beast in a single day than the damming of the river.

The job was forced into the summer schedule by the vagaries of weather and the exigencies of crop production under irrigation. It came during the hottest part of the season, usually, at a time when ditches up and down the valley were exercising their water rights to the fullest and the South Platte was a series of trickles between bars of glistening sand.

Ditches with senior rights could call on newer ditches upstream to close their headgates. Our ditch's rights were junior to those of most of the upstream ditches, so it had to scratch for its water, more or less, in times of shortage.

"We've got to go to the head of the ditch," Father would say at breakfast some morning, and he usually designated the next day as the time.

Men and teams were pulled out of the hayfields or wherever else they might be working, but Father was openly selective. Men past 40, men slow of foot or overweight, any with obvious frailties, didn't get the call.

There was some care in selecting horses and mules, too. Any animal that had been known to panic at the feel of soft, sucking sand was excluded, as were any that didn't work well in four-horse hitches. Among neighbors and tenants who shared the need for more water were men with long experience at this job, and Father usually managed to enlist one or two of them.

When all the wagons had drawn up alongside the main headgate, about 8 a. m., there would be from 12 to 20 horses and mules, half a dozen men, three or four Fresno scrapers and perhaps two slip scrapers. In one of the wagons there would be a large tool box, an assortment of harness leather, rope, wire and some pieces of oak for quick replacement of eveners and double-trees. The job was hard on equipment, especially harness, when animals floundered or fell in the soggy sand.

The main item of equipment was, of course, the Fresno, which at that time was a basic tool of the dirt-moving business across the whole country. These varied in size, but most of those in our neighborhood were designed to be pulled by four horses.

Some of the men had rubber boots to put on as soon as the work required wading in water. Others—including some old hands at the business—insisted that it was better to wear regular work shoes. Sooner or later, they argued, one was going to be wet all over, regardless of what he wore. And for those who took the lead when the going got tough a good ducking in the rising water was almost inevitable.

If Father hadn't cased the situation the day before, he did it that morning while equipment was unloaded and teams put together. Sometimes he brought a saddle horse for his trip over the sandbars and islands and through the cottonwoods to a point on the opposite side of the river.

What he laid out in a rough way was a series of sand dams across the channels and a series of cuts through the bars and islands that would create a rude, but continuous, waterway from the flowing channels on the right side to the dry channel on the left from which our ditch extended. The staggering of the dams took full advantage of the channelized river bed and its natural fall. With each dam about 100 feet downstream from the one above, none of these flimsy sand dikes had to be more than two to four feet high to contribute to an effective diversion from the low side of the river to the far side.

143

The work always started in the high and dry channels. The first channels with water would divert into the new waterway. Then the next, and the next.

Father sometimes spoke wistfully of the possibility that if the job were carried out properly, it just might start a diversion that the river itself could complete. If the barriers across the heavier flowing channels could survive a season or two, they might sprout grass, willows and rosebushes and develop into islands. Thus the whole nature of the river would change, and the heavy flow would be permanently transferred to the left side and made easily accessible to our ditch.

While the cuts through islands sometimes stood up for a season or two, the dams across channels were fragile and temporary at best. They went out with the first rise of the river, usually, but nobody seemed to mind. If the river was up, there was no pressing need for them.

Starting with the relatively easy task of scooping up dry sand and leaving it in neat windrows, the two-man-and-four-horse units would work gradually across the channels and islands. Unfortunately, they had to look forward to their period of greatest anxiety along in the afternoon, when both men and horses would be wading in water most of the time and tiring.

At the end of the curved steel handle with which a Fresno was guided and maneuvered through the loading and unloading process there was always a length of heavy rope with which the scoop would be pulled into loading position after being emptied. Soaked with water and coated with sand, one of these ropes sometimes swung wild and caught a person square in the face.

The horses' hooves and dumping Fresnoes splashed water over everyone. Men strained to hold half-submerged Fresnoes steady as they loaded from the bottom of a flowing channel. There was always the possibility a team might lurch at the wrong moment and send the loader flying toward the horses' heels before he could let go of the handle.

Once in a while a horse's leg would sink suddenly in the sand

and water. The animal might stumble and fall. Most certainly, it would extricate itself only after a wild struggle. This was quicksand, somebody would say, and the drivers would try to avoid the spot on the next turn. It was in just this kind of situation that harness gave way on occasion, and one team would be out of action for a while.

The climax of the day's effort came when a dike had been extended perhaps two-thirds of the way across the final channel—the one with the most water always. The rush of water through the narrowing gap would take at least half of each load of sand, it seemed, before another could be dumped. The pace quickened, and sometimes the Fresnoes would be abandoned for a couple of slip scrapers behind two-horse teams. They could maneuver better in crowded quarters.

Finally, a couple of quick dumpings would block the flow, and several more loads would be added for good measure.

A great stillness seemed to come over the scene. The water started forming a silent pool. Men's voices relaxed, and one

heard the swish of wet horse tails against the especially annoying flies of the river bed. Everybody took a moment to survey the quiet scene and then started a parade in the direction the water had been forced to take. A good stream would be passing through the headgate by the time we got the wagons loaded and were heading for home.

What fascinated me from the first time I observed this mid-summer ritual was that one could look downstream from the new dams and see water seeping up through the sand and developing into rivulets a hundred feet away.

On the day we were laying a continuous barrier of sand across the bed of the river and arresting a considerable flow of water, there might have been a similar dam at the next ditch upstream, and it could have been in place for several days.

The South Platte, flowing on a bed of saturated sand, recharged itself every few miles—not completely, of course, but enough that there could be a whole series of these dams, each absolutely necessary to keep water flowing into an irrigation ditch—and there was sufficient water that all ditches came close to meeting their needs.

What we referred to as damming the river was not exactly what the Army Engineers would fit to the term. But it blocked enough water for the need of the moment. And it was awfully hard work.

# 12. HOG KILLING

## . . . And Other Provisions for Food

Many hours of many days and many days of every year were given over by most of the able-bodied personnel on the ranch to the production of food for home consumption.

On a day-to-day basis there was the milking of from five to eight cows, the feeding of chickens, turkeys, hogs and an occasional lamb or steer that was penned up and put on a special diet just prior to being converted into meat. Through the summer there was the care of two garden plots near the house and patches of potatoes, melons, pumpkins, turnips and such on odd strips and corners of irrigated land elsewhere around the ranch.

But the day we killed hogs seems to illustrate more than does any other occasion the extent to which rural folk of that era managed a lot of their food needs in their own ways. The project called for a concentration of manpower to match the opening of the wheat harvest or the first day of stacking alfalfa. Hired men were drawn off other details, and an outsider or two might be called in. Invariably, almost, there would be one fellow around who was there to help drench and scrape carcasses for nothing more than the privilege of taking home some livers, backbones, kidneys or lungs. (The latter two were considered waste in the eyes of Father and Mother, but others in the neighborhood had uses for them.)

Part of the drama, therefore, was in the assemblage of people, and it started early in the morning, usually in January. The site was adjacent to a complex of pens in which the doomed animals would have been confined the night before. By the time the sun

147

came up, Father would have his fire going and his collection of iron bars and broken castings carefully placed to take in maximum heat. Several railroad ties would have been split for fuel.

The scalding barrel was braced into a slanting position on a crude frame within 15 feet of the fire. Water was carried from a nearby outlet of the hog watering system, and when it filled the barrel to the proper level, it would be brought to the boiling point as red-hot pieces of iron were hooked from the fire and immersed in the barrel, from which a cloud of steam came with the insertion of each iron.

As soon as the water had taken the heat from the irons, they were withdrawn and put back in the fire. Meanwhile, the first hog would have been shot and stuck in the throat with a long knife and made ready for scalding. After two or more duckings, in the hands of two men, each holding a leg, the hair would be tested to see if it "slipped." If it didn't come out easily, there would be another immersion, and maybe even another hot casting to bring up the temperature of the water. Nobody ever thought of testing the water with a thermometer. As with many operations around the ranch, scalding a hog was considered an art rather than a science. And artists didn't need measuring instruments.

When a good scald had been declared, the skin was severed at just the right places above the back feet to permit insertion of gambrels under the main tendons, and the carcass was ready to hang on a four-inch pipe that extended for about 15 feet between a cottonwood tree and a heavy post. If the scald was right, the hair was removed in a matter of minutes and Father was ready to slit the carcass and remove the entrails and abdominal organs, being careful always to save the heart and liver from going with the rest of the waste into the feeding troughs of the hog pens and the chicken yard. We kids usually got hold of some bladders and, using a pipestem, we inflated them and played with them.

One by one, the hogs were killed and dressed until as many as a dozen would be lined up on the pipe.

From the slaughter site the carcasses were hauled in a wagon to the engine house, where a makeshift cutting table was assembled from a couple of over-sized sawhorses and some two-inch planks. In good weather the table was set up outdoors; in bad weather it was crowded into the engine house, alongside the large wooden box into which hams, shoulders and sides were placed after being trimmed and treated with any one of the several mixtures of salt, pepper, sugar and other ingredients with which Mother regularly experimented.

In the trimming process large strips of lean meat and lean-fat mixtures were piled high for grinding into sausage. The pure fat trimmings went into a pile which would be rendered into lard and packed away in jars and crocks.

We of the younger generation were especially interested in the size of the collection of trimmings destined for sausage. We liked to eat sausage, of course, but of all the processes in working up hog meat there was none more fascinating than feeding strips of pork through the sausage grinder. Our grinder was a big one, and there were times when a hired man was assigned to turn the handle. What fascinated the young, however, was the way the meat seemed to gurgle and groan on its way to final emergence in a pattern of thick strings from a dozen or more openings.

I recall Mother's using several different recipes for mixing the salt, pepper, sage and other flavoring ingredients. She seemed never quite content with the flavors she produced. Usually, she packed the mixed sausage in one- and two-gallon crocks and sealed it with layers of lard. There were years, though, when she pre-cooked some sausage and sealed it in glass jars.

The hams, shoulders, and bacon slabs (we called them side meat) remained buried in their salty bed in the big box for the prescribed period and were then put through the smoking process. There were years when Father applied the smoke flavor in liquid form, but later he built a tight room in a corner of the so-called coal house and made it a regular practice to expose the pork to a couple of days of dense smoke from a fire of corn cobs.

As I think back after more than 50 years on the quality of the pork that these processes produced, I must fight off a temptation to declare it superior to the products of the commercial packers to which I have been long accustomed.

The home-made sausage of my boyhood would stand up quite well against today's commercial products. But the hams and bacon could compete only in those circles where, because of some special circumstances, people have maintained or developed a taste for so-called country-cured pork and who cling to the belief that it excels.

Beneath the salty, sooty, greasy, and almost grimy, exterior of a ham or shoulder as it came from the smokehouse there was a surprising lot of character. The lean meat was red, solid and dry. The fat was white, almost as solid and almost as dry. The fat portions of a slice of ham seemed to soften in the cooking. The lean remained pretty hard and grainy. The blackish red gravy was almost as tempting to some as the meat itself. The bacon and the ham—and the gravy—tended to be salty. In the words of the professional wine testers, though, a pan of fried ham had body and bouquet, and there was nothing subtle about either.

The bacon, as a general rule, was less tasty than the ham and shoulder meat. The streaks of lean in a typical slice of bacon were discouragingly thin, and the shrinkage through frying seemed close to total destruction.

An earlier paragraph implies that we killed hogs just once a year. As a general rule, Father tried to get most of the annual supply of pork into storage during January. But there were many years when the prospect of a shortage would cause him to kill a few hogs during the first cold spell of November. It was necessary some years to butcher in March.

Cured pork was our year-round meat. We thought little about the likelihood we might get more uniformity of quality and eliminate a lot of work by buying our hams and bacon in town. In the long run, it might have been cheaper, considering all the man-hours that went into the killing of hogs and the preparation of the meat for curing. But those years of my boyhood were years in which there was still a lot of confusion as to whether farming was a business or a way of subsistence. Father, whose pay as manager of the ranch included housing and board for his family, seemed to presume that he was expected to hold the cash outlays for food to an absolute minimum. And this he did in a variety of ways.

From the cows we milked we got not only the milk, cream and butter requirements of the ranch kitchen, but enough cream to make a shipment to the Sterling creamery as often as once a week.

There were as many as 500 chickens around the place in midsummer, after scores of hens had sat through the hatching of nests of 10 to 15 eggs. Most of the hatching was under Mother's watchful eye in the two henhouses, but a surprising number of hens managed each spring to locate their nests in outlying sheds and barns, and a good number of these brought their broods to maturity.

Fried chicken was a regular relief from cured pork and sausage during the summer and fall, and stewed or baked chicken appeared frequently on the kitchen table in winter and spring. Fried eggs could turn up at most any meal.

Mother was adept at many chores around the ranch, but she was especially skillful in killing and dressing a chicken. On more than one occasion I watched her wring the necks of three or four cockerels at 10 o'clock or later and go through the removal of feathers, the cutting up and the frying in time to have a big platter of chicken ready for the table at noon.

Father's inclination to add mutton to the diet for a spell each winter was one of the many little things, I am confident, that contributed to my progressive disenchantment with ranching as a way of life. I cannot recall ever putting a piece of mutton on my plate without seeming to get a whiff of sheep in the raw.

I developed much the same feeling about raw milk. I could apply raw cream to breakfast foods, fruit desserts and so forth, but the drinking of a glassful of milk was almost nauseating. My only explanation is that it had something to do with my close association with the cows after learning to milk at the age of seven. Raw milk seemed to taste like cowbarns smelled.

While the chickens were on the ranch primarily to provide meat and eggs for home consumption, there were periods when egg production ran high enough that Mother could deliver a 12-dozen case to one of the Proctor stores with every trip she made to buy groceries. The value of the eggs became a credit against the ranch's sizable purchases from each store.

The eggs came from Barred Plymouth Rock hens. No other breed of chicken ever got mixed into the flock, except for a brief period when we children were allowed to have two Bantam hens and a rooster. The latter made some friends among the Plymouth Rocks, and some of Mother's hatchings that spring included birds with feathers far brighter than the mottled gray of the straight Plymouth Rocks.

While we usually produced from 25 to 75 turkeys each year, Mother seemed little interested in serving turkey except in the Thanksgiving and Christmas seasons. The surplus birds were sold in Sterling, usually, and sometimes we killed and dressed them before delivery.

The Powell and Blair families, our predecessors on the ranch, had raised ducks and geese, but their carefully-built pond was never filled in our years there. Neither Mother nor Father had an interest in web-footed fowl.

It would have been considered little short of sinful to buy potatoes at the store. Father made it a practice, therefore, to plant several patches each spring, even after he had quit growing them on a commercial scale, as he tried to do the first few years on the ranch. Rarely did we go into a winter without as many as 50 bushels of potatoes in the basement, usually piled in a corner. In late winter we boys often had to go through what remained of the pile and remove all sprouts. This was far from the top on our list of enjoyable occupations.

Within 300 feet of the house there were two fenced garden tracts, each including about an acre and served by an irrigation ditch. One of the gardens included a row of rhubarb plants that must have extended for 200 feet. In one corner of this plot, sheltered from the north winds by the blacksmith shop, there were cold frames that Father used for starting plants in the spring. By the time I was big enough to help with the gardening, these were abandoned, and our tomato and cabbage plants came from a greenhouse in Sterling.

The gardens produced large quantities of radishes, lettuce, peas, beans, cabbage, sweet corn, cucumbers, squash, and usually the earliest plantings of potatoes. There was an asparagus bed in a corner of the "lower" garden, but its production was fitful.

While a few hills of melons were planted in one of these garden tracts and a few hills of pumpkins in another, our best melons and pumpkins usually came from little spots of irrigated land farther from the house. There were years when we harvested pumpkins by the wagonload and fed them to the hogs. There were years, also, when an early freeze would catch some potatoes before they were dug. These were harvested, nevertheless, and fed to the hogs.

Of all the products of the ranch that contributed to variety in our diet, though, there was nothing to match the fruit and berries. I cannot recall a year when the cherry trees did not produce abundantly. We ate raw cherries regularly for two or three weeks in June and July, and when Mother was through seeding and canning, she could count a minimum of 100 quart and half-gallon jars on the basement shelves. Along with the whole cherries, there were preserves and jellies and, on several occasions, Mother canned a mixture of mulberries and cherries. This took place, as I recall, during World War I, when there was a shortage of sugar. The mulberries, almost too sweet and bland for eating by themselves, offset the sourness of the cherries. Mother also mixed mulberries and rhubarb.

There were about as many red plum trees as cherry trees, and there were years when the plum crop accounted for about as many sealed jars in the basement as did the cherry crop. But in later years on the ranch, the plums were attacked by insects and the crops were slim.

One winter following a bumper plum crop, Mother had concentrated on the making of plum butter. The jars stood in long lines. and we all looked forward to spreading the contents over thickly buttered slices of bread. Then one day Mother came from the basement (we called it the cellar) in a state of shock. Someone had removed all but a few jars of plum butter. Mother and Father may have had their opinions as to what had happened. A lot of people knew about the contents of the fruit room, and everybody knew that there were no workable locks on our doors. It was all very exciting, in a way, but for almost a year Mother would sigh and lament the loss of the biggest stock of plum butter she ever had laid up.

In sheer volume the long rows of black and yellow currant bushes probably exceeded the production of the cherry and plum trees. The word was out in the neighborhood that anyone willing to pick currants could do so on a share basis. Among those who took advantage of this offer for several consecutive seasons was the matriarch of the community, Grandma Colburn, who came with one or more of her granddaughters—all wearing black cotton stocking legs over their arms for protection from the rough bushes. So far as I can recall, Mother planned a quota of jellies and jams from the currants each year, but made no effort to utilize the full production of those prolific bushes.

Some scattered chokecherry and gooseberry bushes contributed to the variety of jellies put up in those summers when Mother and her kitchen help had the time. Some families picked wild grapes along the river. We never did.

The sweetest home product that was on the table for every meal throughout the year was honey. The abundance of alfalfa and sweet clover up and down the valley attracted professional beekeepers to the area, and Father had no trouble working out arrangements whereby one of these men took care of the ranch's bees in return for the privilege of keeping additional bees of his own on the place. The ranch's take from this operation constituted scores of squares of comb honey each fall, along with several five-gallon cans of honey that had been extracted from the comb. The beekeeper took care of selling any surplus.

Food storage facilities were primitive by the standards of a later day. There was the cellar under the house, of course, with plenty of capacity for potatoes, sauerkraut, canned fruits, vegetables (and in some years) canned beef. The sauerkraut, made each fall from cabbage cut just ahead of the first killing frost, was packed in five- and ten-gallon crocks or kegs. Mother usually had a large plate or circular piece of board to lay over the kraut, and on top of this she placed a three- or four-pound rock or a couple of old flatirons. The pressure from this weight had some bearing on how soon the fresh cabbage started "working." By late fall we boys would sample the kraut regularly, lifting the weights and lids and snatching a handful which, because it came off the top of the pack, sometimes carried bits of mold.

There was a large pantry off the kitchen in which Mother stored canned goods, cereals, and various other packaged foods on shelves protected from flies by screened doors. Below these shelves were several bins, one of which was reserved for sugar and was capable of taking the contents of a 100-pound bag. Flour was purchased in 48-pound bags and stored in a bin beneath a specially-built table or "bread board," as we called it, that was reserved exclusively for working bread, pie and cookie doughs.

Among hired men and others there were some comments on some of the peculiarities of the menus which Mother prescribed. For one thing, our meals featured far more hot breads than did the meals of most families of the neighborhood. Following the tradition of her family in Tennessee, Mother considered hot biscuits as something close to essential in our breakfast diet. And there was hot cornbread on the table at half of our suppers, perhaps. We children heard some murmuring against cornbread, and Father talked openly about one hired man who had complained to him that it scratched his throat.

Mother was against some things that others took for granted in planning farm and ranch meals. She had little use for pancakes, though she did break down occasionally, usually on a Sunday, and mix up a batch. Neither she nor Father cared for coffee with their noon meal, and except on occasions when there was someone around who had spoken out in favor of coffee for dinner (served at high noon), the pot sat cool from breakfast to breakfast. I can recall a time or two when I relayed to Mother that a certain hired man had complained of a headache or some other difficulty as a result of not having had a cup of coffee at noon.

The garden products that Mother seemed to relish more than any other were sweet corn and green beans. She loved them, but because of her dentures, she preferred cutting the corn from the cob. This all but ruined it in the eyes of us children.

If there were a single feature of the ranch kitchen that distinguished it from most of the kitchens of the community, it was the big Alaska refrigerator. It was outside the kitchen, actually, in a corner of the enclosed back porch. It was of oak construction, basically, but its interior lining, both in the food storage areas and the ice chest, was of galvanized steel that was beginning to show rust spots long before we left the ranch.

The ice chest had capacity for at least 100 pounds, maybe

more. There was a small pipe connecting the drain board to a removable pan on the floor. This pan had to be emptied by hand. There was a tendency to forget this chore, and there was frequently a puddle of water extending from below the refrigerator to the edge of the slightly sloping porch floor. A small faucet on one side connected to a small tank in the ice chest. This was for cooling drinking water, but we never used it.

All dairy products for table use were kept in one of the two large compartments in the refrigerator. Certain other foods were kept there, too, but it was a general practice of the times to try to minimize the quantity of leftovers from one meal to the next. There were frightening stories about what could happen to such things as green beans or potato salad if allowed to stand around for a day or two in warm weather. Our refrigerator was a convenience, nevertheless, a convenience that few families around us enjoyed. And we had it because the developers of the ranch had arranged for the harvest and storage of ice. That is another chapter.

# 13. FILLING THE ICE HOUSE

## . . . And Reaping the Fruits Thereof

Times of heavy work for adults on the ranch were fun times for us children. One of these times was the annual ice harvest.

The time to cut ice was not fixed by the calendar, but by the thickness of the ice. Father preferred a thickness of about 12 inches, and this usually was available shortly after Christmas. For the young in the family there was always speculation as to whether it would come during our vacation or after we had started back to school. We much preferred the former.

There was a series of three ponds on Skinner Draw, all within a half-mile of the icehouse. Father kept two of these in condition for ice production, but generally favored the upper of the three. All three had been formed by construction of irrigation ditches across the draw. The upper one, however, was on the site of some springs from which there had been a light flow of water before the ditches were built.

Father tried to maintain a depth of at least six feet over enough of an area of the ponds required for a season's supply of ice. When we had to cut in shallow parts the saws sometimes struck the muddy bottom.

There were some cold winters when the ice was 15 or 16 inches thick before Father could fit the ice cutting into his schedule. And there was one mild season when he waited patiently for prolonged cold weather and finally settled for ice that was barely six inches thick in February.

The icehouse was an especially built section of the structure we generally referred to as the bunkhouse. It was, in fact, one half of the first story of this building. The walls were of heavy stone, and the storage area extended four feet below the surface of the ground. There was a floor space of about 20 feet by 12 feet, and the ice could be stacked to a depth of close to 10 feet.

The ice was cut in cakes about 18 inches in width and three feet in length. The third dimension, of course, was dependent on the season.

There was something almost miraculous about the way the big saws cut their way across the pond, their teeth always working through a mound of what would qualify today as superb crushed ice. We watched with bated breath as each cake broke from the surface and went into flotation, its surface rising about an inch above the level of the fixed ice.

The usable ice was cut from near the center of the pond. But before any blocks were sawed for loading, the men cut a runway, so to speak, from the point of loading to the place where the ice was of desirable thickness and cleanliness. Through this canal each cake was pushed with iron-pointed poles to the loading area.

The high point of action at the pond came with the loading. The double-box wagon was backed to the edge of the pond, sometimes with the rear wheels resting on the ice. A wooden chute that fit snugly into the rear endgate opening extended into the hole in the ice. When a cake had been nudged to the foot of the chute, it was gripped by tongs and snaked into the wagon by a man with saddle horse and lariat.

When it was one of the first cakes to be loaded, it would glide the length of the wagon and hit the front endgate sometimes with a threatening thud and a spray of water.

The loaded wagon, with icicles hanging from cracks in the floor, moved to the icehouse, which was about 40 feet from our back porch. A duplicate of the chute used at the pond was used here for unloading.

Placing of the final layers required lifting the ice above the level of the wagon, with the chute slanting up instead of down. The saddle horse came into use at this point. The horse and rider took position outside a window at the side of the building, the rope extending through the window and out the door. At the proper signals from the wagon, the rope would tighten on the saddle horn and another cake would go bouncing up the chute and into the waiting hands of men who had to work in a crouch to keep from bumping heads on the ceiling.

The degree of excitement in the unloading depended in part on the temperament of the person in charge. The more daring of the hired men or neighbors who helped with the work would send the big cakes sliding, uncontrolled, and once in a while this would cause a collision of one cake with another and a good crackup.

A cake of ice thus broken usually was pushed aside to be further broken down for use in filling the crevices between the cakes. The filling of crevices was important, because it eliminated the circulation of air. The end result of a good job of tamping was one solid block of ice, about 18 feet by 16 feet, by 10 feet—insulated from the walls of the building by about 24 inches of wheat straw.

Just how much loss there was from melting between January and the final filling of the back-porch icebox at the end of September no one ever bothered to estimate. My guess is that we took out of the icehouse about two-thirds of the weight we put in. The rest seeped into the dirt floor.

To the best of my recollection, it took from two to three days from the time the pond was opened until the last cake of ice had been lifted into its storage space and the last forkful of straw had been piled on top of the last layer.

Two men with wagons were kept busy hauling. There were at least two men at the pond who handled the saws, and two or three others, including Father, who were occupied with supervisory details. The man-hours required, therefore, were considerable.

But the job involved much more than time. It took a lot of energy and endurance to stand all day on the frozen surface of the pond and pull an ice saw. Wrestling the heavy cakes out of the pond, into the wagon and then into final storage, even with the use of a saddle horse and chute, certainly wasn't light work.

The work aspect didn't fully dawn on me until my freshman year at college. The family had left the ranch by then, but I hired out to the Wiltein brothers, who were operating the place, to help with the ice harvest during Christmas vacation. I volunteered to handle one of the saws. After the first half-day, my aching shoulders told me that this had been a horrible mistake.

What has happened to the icehouse ties in with a lot of other things that have changed in agricultural America. The cutting of natural ice began to disappear at about the turn of the century. The railroads and some other industries stored natural ice until the 1930's.

But with the perfection of ice-making machinery and the growth of the so-called cold-storage business, artificial ice began to reach country stores and some rural homes. It was doing that in our area when we were still putting up our own ice from the pond. The final blow to the country icehouse and all that went with it came with rural electrification and the mechanical home refrigerator.

The central purpose of the ice storage program, of course, was to provide a coolant for the big refrigerator. About once every four days through the summer, someone had to open the double doors of the icehouse, roll back the straw and break out a chunk of ice weighing 100 pounds or more. This was a two-man job, and for the last year or two we were on the ranch I usually was one of the two.

If and when iced tea was served with a meal, the necessary ice was chipped from that in the refrigerator. The same went for lemonade, but this is not to imply that these cooled drinks were an everyday offering.

We drank our water as it came by pipe from the windmill tank or from the hand pump at the well nearer the house.

While ice in the refrigerator was a necessity, by family standards, ice in a drink was a luxury. We drank a glass of iced tea or lemonade slowly, dragging out the pleasures of the coolness as well as the taste. This, on a hot day, was a peak experience, truly.

When we sucked on a piece of ice or watched it floating in a glass of tea, we talked sometimes about the purity of water that came from seepy bogs, water in which cows waded, water that once had carried a considerable load of sediment from a plowed field, and we always reassured ourselves with the old canard about the death of all germs in freezing temperatures. But these discussions were not exactly peak experiences.

A very definite peak of living in a household that could draw on its own supply of ice came with each summer Sunday morning. That was the time of a ritual more regular and better defined than Sunday School. That was when we made ice cream.

Somebody went to the icehouse right after breakfast. And somebody else started preparing the mix for the two-gallon freezer.

We had two systems of crushing the ice. The one that prevailed when I first was conscious of such things involved placing sizable chunks in a gunny sack and then beating it with a heavy stick—a piece of oak about the size of a baseball bat—or with the flat side of an ax.

This always meant the sacrifice of at least one sack, sometimes two. The burlap took a terrible beating—especially if there were sharp edges on some pieces of ice, if the ax twisted slightly at the wrong time, or if the stick available on a particular occasion was not smooth.

Ultimately, as I recall, someone came up with a sturdy wooden box, about three feet square and a foot deep. We placed large chunks of ice in this and broke them down with the flat side of an ax or club similar to the one used on the sacked ice.

Somewhere in the course of events I took over from Mother

the preparation of the ice cream mix, and while the quality may have suffered at times, there was a distinct move toward greater experimentation. Among other things, I wanted to know just how much pure cream could be included.

Thick cream was something we had plenty of, and didn't we boys deserve some reward for milking the cows and putting the milk through the separator? I learned on the first try that there was such a thing as too much butterfat for good texture, but we leveled off with a much richer mix than Mother's basic frugality ever would have permitted.

Grinding out a two-gallon batch of ice cream in a hand-operated freezer would have been pure drudgery for one person, but this was Sunday and there were enough hands around usually to keep the thing going at a brisk pace. When we boys were small, the task generally fell to a hired man. But in due time the main responsibility was ours, and the hired man (or men) came into the act under pressure or persuasion of one kind or another. A young man with the insatiable appetite of one who had worked hard in the fields all week was easily lured with the promise of a generous sampling of the product as soon as the chore was finished.

The procedure was to bring a large pan to the work area—in the shade of a cottonwood tree—and remove the paddle before draining the salt water from the tub and packing with fresh ice. The rule was that all ice cream that came out with the paddle was for eating on the spot. A certain deftness in withdrawing the paddle could bring out a generous quantity, and I detected in my first experiment that ice cream with high butterfat seemed to stick to the paddle better than did the thinner mix Mother had been providing.

And so a peak experience of summer Sundays was the making and eating of ice cream. Whatever thanks were offered for that blessing should have included a word in behalf of the builders of the place whose foresight had provided for a sturdy icehouse along with the other buildings.

In a rather vague way, we children began to sense that our stock of ice was a privilege—almost a status symbol. Few families in the vicinity enjoyed the luxury of home-stored ice, and the nearest commercial ice plant was at Sterling, 20 miles away. One of the stores in Proctor put up ice during the earliest years of my memory, but eventually it abandoned the practice in favor of taking ice off a route truck from Sterling.

Frequently someone would drive up in a wagon, buggy or car and seek to buy enough ice for a batch of ice cream—or sometimes just enough to provide a round of cool drinks for some special occasion. These requests were disconcerting.

Experience had shown that a full icehouse contained just about enough to carry the ranch household from May through September. To put a price on the ice would invite more requests. And so there were long and careful explanations to those who who came asking for ice. No, it was not for sale. What use was to be made of it? How much would do? Usually, the party left with a dripping burlap bag and a rather polite reminder that it was easier to give away a little ice now and then than to create the impression that there was enough for everyone who might call.

On a few occasions the seeker was a distressed parent in search of anything to relieve a sick child at home—something to cool feverish lips or to provide a pack for an aching head. There was ice for these, with no questions asked and no hints as to the possible futility of another visit.

I faintly recall an occasion when Father actually took money for ice, and it seems to have been related to somebody's plan for celebrating the Fourth of July. A sale for that occasion was a once-a-season precedent that would cause no problems for at least a year.

And so go memories of those warm days of summer when a little bit of coolness could mean so much, and of the hard work in winter that made it possible.

# 14. WE KNEW A LOT OF ANIMALS

## ... And Could Almost Talk with Some of Them

The animals we came to know in our 18 years on the ranch would have made a much longer parade than the people who figured in the life of the community during that period.

We were in daily association with hundreds of creatures—fowl included—and with some of them the association was quite intimate, as in the case of the cows we milked and the horses and mules we curried, harnessed or saddled and worked or rode.

For the most part, there was a quite casual relationship with the beef cattle, the hogs, the sheep, the chickens and turkeys. There were exceptions in the calves we taught to drink milk from buckets and lambs and runty pigs we fed from bottles. Of the hogs that got special attention, none fared better than the purebred gilts Brother Dave and I raised as members of what later became the 4-H movement.

For several years we looked with pity and affection on a splotch-faced cow that limped at the rear of the herd whenever we moved the cattle. She had been born in a blizzard and one of her feet was so badly frozen that it developed in to a clumsy mass of hoof. We called her Old Crip, and there was genuine sorrow among us boys when Father finally decided she should be stuffed into a car of fat cattle and sent to the Denver market, where she sold as a "canner."

There was hardly a spring when Father failed to bring lambs to the house for bottle feeding. In most cases it would be because the mother ewe had refused to accept one of her young or had died. One year he came carrying a lamb with a broken front leg and expressed some feeling we would be lucky to save the lamb, let alone the leg. The ends of the bone were visible and mud-stained; there were definite signs of infection. I washed the bone ends and put them together, applied whatever disinfectants we had and then laid heavy gobs of an all-purpose salve (good for man or beast) over the whole area and bound it with strips of muslin.

Outside the first bandage I fitted a couple of sticks that extended a half-inch or so beyond the hoof and bound these to the leg. With the inner stick fitting behind the shoulder joint, the arrangement allowed the lamb to limp around the back porch where he was quartered. His willingness to take milk from a bottle enabled him to gain strength, and in a few days he was hopping across the yard. I replaced the bandages once, as I recall, and when I removed them the second time, the break in the skin was healed over and, except for a sizable lump, the leg was normal.

In the meantime, two more dependent lambs had come on the scene, and we had taught all three to take their milk direct from a cow. This eliminated bottles and nipples and, more important to us boys, it was taking care of just about all the milk we could expect from Old Creepie, a short-teated cow that nobody liked to milk.

In due time these three lambs were going to the pasture each morning with the cows and bedding down with them in the barn lot at night. In June that year, we sent Creepie and the lambs along with the beef cows to the north pasture, some six miles away, and she and her three charges stayed together there all summer. Three young sheep, by themselves, would have been easy victims of coyotes, but these three managed a sort of one-way defense pact with the cows and survived the summer.

It was our practice on the few occasions when we had to bring in the milk cows without benefit of a saddle horse to manage a ride on one of the cows as soon as we got them headed for the barn. We tested the readiness of all the cows to accept a rider by getting astride them while their heads were locked in the stanchions at milking time. We learned early in her first milking period that Creepie would have none of this. The result was that we were soon treating her as a rodeo performer as well as a dairy cow. We would put a rope around her belly and hold onto this as we rode her out of the barn. (We picked our times, of course, because Father would have put a stop to it the minute he heard about it.)

One day when Father and Mother were going to be in Sterling overnight, we invited anyone in school to go home with us and, as soon as the cows were milked, join in a milk-cow rodeo. Mine was the first and only ride of Creepie. She came out of the barn running and headed down the edge of a high woven wire fence. When she finally dislodged me, I fell on the side of the fence and was dragged several feet along the wire.

My injuries were mainly to my left arm above the elbow, and I managed to bandage the worst abrasions with some strips of

*Getting to know Old Tom*

flour bag from Mother's collection. So far as I could tell, the wounds were healing, and only those who had seen me get tossed into the fence were aware of my injuries. But within about four days of the incident, a woman showed up at the Proctor school and announced she was the county nurse on a tour to check the extent pupils had been vaccinated for smallpox. Thus the order was for all who had ever been vaccinated to bare arms and march by for a close inspection. My vaccination was at almost the very spot of the worst cut on my arm. The nurse took one look and started cutting off my bandages. I mumbled a few explanations of what the injury was, but she had lost interest in anything but the horror of finding anyone in civilized society who would bind an open wound with such "dirty rags."

Sister Ruth took this as an insult to the family. I had disgraced all the Hamils, she argued, and the whole matter would have to be aired that night. I pleaded with her all the way home, but she went direct to Mother with the story, and I had to confess my part in the cow riding episode as well as take the heat for having set up the whole show. To the best of my recollection, Mother accepted my apologies and regrets and chose not to inform Father of what had been going on at milking time when he was not around. She and I worked out several deals of that kind over the years, but there was never any question as to her disappointment in me or her firm injunction against any repetition of the deed in question.

Father's method of choosing cows for milking was without much concern with the usual standards and practices of a professional dairyman. I suspect, though I could not prove, that he looked upon the milking herd as something to keep his young sons busy almost as much as a source of food or a generator of modest revenue for the ranch owners.

The milking barn had stanchions for about 12 cows, but the number we milked at one time rarely exceeded eight. My earliest recollection is of one Holstein and one Jersey in the

168

milking herd. But by the time I learned to milk, the cows were mostly red in color and of obvious Shorthorn or, as Father insisted, Durham ancestry. Once in a while Father would spot a heifer with markings indicating Jersey blood. Old Creepie, in fact, was one of these, but somewhere in her breeding there was a strain that worked against her development of an ample bag and teats. But once Father marked a cow for milking, we usually were stuck with her. Nobody was weighing milk or testing butterfat to determine which cows were efficient producers.

We boys had one measurement of the worth of a cow, and that was the ease with which we could take her milk. The champ of champs was a red cow with long, tapering teats from which milk seemed to flow at the first touch. She could be called by no other name than Easy. The only problem we had was in making sure that the privilege of milking Old Easy was equally distributed. She was a natural, of course, for training Sister Edna to help us with the milking—when Edna was perhaps six years old—and Brother Don, two years behind her. As a matter of fact, we trained each of them to milk when they were too small to carry a bucket without its dragging on the ground. Mother and Father accused us of taking unnecessary advantage of the younger children's desire to be where the action was and took steps at times to hamper our on-the-job training programs. But for Dave and me this was what we were looking for—anything to reduce the burden of twice-a-day milking that seemed to weigh on our shoulders. In our juvenile way, I suppose, we were practicing the basics of good management— getting somebody else to do our work for us.

It would be unfair to leave the subject of cows and milk without noting that there was a payoff in the steady demand for milk among families in Proctor. During the school years we children carried from one to two gallons of milk as we went to school and delivered it in the customers' pails at the front doors of their homes. The price at the beginning was five cents a quart, but it did go up to 10 cents during the inflation of the late teen years. The one who delivered the milk got the money, Sister Ruth included, even though she helped very little with the milking.

There were quite a few lessons in the experiences of an eight- or nine- or 10-year-old milk distributor. We soon knew where the sure pay was and where the fresh pail we picked up with each delivery didn't always rattle with coins on Friday morning. Then there were the lessons in the high cost of dalliance. Along the roadside ditches in winter there were long strips of ice. Who couldn't resist stepping down there and sliding a bit? Every once in a while one of us went down on the ice with milk or lunch pails in hand. Sometimes we lost a pail of milk in this way, and there would be a hurried trip home for a refill from Mother's supply. Once when I fell on my back, the pails of milk in each hand hit the ice with enough force to snap off the lids and shower me with milk from both sides. I had to go for fresh clothes as well as milk.

Near the end of World War I, Father took steps toward conversion of the beef herd from its dominant Shorthorn (or Durham) strains to more Hereford blood. The process was gradual and was marked at the beginning by the purchase of two Hereford bulls from the Len Sherwin ranch near Winston. If we had stayed on the ranch long enough, this could have brought an end to the practice of locating potential milkers among the run-of-the-herd cows. Hereford cows were not for milking, or so went the wisdom of the time, but Shorthorns, or Durhams, as Father preferred to call all red cattle, were—even when they turned out to have short teats and low production.

One of the new whitefaced bulls was what we called a muley (without horns). He was quite gentle and friendly, and we boys decided he needed a name to match some of the names one saw in the advertisements of purebred cattle producers. Either Dave or I had been reading about Izaak Walton in school, and one of us applied the name that stuck. The second of the two

170

bulls had horns but was devoid of personality to the extent we never bothered to name him.

The horse and mule population varied, but there were times when the total approached 100, including the work stock at the so-called lower place, where Charlie Morton farmed on shares for several years. With as many as 20 mares dropping foals each spring, there was an on-going question as to which animals were to be disposed of—colts ready for breaking, animals of demonstrated physical or temperamental weaknesses or a really desirable team for which somebody was willing to pay a good price.

The brood mares included several that were no more than half-broke and were excused from all work. One of these carried the Box-J brand and produced a colt as regularly as the spring rolled around, provided she had been granted her annual appointment with a stallion. Her past was a little hazy, but Father referred to a time when somebody had tried to break her to ride and had given up. She had all the characteristics of an animal in constant defiance of man. On the occasions when we had to round up the herd with which she ran, she was always the first to respond to our appearance and made it a point to keep out in front as soon as she determined the direction she would be forced to go. Sometimes she tried to choose her own direction. The general presumption was that she was of Morgan breeding, but had run with half-wild herds until she was two or three years old. Her colts from a Percheron stallion were deceiving. At the age of two they looked like ideal saddle horses, and several were ridden for a year or two. But by the time they were four years old, they had taken on enough size to be put in harness. Weighing about 1,400 pounds each, two of these were put together when they were four and five years old, respectively. Light bays with black manes, they made one of the best-matched teams we ever had. They were especially good on a buckrake or beet cultivator. They were the favorite team of Rudolph Wiltein, who with his brother, Bob, farmed beet and wheat land on shares the last few years we were on the ranch and took over when Father gave up the managership.

One of my last recollections of John Wiltein, father of Bob and Rudolph, was seeing him ride from his barn on the edge of Proctor on Old Prince, one of the largest horses on the ranch and for a dozen years or more the true prince, if not king, of the work stock.

Both John and Prince were showing their age on this occasion (about 1925). Both were slowing down. But it struck me that they made a fine combination—a man who had been one of the strongest, hardest working individuals I had ever known, and a horse that had been strong, willing, faithful and responsive in every situation. John was a short-legged man and Prince was a broad-beamed horse, but John sat straight in his saddle, reins grasped in one hand, and Prince arched his neck and set off in a proud walk. It was only the second time I ever had seen Prince under saddle, because he was a work horse. But such was his style that he and John Wiltein could go down the road like the pair of aristocrats which, in their individual ways, they truly were.

Prince was one of a team of bay geldings Father bought from a farmer near Fleming in about 1912. The two were almost perfectly matched in color and size, but it was soon apparent that while Prince was a super-excellent horse, his mate was a mediocrity. The latter left the ranch at about the time Father was selling horses to buyers for the British army. For the rest of his years with us Prince found himself hitched with horses of all colors, shapes and sizes, but never did anyone take him to the field with a horse that matched him in all-around performance and attitude. His partners in harness included two stallions, a couple of big mares, a mule and a raw-boned gelding that matched him in weight but not in appearance or reliability. Toward the end of his career John Wiltein worked him with a smaller sorrel. He was the stacker horse for several hay seasons and was Father's choice to put on the one-horse plow and cultivator that we used in our garden plots. Weighing 1,600 to 1,700 pounds, he had the broad back of a circus horse and he was immensely tolerant of my jumping on and off him (in tennis shoes) and standing on his rump while he trotted around the corral. He had some white on his face, a beautiful head and black mane. When he arched his neck, as he did more often than most geldings, it was hard to believe he was not the equal, in equine masculinity, of the stallions with which he was often hitched to a mowing machine or wagon.

My first ride on a saddle horse was in Father's arms, with my legs on either side of the horn and the long ears of Old Tom bobbing in and out of my view of the road ahead. Tom was Father's favorite horse during our early years on the ranch. They went together to the far corners of the place and on long jaunts to distant ranches and construction camps. Each spring Father spent at least a day on Tom in the lower corral, where the new calves were branded and vaccinated and the bulls among them castrated. Tom was considered a good roping horse, unexcitable and steady and trained to keep the rope tight if left alone while his rider was wrestling with the animal on the other end.

By the time I started riding Tom alone, he was getting a bit stiff and Father was riding a new bay gelding that was younger, more restless and excitable, but the easiest riding horse that ever darkened our barn door. In two or three years Tom was in full retirement and in a year or so after that he breathed his last, after lying for a day or two on his side in a corner of the hog pasture. His retirement years were no more than two, but there was never any question in Father's mind that Tom should live out whatever years were left after he could no longer carry a rider. Few horses were allowed to die on their own terms this way, but Tom was a little different. At some time in our early years on the ranch, Father and Tom were caught in a blizzard. Father lost his sense of direction, but Tom didn't, and when he pulled up at the corral gate, Father, I am sure, made some kind of vow as to Tom's future. He was never offered for sale, and there was never any talk about shooting him after it was clear he would be of no further service.

Father's new horse was named Bird, and he came to the ranch as the possession of a hired man, Adolph Hoelscher. How much of the ranch's money went into the purchase of this long-legged, hog-backed bay was never discussed, but this was no ordinary deal. Father had ridden Bird a time or two and was so taken by his easy gaits and quickness of movement that he probably paid the asking price without a quibble.

Bird was the fastest running horse we ever had, and he was the only one with a pacing gait that was in direct contrast to the hard trots of most saddle horses. It was like "riding in a rocking chair," Father often said in describing Old Bird and his so-called pacing.

He was too nervous ever to have been a good roping horse, and he took a lot of room to turn around when chasing a cow or steer that was trying to break from a herd. He preferred a running turn to the stop-and-start turn of most cow horses. One story was that he came from racing stock and was disposed of as a colt because his owner was discouraged by the way his back bone arched up from his hips. Bird was sure of foot and could run, and would run, at the slightest urging. On more than one occasion he started running with Dave or me and didn't stop till he drew up at the corral gate.

In the summer of 1925, when I was working on the ranch for the Wilteins, he slipped and fell with me while turning to head off a cow. It was the only time I ever saw him go down. There was a look of fright in his eyes as I gathered up the reins to remount. But there was something else he seemed to want to say as he stood there trembling. The desire to please ran strong in his makeup, and he seemed to know that no rider was pleased with a stumbling horse.

His desire to meet the requests of a rider was something on which Father commented frequently. The subject would come up in talk of horses and their homing instincts in such situations as the time Father and Old Tom were caught in swirling snow. "I would be afraid of Old Bird in a storm," Father would say. "He would turn in the wrong direction if he felt the slightest pull on the reins. But Old Tom wouldn't have done that. He knew when he knew more than his rider."

If we had a single horse on the ranch that displayed the qualities that have been developed and refined in the modern Quarter Horse, it was Old Jim, a buckskin with some white on his face and a quickness of movement that was the talk of all who ever rode him. He was over the hill by the time I was able to ride by myself, but I am confident Father would have disqualified him as a horse for learners, even in Jim's final years. Once, when Jim was the favorite horse of Charlie Brecht and Charlie was Father's favorite hired man, Charlie responded to Sister Ruth's appeals for a ride on a horse. Whether he took her in the saddle with him or placed her there by herself, I cannot remember, but Jim jumped and Ruth fell to the ground. About all I recall was the excitement and anxiety of the occasion and the considerable blood that flowed from a cut Ruth suffered.

Both Jim and Tom had been part of the saddle string during the Powell and Blair ownership of the ranch, and I have wondered if either of them might have come from Oregon with the big herd of cattle Mr. Powell brought from there in 1896.

There was never any question in Father's mind about the importance of teaching his children to be at home on the backs of animals. We had been on the ranch not more than a year or two when he bought a burro. The story of this poor brute is told in two pictures from the family album. One shows Ruth Eleanor Blue from Cedar Rapids, Iowa, with Sister Ruth and me on the burro. The other shows a hired man on him while another man pursues with a pitchfork in hand. The explanation of the second picture, of course, is that young men around the place couldn't resist getting somebody on the burro and then making him buck. A jab from a pitchfork apparently brought

175

the right response, and eventually this treatment ruined the burro's disposition. And so Father sold the burro, and started looking for a pony.

As Christmas approached in 1912 or 1913, Father and Mother started slanting their recommendation as to just what we should be asking for in our communications with Santa Claus. Much of what we had asked for in times past had never materialized, and we never had mentioned anything as pretentious or ambitious as a live pony. We must have seemed disappointingly indifferent to the idea of a pony.

In any event, Santa Claus did stop at the barn, and in the first light of dawn we went out to inspect our gift. There was some disappointment in the fact that the word "pony" to us denoted a Shetland. Old Buster, as he was immediately named, was a slightly under-sized cow pony. He was a light bay, with a black mane and a star on his face. Spots of white hair on his back suggested his maturity of years and the fact he had been ridden enough to have had saddle sores.

For the purpose he served, Buster was just about ideal. He was gentle to a fault and responsive to the pleas of riders or drivers (he pulled a buggy sometimes) only in minimum measures, or when hearing anything that sounded like "whoa." When one persuaded him out of a walk he offered a reluctant trot and would go beyond that only after a hard kick in the ribs or a tap with a quirt. Once forced into a gallop, he was ready to drop back with the slightest change of position on the part of the rider. Keeping Buster moving, in other words, was hard work.

Our only one-horse buggy for several years was a heavy phaeton. It was too heavy, really, for a horse of Buster's size, but he was so much easier to deal with than any of the other horses, and, as a matter of convenience, he became Mother's driving horse. Fortunately, she had few trips of more than a mile or two.

Once when Brother Don was between two and three years

old, he found himself as the only person in the buggy behind Buster and, gathering up the lines and whip, he started for Proctor. The whip taps kept Buster going, but not so fast that I didn't have time to get on another horse and catch them before they had gone half a mile. Even as I caught up with them, it was obvious that Buster, despite his blinders, had got the idea there wasn't much force behind him, and he was setting his own pace.

At least five of us rode and drove Buster. The older of us saddled him, bridled him, harnessed him and went on cattle drives with him, but there was never a case of accident or injury in which he was involved.

As younger children came along to ride Buster, the older of us were assigned to other horses. For several years my horse was a sorrel mare named Daisy. It so happened that Father was dealing extensively at that time in mules. Since this was a sideline for him, he did a lot of his work with the mules on weekends, and when he was moving the mules from one pasture to another, it was my job, on Old Daisy, to ride ahead of the mules in whatever direction we were supposed to go. Old Daisy had seemed especially attractive to young mules, and they would follow us wherever we went. A mule would run up to Daisy, sniff a bit, nuzzle her, then kick up his heels and dart away. On more than one occasion I saw flying hoofs within a foot or two of my face. There was one thing about moving a bunch of mules, though; there was lots of action. With Daisy hurrying to keep both her and me from too many close encounters, we got to the next pasture at nothing slower than a fast trot.

One cold March day we moved the mules all the way from the Will Logan place east of Atwood to a pasture near Proctor, and we did it in about six hours of the hardest riding I can recall. Instead of crossing the river and following the highway on a diagonal, we stayed on the right, or south, side of the river. This meant following section line roads with which I was unfamiliar. It was a trip of considerably more than 30 miles. Fortunately, the mules were as curious as ever to know where Old Daisy was going, and we had little trouble with stragglers. There was no stopping to eat, and my most vivid recollection is of an intense hunger that set in about one o'clock. When we finally got to the ranch kitchen at about three o'clock, the only left-overs from dinner were some pieces of boiled beef and a kettle of cabbage. I never had liked cooked cabbage, but I wolfed it down that day, and I have eaten it with some relish ever since. The most amazing thing about that trip, perhaps, was the durability of Old Daisy. She hadn't worked all winter, and her feet were unshod. But she was still going strong at the end.

Any pay I got for my many long excursions with Father and his mules was never discussed as such. But there was considerable compensation in the fact that when he finally got out of the mule business there was a small horse business tied in with it, and the horses were mine. I had paid $35 for a yearling mare that ran with the mules and eventually produced two colts. I sold the three in 1924 for something more than $300, and this was about what I needed to get through my first year of college.

There was never a word said in explanation of Father's decision to get into mules at just about the time the war was starting in Europe. I often wondered if he had not been discouraged by the ranch owners when he suggested a new emphasis on mules. He may have bought his first mules to prove a point. The truth is that his rather awkward dealing in mules through the war was highly profitable. When he proposed in about 1919 that the ranch should put new emphasis on mules, he got a ready response from Cedar Rapids, and what followed will be covered in a separate chapter.

Meanwhile, it should be noted that there were mules among the work stock for almost all our time on the ranch. Two teams are well remembered. One was a male and female combination known as Sampson and Jenny. The other was a pair of males called Tom and Jerrry.

Sampson was a big mule. In good condition he weighed more

than 1,500 pounds. Jenny was about 100 pounds lighter. The two of them were versatile, manageable and gentle. Tom and Jerry were almost perfectly matched in color, size and temperament. They were as unflappable as any pair of mules could be, but that characteristic itself helps explain other traits. They were unresponsive when response meant speeding up, and they knew how to reduce speed in unison. They would start pulling a mowing machine at normal walking gait, but gradually they would slow down to the point the sickle was moving too slowly to clear out the hay. These slowdowns were so gradual that the driver would hardly notice it if he were not aware of his team's tricks and traits. And Tom and Jerry treated any sound from the driver's seat as "whoa."

One day Father drove into the yard with a half-grown billy goat in the back seat of the Model T. There was no explanation that I can recall, but there were those who said that a billy goat was good to have with sheep because it would fight off coyotes.

It soon developed that our Billy had little use for the sheep. He preferred people and would jump over or crawl through any of our fences to get away from the sheep and renew his acquaintance with the family and our two dogs, Bob and Ring. As a matter of fact, his ways seemed more those of a dog than a goat. He followed us wherever we went and he loved to stretch out on the concrete outside the back door. He climbed over cars, buggies, wagons and low buildings. He ate his share of overalls, shirts and dresses until Mother learned to pen him up on wash day. Gradually, though, he advanced from youthful playfulness to fits of adult temperament. He got to butting us when we weren't looking. In fact, he seemed to have staked out the backyard as his special domain. His downfall came when he started urinating on the pump handle in what some said was a warning that he was adding this spot to his little kingdom. There were no family conferences from this point. Billy had sealed his own fate, and there were few regrets when Father loaded him into a railroad car with either hogs or sheep and sent him to the Denver stockyards.

There were dogs on the ranch from my first recollection, and the recollection is rather vivid, because those early dogs were bigger than I was and they tended to rough me up once in a while. One was a slim greyhound named Queen and the other was larger, with long hair and whiskers, and was never identified as anything but a "hound." We called him Bosco. The two were taken sometimes to chase coyotes, and Father explained how the smaller and faster Queen caught a coyote and held it until the big fellow came along to handle the kill. They chased rabbits, too, and forgot sometimes about the barbs on the wire fences. Both dogs came in with fence cuts several times, and Father finally decided they should go.

After the hounds there was a whole procession of dogs, some with collie breeding, some with shepherd breeding and some with breeding that nobody tried to explain. One of my favorites, with long reddish hair, was caught sucking eggs, and was taken away very much against my wishes.

One day Father came home from Sterling with a half-grown, short-haired bitch terrier with a brown body and a white collar and white feet. We named her Ring, and she fitted herself into the family at once. Being small, she enjoyed more house privileges than bigger dogs had, and while Mother tried to limit her time in the house, we found various ways to sneak her in on cold days. Ultimately, she had two litters of pups. In the second litter was a male that almost matched her in color, and we children, after some pleading, convinced Mother and Father that we could have two dogs. We had called the mother Ring because of her white collar, but we abandoned descriptive language and named the pup Bob. Ring went to the veterinarian for spaying before there were any more pups, and for the next five or six years she and Bob roamed the ranch together, catching an occasional jackrabbit by working in shifts. Bob, the slower and lazier, often made the catch from a hidden position he had taken while Ring kept the rabbit going in circles.

The many granaries, feed bunks and open feeding floors around the ranch attracted rats and mice. It was a matter of policy, therefore, that we maintain a few cats. There was a period when there were a half-dozen or more cats in the vicinity of the lower corral that were totally self-sufficient. They were as wild as the rats themselves.

We boys acquired a couple of pairs of rabbits about 1917, and within a year and a half, the place was literally overrun by their progeny. As in the case of the cats, some rabbits struck out on their own and eventually started mingling with cottontails that had their homes among the ruins of sheds and fences. When we left the ranch there was a sizable rabbit population that showed the crossing of cottontails and domestic breeds.

Mention has been made of a decision to take the ranch into the production of mules. That is the story of an unforgettable animal and it merits a chapter by itself.

# 15. THE RELUCTANT JACKASS

## . . . or What's In a Name?

The most pampered animal on the ranch in our time was, without question, a jackass. He could have been referred to as a lowly jackass, perhaps, but there was nothing lowly about Jeffries Longfellow.

He was the only creature we ever had around that came with a registered name. His records, from a Kentucky-based breed association, traced his ancestry through a long line of jacks and jennets. And he cost $900.

Many who saw him were quick to comment on his size. I doubt that he ever was taken to the scales, but he must have weighed considerably more than 1,000 pounds when at his heaviest.

From a distance he seemed almost solid black. A closer look showed a brownish tinge in the ends of the longer hair on parts of his body, and there were flecks of gray around his flanks and inside his legs.

His quarters included a stall at one end of the old horse barn that opened into a solid-plank enclosure about 20 by 40 feet. The wall was about six feet high, but with his long neck he could extend his head over it and nip at passersby. Once he clamped his jaw over the neck of a yearling mule that got too close to the fence, and the young animal was so surprised and shocked that it made no attempt to break loose. Instead, it stood there crying like a child in distress until somebody cracked Jeff across the nose and made him loosen his grip.

Jeff, of course, had a cry of his own. It didn't come forth often, but when it did, there was no mistaking the origin. Country musicians now and then simulate a braying mule with fiddles and banjos. But no such sound I have heard comes close to the call of a jackass in good voice, and Jeff was in good voice most of the time. He started on a low note, somewhere in the range of a baritone horn. Then he slipped into a grating squeak, somewhere between the scrape of chalk on a slate blackboard and the screech of a violin when the bow hits the E string on the wrong side of the bridge. From a bar or two of this, Jeff fell back into horn notes, lowered his volume and slid through an easy finish. The whole orchestration seemed to run for at least eight seconds, maybe longer. For anyone within 100 feet of his pen, of course, time almost stood still.

Father had kept at least one Percheron stallion in residence for most of our years on the ranch, and the progeny had brought new blood into the work string and contributed to the surplus of horses from which some were sold every year. There had been no means of supplying new mules from within the ranch operation, and Jeff's arrival was supposed to change all that. (A mule, as some readers may not know, is the product of breeding female horses to male asses.)

Father had been dealing personally in mules for several years. It was a moonlighting enterprise, to borrow a term that has come into our language since that day. He bought young mules, ran them on rented land and sold them off when they reached breaking age. He had made good money through the war years, and his success was, I am sure, a factor in the decision of the ranch ownership to permit his investment of $900 in a jack that could add mules to the annual production schedule.

In retrospect, this move must go down as one of the few major judgment errors Father made in his 18 years as ranch manager. For one thing, those years following World War I marked the beginning of the end of both horses and mules as primary sources of farm power. The days when two well-matched four-year-old mules would sell for $600 to $800 would be gone by the time the ranch's first crop was ready for market.

But the heart of the disaster, so far as Father and the ranch were concerned, was in the temperamental, and possibly physical, constitution of Old Jeff himself. He was barely into his first breeding season with us when he started building a reputation that brought out all sorts of coarse and humorous allusions. What these boiled down to was that Father had invested $900 in a most reluctant jackass. But this gets us ahead of our story.

Father bought Jeff from a farmer living north of Sterling. He liked the size of the beast, but he also liked what he saw in the three or four young mules that were pointed out as being of Jeff's siring. Then there was the matter of registry; there weren't many registered jacks around. The importance of the acquisition was underscored by the fact that Father himself drove the team which pulled the specially-built stock rack, as we called it, in which Jeff came riding the 18 or so miles to his new home.

His arrival was in early spring, and it was only a matter of days until Father was scheduling appointments with mares from within the ranch herd and the mares of some in the neighborhood who were ready to pay the fee of about $15 for standing colts from this noble creature.

Jeff's quarters adjoined a corral which in turn adjoined the portion of the old barn that was used for milking. There were no cows around in daytime, so this corral became the designated trysting place. There was a high board fence that made for seclusion. At an earlier time, this had been the place where mares and stallions met, and the special equipment for those occasions was a small telephone pole suspended between two posts. This was a measure against a stallion's being kicked in the legs or the head as the receptiveness of the mare was being tested. In barnyard vernacular, it was known as a snorting pole.

For the protection and convenience of Jeffries Longfellow there had to be a much more elaborate arrangement. Two round poles, bolted to posts, paralleled each other on a slant from about two feet above the ground on one end to some four

184

feet on the other. The space between the poles was barely enough to permit a large mare to stand. Most certainly she was without freedom to move in either direction, and her rear feet were pretty well immobilized by being in a slight depression in the ground, with heavy planking behind that. Once backed into position, a mare had a sort of trussed-up look, and most certainly she must have felt that way.

For many mares there was an obvious sense of fright at being placed in so helpless a position. For some there was a sense of rebelliousness, too, and they often asserted it at the sight of old Jeff lumbering out from his stall. His appearance was surprising, of course. With his long ears and neck, he must have looked to the mares more like a clown than a lover. There was no arched neck, no flying mane and none of the romantic graces of an aggressive stallion. Jeff always came out under leash, and his handler—usually Father—took hope from that first lunge into the open air. Then came signs that Jeff was interested in the air, the freedom from his stall and all sorts of things besides the mare into whose presence he was being led.

After the first few occasions, the orders went out that there was to be no talking once the time had come when the next move had to be Jeff's. Persons not involved at the scene were fully aware that there was to be no opening of the gate by which the corral was normally entered. The gate had a noisy latch, and the sound of it would break into Jeff's reveries.

While all seemed pretty quiet around the ranch in daytime, it became painfully apparent that noises none of us had paid attention to had a killing effect on the jack's emotions. The rattle of a Model-T Ford pulling up in the yard outside the corral was almost a disaster, as was the crow of a rooster. It became a stock joke that a few faint notes from a songbird could cause him to shift his ears and his interests and disrupt all visible preparation for the job at hand. All this was so contrary to the expected nature of such a lusty-looking brute that if we had known about Ferdinand the Bull, we undoubtedly would have drawn a parallel. Jeff may not have been interested in flowers, as Ferdinand was, but there were times when he seemed to attach more importance to the distant call of a meadowlark than to the scent of a mare in heat.

On most occasions Jeff finally carried through, but almost always there was that exasperating wait and all sorts of worry about the vast assortment of potential sounds and other distractions that would prolong the proceedings. On some occasions time ran out, and Jeff was led back to his stall and the mare turned back to pasture or led home. Father would enter a zero in his record book and break a few eggs into Jeff's next feeding of oats. Someone had said the jack needed lots of protein.

But Jeff's problems didn't end with his indifference to duty. If there had been a disposition on the part of anyone to relate the affairs of jackasses to baseball players, Jeff would have been a candidate for the batter with the highest number of strikeouts. By the end of his second year on the ranch the records showed he was producing about one mule for every five or six visitations. The highest number of mules for a single season, as I recall, was about 11. Fortunately, Father still had a stallion, and this animal, getting second-rate treatment in comparison to Old Jeff, was batting close to 1,000 as a mere back-up hitter.

The crowning humiliation in the affair, so far as Father was concerned, probably was the experience of our good neighbor, Jesse Stewart. Mr. Stewart bought a jack a year or so after Father bought Jeff. He tried Father's system of keeping the animal in close quarters and supervising every relationship with a mare, but in due time he turned his jack loose with the rest of his horses. This was not the prescribed way to handle a jack. There was a general assumption that a jack in a herd of horses was bound to get kicked around and injured. There was the additional assumption that a jack needed men around if he was to have maximum success with mares. Jesse Stewart's jack, smaller and wirier than Old Jeff and unencumbered by the

status of being registered, refuted all the theories. His one year of free-lancing with the Stewart mares, and the mares of some neighbors whose pasture fences were not always enough to keep him out, produced more than double the number of mules Old Jeff could claim for the same season.

The single saving feature of Jeff's career was in the fact that while his production rate was terrible, his record for quality was unexcelled. The mules that came from him were outstanding in almost every instance, and if mules hadn't started going out of style at about that time, he might well have paid back the initial investment and his upkeep.

Commenting on those few fine mules, Father would hark back to his decision to purchase Jeff.

"They look just like the mules the man showed me—real good," he would say. "The trouble was, I didn't ask how many there were."

# 16. THAT FIRST MODEL-T

## . . . And How We Entered the Age of the Auto

One summer day in 1912, Father, Mother and the three older of us children went to Sterling to see a circus. To the best of my recollection, we went by train, but the return trip was by automobile.

Instead of going to the circus, Father spent the afternoon at Mr. Applebaum's "garage" and made a deal for a new Model-T Ford.

Father never had driven an automobile and knew nothing about the care of one. It seemed only proper, therefore, that one of Mr. Applebaum's men drive us to the ranch and spend the night there. A few miles out of Sterling we were caught in a sudden shower. There was a hasty search under the seat for side curtains, and some of those had been put in place when the rain ceased with as much suddenness as it had hit us. There had been enough moisture, though, to leave the dirt road soft and slick.

The experience of the next few minutes was the first of a lifetime of reminders that the automobile has never been any better than the road systems we have built to accommodate it. The driver managed to keep the car on the grade, but he didn't progress very much until there had been time for the water to soak into the packed roadbed or be evaporated by the late-afternoon heat and wind.

That first ride in a Model-T was a fitting preview of events ahead for five Hamils who, on that day, wittingly or unwittingly, moved into the age of the automobile. In a matter of an hour and a half, over a course of some 20 miles, there was occasion for exhilaration, fright, anxiety, disgust, despair and a great feeling of relief that came when the wheels quit spinning and skidding after the rain. Our respective affairs with cars of all kinds would be that way for the rest of our lives.

Father was elected county commissioner the next November, and the Ford became his conveyance in getting around his district and to meetings of the board in Sterling. It helped him appreciate the fact that roads which seemed adequate for wagons and buggies didn't always suffice for those who were driving Buicks, Brushes, Metzes, Appersons, Ramblers and Dodges, as well as Fords. He started putting gravel on the road between Proctor and Iliff, against considerable local complaint, but by the time he went out of office in 1916 there was gravel on most of the road from Proctor to Sterling, including the stretch where our driver almost had to give up with the Model-T after that light rain.

The 1912 Ford gave way to a 1914 model and that one in turn to a 1915 or 1916 version, which differed from the other two mainly in the fact that a molded metal shield had been fitted between the hood and the dashboard panel. In the earlier models the wood paneling of the dash was exposed.

This third Ford was with us several years, and it was the one I drove on many errands by myself before I was 11 years old.

Those first three cars had no starters, and one of the first tricks one had to learn was to handle the crank in such a way as to get a positive response from the engine without risking injury from a backfire, or kick, as we called it. There were a lot of broken wrists from mishandling an auto crank.

The third Ford served through the spring of 1919, at least, because I recall having driven it in the spring of that year across the river to a neighboring school with which our school was having an all-day picnic. The privilege of taking the car was extended by Father and Mother not as a favor to me, but as a gesture to save eight-year-old Sister Edna from having to walk. The rules were very clear: There were to be no boys among my passengers. The two young teachers (both roomed in Proctor), Edna and three other small girls—that was my load.

School took up as usual that morning, but only for the purpose of last-minute instructions as to where to go and how to conduct ourselves. We who were to ride in the car remained at the school until the entourage of horseback riders and walkers had moved out. Then we waited some more, probably because our teacher, Miss Calvert, wanted to come up on the others at about the half-way mark.

I recall faintly that Mrs. Pashby, mother of one of the little girls, was not too happy with the idea of her daughter's being in my charge that day. She lived near the school and hovered over us until we were ready to start.

She probably didn't know that her daughter would be riding with one of the most thoroughly briefed 12-year-old pilots ever to guide a Model-T. Father had seen to that.

We would skirt Proctor's two-store business center. We would approach the railroad grade not too fast, but fast enough to avoid killing the engine on the tracks. And we would look both ways and be sure no trains were in sight. We would stay square in the middle of the road when crossing the new drainage ditch. It was eight to ten feet deep, and there was no railing. There was to be caution at each of the river bridges. They were too narrow to permit two vehicles to pass. And there could be loose and treacherous sand on the fills between bridges.

Loose sand could tear the steering wheel of a Model-T right out of your hands and bring you to a jolting stop. It could halt progress in another way, too. It could prevent the rear tires from gripping and leave you as helpless as if you were in deep mud. And so our instructions were very explicit about staying away from the blow sand in the vicinity of the host school.

There was a stretch of road that was no more than parallel ruts in the virgin prairie. This was something to watch. Sometimes the ruts were so deep that a Model-T could hang up on the center ridge. We were to avoid anything like that.

Anyway, we made it—past at least one house in town from which an anxious mother watched; past the lumber yard; past the blacksmith shop and the elevator; over the track and across the main highway from Sterling; across the little bridge at the river; then the middle-sized bridges and finally the big bridge under which most of the water flowed. Past familiar cotton-woods and willows; past corner posts and gates, alkali spots and abandoned bits of rusty machinery—familiar landmarks every one.

As we moved through the foot-and-horseback contingent, I couldn't help thinking they were having more fun. I listened for somebody to taunt us for being too good to walk or ride a horse, but the presence of the teachers probably discouraged the words some were thinking.

We gave the sand around the school a wide berth and parked on solid ground at the nearest farmhouse, about 300 yards from the school. In no time at all we were engrossed in the fun and games of the day, and I forgot all responsibilities so far as the car was concerned until we were ready to start home in mid-afternoon. The role of driver of the day was old stuff by then and it is significant, I guess, that I have not a single memory of the trip home.

There is a tendency among those who recall the days of the Model-T to picture it as rugged, reliable, shock-proof and given to none of the moods and sensitivities of later versions of the automobile. The truth is that one of those simple Fords could be more of a prima donna than the most exquisite Cadillac or Continental that came along 50 years or more later.

At the left of the crank was a steel wire loop with which one choked the carburetor. The amount of choking varied from car to car, and woe to him who took lightly the instructions of the owner of any given vehicle.

"Choke it on the first turn only," would be the advice for one car. "Hold the choke out and pull the crank three times. Never spin it." That advice would apply to the next car. "Don't choke

191

it at all," some owners would say.

Then there were very delicate adjustments to be made to small levers on the steering column, just under the wheel. For some cars you set the accelerator (we called it the gas feed) about five notches down. For some you set it wide open. Opposite the gas feed was an identical lever that set the spark. Where you set this had a lot to do with the possibility of getting kicked by the crank. With the minimum of spark, one took little risk with most cars. But some wouldn't start without a lot of spark and a lot of risk. And so went the many little things we learned about each car.

The real test of temperament in both the car and the people around it came in the dead of winter. On a cold day we went through a ritual that required more time starting the engine than we would need to spend in a trip to town and back.

The first requirement was a lot of hot water—at least four gallons of it. One gallon (usually in the teakettle from the kitchen stove) was for pouring over the carburetor and the manifold. These were sensitive areas that would not be warmed by the three gallons of hot water that went into the radiator opening.

With the radiator filled and the engine warming, we could close the hood and place a blanket over it while the heat from the water was being transferred to the cold metal of the engine block. When we boys were doing this at the ages of 10, 11, 12 or 13, we used the waiting time to jack up a rear wheel. Before we started cranking, we released the lever that put the transmission in high gear. With this arrangement, the free wheel served as a flywheel and enabled us—so we thought at least—to get more action, faster turning of the cold crankshaft, more possibility of the right mixture of fuel fumes and spark to bring the first combustion. (There was no such thing as winter-weight oil then—or at least we didn't know of any.)

To this point the ritual consumed at least 20 minutes, provided there had been no waiting at the kitchen stove for the

*Family and Ford* circa. 1913

heating of the water. Just how much time would be spent on the crank was largely a matter of luck. There still remained the hazard of flooding the carburetor. The cranking often dislodged the jack. And there was always the danger that the cranker might be caught by a kick of the engine. In truth, though, there was something encouraging about a kick. It was a sign of life—and any sign of that was always welcome.

And what if the cranking was to no avail? On the ranch in those days there were always alternative flight plans, as they say in aviation circles. These alternatives, of course, involved horses. If the trip wasn't too long, you saddled one and rode. Or you could hitch one to the buggy or two to the wagon. But before going all the way with a team, there was one final resort. That was to tie the Ford behind the wagon and see if it could be started after it got rolling at the pace of a brisk trot.

If the only problem was a cold engine, the pull usually paid off. And away you went, the engine coughing along on three cylinders perhaps, and the cold breezes whistling under and around the oilcloth side curtains with their isinglass peepholes. But there was life and movement and a tremendous feeling of accomplishment. This was warmer, faster and more exciting transportation than the only other ways we knew. Looking back, one has to concede that the sense of victory, security and comfort was only relative. But what in this life really isn't?

After that much effort, one was most wary about allowing the engine to cool off until it was back in its accustomed place in the machinery shed, alongside the Van Brunt grain drill and the McCormick binder. It was not uncommon, therefore, to see our Ford and a couple of others standing in front of the general store and postoffice, with engines running while the drivers warmed themselves before the coal stove and exchanged comments on the weather and those things treated in red headlines in the Sterling *Advocate* and the Denver *Post.*

When the day's travels were over, the car was maneuvered into the fixed spot that permitted draining the radiator into a small pit that was dug in the dirt floor at the beginning of each winter. Once the petcock was open, it was time to cover the hood with a heavy blanket in what seems now to have been a vain effort to preserve some engine heat against the time when we would come again with hot water, fresh arm muscles and the hope that sprang eternal.

The years passed, and there came the self-starter and eventually a Model-T sedan with glass all around and what passed as a heater.

And there was stuff to put in the radiator that would not freeze. Mostly, we used alcohol. But someone in the neighborhood recommended a lightweight lubricating oil, the kind made for cream separators.

One of the memorable experiences of my high school days was the time the oil-filled radiator in the Overland Model 90 sprang a leak on the road. The oil poured onto the hot engine block. The smoke poured from under the hood. Al Stewart and I jumped out of the front seat and ran about 30 feet before stopping to survey the situation. The smoke subsided in due time, and when we were certain there was to be no fire or explosion, we determined what had happened, then traveled on, with a stop about every mile for stuffing snow into the radiator and fresh bits of handkerchief into that persistent leak.

There was no water along the road, because it was—as it seems always to have been when we had car trouble in those days—about five degrees below zero.

One of my earliest memories is of the first automobile to visit the ranch. I could not have been more than two and a half years old, but I never lost the picture of that huge black contraption, with its brass radiator, its other brass fittings, its fully exposed white tires, its flat top and the wheel which men grasped in maneuvers that had something to do with the over-all movement of the thing.

The machine belonged to George Henderson, Sterling's leading banker, and the trip of some 20 miles was an undertaking of such significance that a qualified mechanic came along as driver and back-up man in case of mechanical difficulty.

About the time we got our first Model-T, the local storekeeper, Mr. Fedder, came home with a Buick, and this brought something that has plagued millions of American families for 60 years—the role of the automobile as a status symbol. The neighboring Stewart family came up with the community's first Dodge which, like the Buick, was distinctly larger than the Ford. The younger Hamils were pretty much on the defensive until a 1918 Overland was parked in the machinery shed alongside the Model-T.

One of the biggest and seemingly awesome vehicles to hit the neighborhood was an early-day Rambler. There was a Moon in the neighborhood for a while, and a Moore, owned by my Uncle Bob Hamil, was generally classified along with the Maxwell among the bigger mistakes of the automobile industry of that period. The Moore came and went in a hurry, but the Maxwell became the Chrysler and went on to greatness.

A bachelor neighbor, Arthur Conrad, drove a Metz that was a distinct novelty because of a power train that included an open friction transmission that drove a sprocket shaft from which chains connected to the rear wheels.

When District Judge Munson drove up to the general store in a new Oldsmobile one day, there were all kinds of exclamations as to its size and beauty, but the one that stuck with me came from a woman who said, "Some boat!"

The variety of motor cars that came into the community between 1912, say, and 1922, seems most unusual in retrospect, but it was obviously a reflection of the great variety of name plates appearing on cars until General Motors, Ford and Chrysler emerged as the big three of the industry.

The dawning of the automobile age was interrupted one day when a beautiful horse-drawn vehicle pulled into the yard.

The driver was a farmer from Nebraska, and with him was a son several years older than I. After Mother had agreed to provide a room, an evening meal and breakfast, the farmer's story unfolded.

He had had a series of good years and had decided that he and the son would take a trip. Their outfit included a beautifully matched team of Morgans and a brand-new buggy that had everything. There were oil lamps, inside and out, an oil heater and curtains with which the occupants could completely enclose themselves in bad weather.

Here was a line of talk quite contradictory to much we had been hearing. There was no future for the automobile, as this man saw it, and one reason for his trip was to demonstrate to himself and to others that with a good team and buggy he could go everywhere and go better than could anyone in an automobile.

After the formalities of departure the next morning, the team broke into a sharp trot, the buggy wheels glistened in the sun, and our overnight guests drove into an oblivion which seems now to have been a fate for which the farmer had deliberately prepared himself. He was one, at least, who chose not to hope for the day when one couldn't live without worrying about the possibility of muddy or slick roads, flat tires, or engines that wouldn't start on cold days.

# 17. THE DAY I THREW AWAY MY HORSESHOE

## . . . But Didn't Kick the Habit

In our part of Colorado in the first two decades of the century, the chewing of tobacco was considered a manly art—among men, that is.

Father chewed, as did a high percentage of the hired men. It goes without saying that among boys of the neighborhood there was a powerful hankering to learn to chew, even though we may have been promising our mothers we would never make a habit of it.

There were little gatherings behind barns and in other out-of-the-way places where one was tested by the casual offer of a bite off of someone's hunk of Star, Horseshoe or Peachy Plug, or a pinch out of a can of snuff. The ritual had almost as much standing among the participants, I would venture, as some of the puberty rites of so-called primitive societies. It relates to some extent certainly to the way young people of later generations have been tempted to try certain narcotics. It was exciting and rebellious.

For those households, ours included, where the prevailing brand of chewing tobacco was Horseshoe, there was an offset to some of the built-in objections to chewing in the form of material rewards. The makers of Horseshoe were pioneers of what might be called the green-stamp syndrome of the merchandising world. They offered premiums in return for given numbers of the tin horseshoes that were stuck to every ten-cent cut of their product.

Father always chewed Horseshoe, but I never was certain as to whether he chose the brand because of the value of the tags or the flavor of the product. His consumption rate was such that we could count on an average of at least one tag a week from him. Those times when two or three men in the bunkhouse were also Horseshoe chewers were veritable harvest seasons.

There were things in the Horseshoe catalog for women and girls, but my recollection is only of the knives we ordered. By the time Brother Dave and I were both allowed to carry knives, the loss rate was such as to require use of all the tobacco tags we could hoard, if we were to have knives in our pockets.

My first recollection of a trip on a saddle horse without the company of another person was when Father put me on Old Tom, set my feet in some makeshift stirrups he had tied to the horn of his saddle and sent me off to Fedder's store for a plug of Horseshoe. It was understood that I was not to dismount, but to ride to the front of the store, make my presence known and ask Mr. Fedder to hand me the tobacco, for which I was to produce a dime from my overalls pocket. This worked out quite well, and the privilege of going on a tobacco-buying trip was accorded me several times before I was big enough to get on and off a horse by myself.

It was my privilege on these occasions to remove the tin tag from the plug before giving it to Father, and on one trip I licked the back of the tag and discovered something enticing about the taste of the syrup with which chewing tobacco was flavored. It might be said that this was the beginning of a habit, because by the time I was 12 or 13, I had—with the cooperation and advice of several hired men—learned to chew.

While the arguments over the pros and cons of smoking the so-called weed have gone on at the highest levels of the scientific and political worlds, the arguments over chewing tobacco have been held largely to family circles. The women of several generations have aligned themselves against tobacco chewers with a ferocity that certainly would stand up to that of the W.C.T.U. in its finest hour against liquor.

That the chewers have lost is attested by such things as the consignment of tens of thousands of brass and silver spittoons to the shelves of antique dealers. As objectionable as many persons considered them, they were essential to indoor chewing.

When I was in college in Nebraska, I did a turn as janitor for a law office. There was a spittoon at every desk, and it had to be cleaned every night. It was my observation then—in the 1920's—that these receptacles served cigar smokers to a far greater extent than they served straight chewers of tobacco. But chewing lawyers had started here.

As a newspaper reporter I was fascinated by one of Nebraska's better-known trial lawyers, then approaching 70, I would estimate. His arguments before judge or jury were punctuated by occasional gestures toward the spittoon. The process included lifting of his mustache with two fingers, but there was grace and fastidiousness in his actions that added materially to the drama of any courtroom scene of which he was a part.

Not all chewers were able to make their diversion interesting rather than offensive, and Father was no exception. Mother was patient and long-suffering, but her position in principle was clear to everyone. It was restated now and then when she caught the slightest hint a son of hers might fall for the habit.

I have never been psycho-analyzed, but it just could be that an analyst would find in my psyche the scars of a sort of schizophrenia born of the fact that during my years on the ranch I shared the joys of chewing while knowing all the time that I seemed headed for a life and time with which it just wouldn't fit. The following incident could tell something.

I was in my second year of the eighth grade. (Our parents had insisted on two years there as a sort of additional tempering for living away from home while attending high school.) My older sister was in her second year at high school, and she had arranged to bring three classmates and three teachers for a weekend at the ranch.

They came out on the Friday evening train, as I recall, and they took over three second-floor bedrooms. We boys were uneasy occupants of the fourth.

It had been established in advance that the principal recreation would be horseback riding. Some of the guests knew about horses, and some didn't. But all were equipped with their bloomers, jodhpurs and high shoes, and early Saturday morning they were ready to ride.

Our saddle stock included at least one phlegmatic pony that was safe for anyone, two others that could be trusted to persons with a minimum knowledge of horses, and one spirited gelding that could jump out from under an inexperienced rider.

It fell my lot to saddle the horses, assign them in accordance with the skills of the guests and, generally, to make sure that everybody got to ride and nobody got hurt. I approached the assignment with some misgivings, a bit of boredom and considerable shyness. Three "town" girls and three graduates of big universities with degrees that qualified them to teach things like Latin, French and English—these were formidable charges.

I couldn't see how they could have anything but disdain for a hostler in overalls who was just finishing the eighth grade. And somewhere along the line I got to wondering what they would think if they knew that in the right front pocket of those overalls there was a plug of Horseshoe chewing tobacco.

Somehow I sensed that I was in the company of people who would not be impressed, as some of the boys in the neighborhood were impressed, by the fact that I had managed to carry my own plug of tobacco and could turn to it whenever or wherever there was little prospect of being caught by my parents or somebody who might report to them. I began to feel uncomfortable.

These teachers—these town girls—these people with whom I would be associating to some degree when I started to high school in a few months—were representative of the refinement, the taste, the ambition Mother talked about when she lectured us on the evils of tobacco.

The teachers proved not to be the aloof individuals I had

pictured as the presiding personalities of classrooms in the big high school. They repected my knowledge of horses, and they didn't talk in Latin or French or do anything else that might tend to exclude me from their company. And the three girls—sophomores of 15 or 16—well, they were just plain interesting.

My vocabulary at the time would not have enabled me to describe it in these terms, but actually I suddenly found myself squarely caught between two cultures. That plug of tobacco in my pocket was a symbol of something that stood between me and this fine group of feminine visitors.

In the late afternoon, with everyone having had enough riding, I unsaddled the horses and headed for the house. By that time the tobacco was weighing heavily on my conscience as well as my pocket. On a sudden impulse I drew it out, took a quick look to be sure I had no witnesses, and aiming between two cottonwood trees and over the fence into the orchard, I drew back and sent that small brown object to a landing in the coarse grass and alfalfa stubble.

Our guests headed back to town the next morning, and life at the ranch soon was back to normal and just a little dull, perhaps, after all the excitement. Late that Sunday afternoon, with an hour or two of chores ahead, I suddenly realized that in the quiet of a ride to bring in the cows, I would not be able to sneak a chew.

Checking again to be sure I was not under observation, I climbed the fence and strolled back and forth through the orchard. I found what I had thrown away 24 hours earlier, but because of a heavy dew the night before and the fact that it had been trampled under the muddy feet of at least one hog, it was beyond redemption.

The proper end to this account should be a statement to the effect that never again did I touch tobacco. This would be contrary to the truth.

# 18. WE WORE BIB OVERALLS

## . . . Most of the Time

When my first grandson was about three years old, his grandmother presented him with a brand-new pair of authentic bib overalls. He refused to wear them.

This came as quite a shock to me. I had worn bib overalls almost every day of my life between age four and age 14. I had to concede, though, that the grandson's response might well have been expected. He probably never had seen a pair of overalls before. The heavy blue denim was a strange fabric. It was rough and stiff, and its smell was unlike anything he ever had associated with clothing.

In him there was no appreciation whatsoever of the fact that these overalls were cut exactly as those his Daddy would wear—if his Daddy would wear overalls. The bib was more than ample, and so were the suspenders. The brass fasteners glistened—somewhat frighteningly, we suspect. And there was a watch pocket over the breast and a pocket on one of the legs. These were real he-man overalls—much more he-mannish than the ones I first wore. And they cost about six times as much.

The whole episode started some speculating on the true significance and symbolism of bib overalls in rural America. I went so far as to reason that if the six-shooter was the thing man had to have to win the West, it could be said that the bib overall was what he had to have to break its virgin sod, build its homes, its railroads and its towns and cities.

Some people don't realize that the word "overall" was so firmly implanted in our language that trousers made of blue denim, and commonly known in later years as jeans or Levis, once were called "bibless overalls." It would be an oversight to touch on semantic relationships without offering a horseback opinion that there was a time when at least six out of ten persons wearing overalls would have spelled the word "overhaul" if they had been put to a test.

The bib overall was (and still is) common, prosaic and taken for granted. But we doubt that any other single garment has come nearer meeting the practical needs of men and boys when engaged in hard physical activity and coming in close contact with dirt, grime and grease.

While the so-called bib did serve now and then to catch the egg or gravy that otherwise might have made a shirt unwearable, it was essentially a protection against things other than the drips and crumbs of mealtime. It was an armor and shield against flying sparks, chips and gravel and the things working men sometimes had to lean against. And it provided a wonderful place to carry a watch.

An interesting fact about the bib overall is that it lends itself to easy shaping. Fat men, thin men, big men and little ones can get a reasonable fit with a minimum of compromise of one dimension with another.

Tall, thin men (and boys) often have to accept some looseness about the waist in order to get the proper length, but extra inches in the girth are hardly noticed. Short men have to accept long legs, sometimes, but with blue denim, more than any other fabric from which work clothing is made, it is easy (and in my day it was stylish) to turn up the cuffs. As a matter of fact, it was considered absolutely essential in the days before some of the shrinking tendencies had been taken out of cotton fabrics that one buy his overalls big enough to take care of a substantial shrink in the first washing.

During my growing-up years in Colorado, I usually had three pairs of bib overalls on hand. Two pairs were already washed and faded, and were first choice for work. The other pair—the first washing of which was delayed as long as possible—was for a

sort of second-degree dressing up. During the summer that best pair of overalls was for Saturday night, when we went to town and loitered among the shoppers and idlers around the stores and pool hall. On Sunday, when there was a church service in the school house, I put on my detested knee-length pants, usually with jacket to match. But the overalls were back on by the time of our noon meal. There was a brief experiment with khaki pants, but I was too thin for the pants available, and I got tired of folding the extra width under my belt.

Overalls came in different weights and qualities, and we boys moved up to the brands that had status as soon as we had money of our own for buying clothes. Mother tended to favor those that cost about 80 cents a pair. A high-ranking brand of the overall trade was Oshkosh B'Gosh—made in Oshkosh, Wis.

And a pair cost in the neighborhood of $1.25. This was Hart, Shaffner and Marx and Hickey Freeman rolled into one, and we paid the price.

If anyone thinks one could have disguised a pair of cheap, low-rated overalls, he has a second guess coming. One thing about bib overalls was that the labels were made to last about as long as the garments themselves. And they were large and conspicuous—and still are. When one wore Oshkosh overalls, there were markings front and back and on all the buttons to tell the world where you rated as a buyer of clothes.

While there was status in the brand names of certain overalls to those who wore them, there was, for some people, an obvious lack of status in overalls of any brand. While we boys always wore bib overalls, and the hired men wore them, as did the brakemen and firemen and engineers on the freight trains that stopped on the local siding, it became obvious quite early that some men didn't wear them. Father never wore them, and neither did some of the other heads of families and managers or owners of farms and ranches. Father never offered an explanation, but I suspect that he chose to distinguish himself from the hired men he supervised. But there is another theory that has some validity. In his younger years Father had spent a lot of time on horseback working with cattle. There was a tendency among the cowman type not to wear bib overalls. This came home to me in later years as I viewed the Marlboro cigaret ads for months on end and never saw a man in bib overalls.

Be that as it may, the garment has a place in American history. And just for the record, it should be explained that while our first grandson disdained bib overalls, his younger brother donned them without question after they had been washed and softened and laid away for about a year.

# 19. OUR ONE-ROOM SCHOOL

## ... Center of Culture—or What Passed for It— As Well As Learning

The society of which we were a part during our years at Proctor was a working society. In some respects it was a society in which the struggle for survival involved just about everyone beyond infancy.

There was no leisure class in the historic sense of that term. There were the usual lazy and shiftless, to be sure, but there was nobody whose freedom from making a living left much time for constructive contributions to community uplift.

The highest level of professionalism was that of the men and women who came to teach school. Few of these, as I recall, had had more than a summer or two of study beyond the twelfth grade, but for whatever passed as organized intellectual or cultural activity they had primary responsibility.

For one thing, the teacher presided over the only public meeting place in the neighborhood. Besides that, he or she was supposed to supervise entertainment as well as learning.

Our austere one-room school, therefore, without electric lights, without central heat and with fixed seats for no more than 30 persons, was the center of the only organized entertainment we knew until we went to Sterling to attend high school. There was an occasional movie in a makeshift theater over a store building at Iliff, and in my own case there was a three-day orgy of movie-going in Denver once during Stock Show week. But these experiences were extraordinary.

Most of the entertainment at Proctor was home-grown, so to speak. One memorable exception was the time a man-and-wife

207

team put on a musical show that opened a whole new world. They hauled their instruments in a wobbly truck and when they set them out at the front of the room, they occupied fully a third of all the space within the walls. There were accordions, horns, guitars and a harp that the lady played with sparkling fingers.

When I think back on this occasion, I am forced to conclude that these people booked themselves into our school without knowledge that it was a one-room institution. They probably were deceived by the fact that Proctor was a postoffice town and a regular stop on the railroad. At 25 cents a ticket—and twice that for adults—the take could not have exceeded $20.

But whether they made money or not, these musicians treated us to some mighty rich fare when compared with what we got at the two or three "programs" that were presented each term by the pupils themselves.

The basic plan of a "program," of course, was that the teacher would line up some recitations, dialogues, singing (within the bounds of the talent available) and anything special that might come to mind. One of our more enterprising teachers trained us for a flag drill that seemed at the time to involve much precision. We marched in circles and figure eights; we reversed on signal; and we raised and lowered our flags in unison. This was quite a spectacle, and it stood as a sort of high water mark until a young teacher at a neighboring school did the same thing with sparklers in a darkened room.

For all this the school expected community support of the money-raising project—the box supper or the pie supper that came at the end.

Box suppers, it seemed, ranked much higher on the scale than pie suppers. Boxes (of food) sold at auction for around 50 to 75 cents, with an occasional one going above a dollar under the pressure of some inside knowledge as to whose it was. Pies went for 15 to 25 cents.

One or more of these suppers raised enough money for the

purchase of the 20-volume set of "The Book of Knowledge." This was a landmark event, because until those wonderful blue and gold books arrived about the only reading available was in the books from which we recited.

The teacher at the time was W. L. Strickland, a prolific reader by Proctor's standards. It was a tribute to him and to the institution of the box supper that when he left after two and a half years, the "library" included "Black Beauty," "Swiss Family Robinson," "Gulliver's Travels," "Two Years Before the Mast," and other works that we never would have read had they not been there for our entertainment and pleasure during the hours when the teacher was occupied with seven other grades, including an almost continuous stream of youngsters from families of European origin who had to be taught the rudiments of our language.

About the time I had reached the seventh grade, I could boast having read "Swiss Family Robinson" five times and every page of the 20 volumes of "The Book of Knowledge" at least once.

For a period there was some adult intrusion into the planning of the "programs." Memory does not supply clear explanations, but it does bring back some names and faces of individuals who were known as "talkers" and who obviously yearned for some kind of forum.

In any event, there was an interlude when the "programs" featured a debate. The topic on one occasion was something like this: "Resolved that fire is more destructive than water." The star performer, we concluded at the time, was the patriarch of the Correll family. This man was on the "fire" side of the argument, and his most devastating point seemed to be his first-hand description of an area in Michigan that had been swept by a forest fire. He struck me as a man who really had been around.

There was considerable talk at home about a topic that may or may not have been openly debated. A hired man—"Old

George," we called him (not so much because of his age but because of his heavy black beard)—wanted to have it settled once and for all that California was the greatest state in the union.

Being a native of California who had taken up residence in Colorado while proving up on a homestead, "Old George" just knew that he could develop an air-tight case. Father suggested that if he were debating the issue, he would have to favor Illinois. He had been there, but he knew nothing of California.

"Old George," if he lived that long—and I haven't heard of him for 50 years—would have been a most happy man when the federal census showed that California was ahead of New York in population and Los Angeles was creeping up on Chicago for second place among the cities. While he had a fixation on California, he was nevertheless a pretty knowledgeable fellow. His own copy of the Denver *Post* came to the ranch; and he read it, line by line, seemingly, in his leisure hours in the bunkhouse.

The *Post* was pretty important to me, too. The big, glaring type of its front-page headlines fairly shouted for my attention as I was learning to read, and my first impressions of many common words came from seeing them in the *Post's* red ink and all-capital letters.

I had become a fairly proficient reader by the time war broke out in Europe in August 1914, and the combination of dramatic headlines and pictures of marching men attracted me to almost every line of every dispatch from the battle zones. Father took me with him to a meeting of the county commissioners a few weeks after the war broke out, and I recall a flash of embarrassment when he remarked to his fellow commissioners, "Harold has been reading the paper, and he thinks Germany will win."

We were taking the Sterling *Advocate* at the same time, and its weekday issues seemed a lot like the *Post's*—probably because the *Advocate*, along with many other small Colorado papers, copied the *Post* in liberal use of red ink on the front page. But when Sunday came, it was the *Post* all the way. One reason, of course, was the comic section, with the Katzenjammer Kids, Happy Hooligan and other popular features. The Sunday *Post* was attractive in other ways. It featured paintings of mountain scenes in color, and then there was the rotogravure section with brown-toned photographs that stood out in clear detail, in contrast with the muddy pictures of the regular news section. There were pictures in the roto section by a photographer at Pitchfork, Wyo.

The arrival of the Sunday *Post* was a big event at Proctor for the simple reason that it constituted a big segment of the weekly flow of news, ideas, concepts, thoughts, or what-have-you, into a community where new knowledge was rather hard to come by.

There was none of the constant stream of reportage, opinion and entertainment that subsequent generations would take for granted. The daily papers were extremely important, of course, but we rarely saw them until their news was at least 24 hours old.

Long before we could read its contents, *The Youth's Companion* was important in our lives. It came each Tuesday, folded flat and wrapped in a belt of brown paper. There was a children's page that Mother read aloud on Tuesday nights by the light of a Rayo oil lamp and, later, a Coleman gasoline lamp. In due time I was reading the more "mature" fiction pieces on my own. I recall particularly one author, Albert W. Tolman, who specialized in stories that ended with somebody's doing the right thing just in the nick of time.

I had reached the age of 10 perhaps when I convinced Mother I should be reading *The American Boy* (which later merged with the *Companion* in a move that saved neither from extinction). *The American Boy* exuded action. There were sports stories, outdoor stories, stories about boys involved in all kinds of innocent intrigue and Robin Hood-ish exploits. What stands out in my recollection is the amount of advertising directed at boys in rural environments. In fall and winter one could find the advertisements of several firms appealing to boys to ship them their mink, muskrat, fox and skunk skins.

In the late fall of 1918 or 1919, when fur prices were still pretty high, we heeded the ads of Hill Brothers in Chicago and sent them about 35 muskrat hides. We fully expected an average of more than a dollar a hide, but when our check came, it added up to a little more than $12 for the entire shipment. The hides were of poor quality, the accompanying note implied. The following March we forgot the ads in *The American Boy* and sent all our skins to an outfit in Denver to which Father had sent horse and cow hides. We got as much as $3 apiece for our skins, and Dave and I divided total earnings of at least $100 for the late-winter trapping season. In all likelihood, our February-March catch was of better quality. There was a lot of talk around the house, though, about companies with slick advertising as opposed to companies with which one had had experience. Mother, through it all, defended *The American Boy* as a reliable publication that would not have taken the Hill Brothers ad without checking on the firm's reputation for dealing fairly with boys.

When I was about 12 years old, J. D. Blue, out from Cedar Rapids for an inspection of things at the ranch, observed that *The Youth's Companion* and *The American Boy* were pretty childish stuff for me to be spending my time on, and, with Mother's consent, he entered a subscription to *The Saturday Evening Post* in my name. I don't recall how many renewals he paid for, but the *Post* continued to come in my name until I was through high school.

I met a lot of authors in the *Post*. Some were already famous or well on their way to fame. They came to me as strangers, though, and I took them all on face value. One was F. Scott Fitzgerald, and while I read some things of his in the *Post*, I had to wait until I was through college to really appreciate him. Stories by Booth Tarkington, Mary Roberts Rinehart, Irvin S.

Cobb, Edith Wharton and others began challenging my attention. I had read the stories of Clarence Budington Kelland in *The American Boy*, and I took it for granted that I should read all of his accounts of the adventures of Scattergood Baines as they appeared in the *Post*. Joseph Hergesheimer and Arthur Train (the latter's stories were about a lawyer named Mr. Tutt) were *Post* regulars, and I don't recall ever reading anything by them in other publications.

I found the *Post* deadly serious and, to me, deadly dull in its non-fiction articles about the League of Nations, postwar tariff policies and the like.

The real bright spots in the magazine, so far as I was concerned, seem to have been missed in 1954 by Roger Butterfield and the others who put together a compendium of the *Post's* best stories. This book of some 500 pages carries not a single story by Ben Ames Williams or Hugh McNair Kahler. Both were inclined to find rural settings for their fiction, and they may have got hold of me through illustrations of scenes I could relate to. One of them wrote about a farmer who seemed obsessed by the notion that his hot-tempered bull was more masculine than he was. Critics today would say there were Freudian overtones in the sequence of events leading to the day when the two faced each other in what had to be a fight to the death. I don't recall which died—probably the bull—but it was a gripping yarn.

For many years Mother subscribed to *American Motherhood*, a slick magazine with pictures of babies on its covers. In my early reading years I kept hoping to find something in it that would interest me. I thumbed through issue after issue before I finally was convinced that there were no stories—just a monotonous series of discussions of bottle feeding, breast feeding (in very delicate and euphemistic language), the various types of nursing bottles that were coming on the market, the treatment of colic, rashes and so forth. This was one of the several publications of that period that seemed to be dominated

213

by Cream of Wheat ads.

Our bookcase included a copy of "Pilgrim's Progress" (illustrated), a children's Bible (also illustrated), a G. A. Henty book, "Grimms' Fairy Tales," "Hans Brinker," a home remedy book, "Before the Doctor Comes" and a small collection of volumes that seemed to come and go. Among these circulating books there was usually at least one of Harold Bell Wright's novels. Mother seemed to like Wright's stories, but I can't believe she ever had time to read one during those 18 years when she was never without at least one child under the age of five.

*Capper's Weekly*, the *Weekly Kansas City Star*, the *Record Stockman* (from Denver) and the *Nebraska Farmer* were among the publications we received regularly. For many years a feature of *Capper's Weekly* was a newsprint version of what became in the days of television the serialized situation comedy. Its major characters were a wife and husband. Father never read such stuff on his own, but he usually listened as Mother read aloud the better episodes in the "Married Life of Helen and Warren." We children were supposed to listen, too, but sometimes we failed to get the humor that Mother seemed to see in these upheavals in the lives of two adults.

In our second reader at school we were introduced to Longfellow and Whittier. The third reader had James Russell Lowell's poem, "The First Snowfall." It was in the fourth reader perhaps that we read Oliver Wendell Holmes' story in verse of the wonderful one-horse shay. We heard very little mention of Shakespeare, but Tennyson's "Crossing the Bar" was in one of our readers. Somewhere in the advanced reading schedule we read all of Scott's "Lady of the Lake" and Longfellow's "Evangeline" and "Hiawatha."

It would be a fair guess that two-thirds of all the poetry we read from textbooks was by authors who had lived within 50 miles of Boston. There was, in fact, a New England flavor to much of the content of our textbooks—especially the illustrations. I can't recall a single picture in any but the history and geography books that took note of the fact that Americans lived in mountainous areas, on prairie farms and in the fertile valleys of California, Oregon and Washington. We saw or read little about the slums of New York and other cities.

A picture in one of our geography books showed a railroad snowplow pushed by three or four locomotives through deep drifts in a mountainous area. I was to learn many years later that the story of the failure of the Colorado Midland Railroad (whose equipment was pictured) was pretty well summed up in that picture. The Colorado Midland crossed the Continental Divide at high altitude, and the high cost of snow removal was a factor in its failure to make a profit.

W. L. Strickland, second in line among the seven teachers I knew at Proctor, sought variety in our reading lessons at about the fifth grade with a collection of stories from Greek mythol-

Dist. 50, Proctor School

ogy in a book titled, "Gods and Heroes." One of our more irreverent boys was quick to rephrase the title into "God-Damn Heroes," but we read those stories with considerably more enthusiasm than we had for most of the stuff through which we were expected to broaden our acquaintance with the English language and what skilled writers could do with it.

Our lesson one day was the story of the Augean stable and how Hercules cleaned it of 30 years of filth. I read the story carefully before time to recite and discovered a new word, m-a-n-u-r-e. I decided it should be pronounced with the emphasis on the first syllable. Mr. Strickland asked me to stand and read at just about the point where this word came in. I pronounced it as I had been pronouncing it to myself at my seat. Mr. Strickland corrected me. I was the victim of a kind of shock, I guess, for having failed to recognize in writing a word I had been hearing and using around the ranch and elsewhere since babyhood. In any event, as I read on and came to that word again, I pronounced it my way again, and Mr. Strickland snapped an impatient, "Sit down." And so for several days I heard from schoolmates and from Father and Mother (to whom Sister Ruth seemed to report all my embarrassments) sly remarks about a farm boy who couldn't pronounce "manure."

Thinking back on the incident, I know that my failure to recognize the word in print could be explained by the fact that around the ranch the word was pronounced not as Webster specifies, but as "manurah."

It dawned on me years later that I could well forgive Mr. Strickland for his put-down and thank him for having introduced me to Greek mythology. If he hadn't done it, I might well have gone on through life without any basis for understanding the many references of writers and speakers to the characters who were supposed to have populated Mount Olympus. Never in my high school or college courses would I encounter as thorough a review of the Greek myths as we got in about the fifth grade.

Our first teacher at Proctor was Miss Minnie Mathinson, who had come out from Phelps County, Nebraska, and had lived for a time on a homestead near Willard. She was in her mid-20's, a trim, precise woman of Swedish ancestry. She had attended Nebraska Wesleyan University and had taught other schools. Her pupils ranged in age from six to at least sixteen, but she was always in firm command.

She had a variety of devices for keeping six-year-olds occupied, but the two I remember best were a can of dry beans and a collection of colored sticks. With the sticks, not much larger than toothpicks, we were allowed to build things on our desk tops. She wrote words on our desks with chalk and then gave each of us a handful of beans to be placed end-to-end on the chalk lines. She drew a hat on my desk once and then wrote the word "HAT" below it. The placing of the beans on all that chalk probably kept me busy for half an hour.

Just in front of my seat was a wastebasket, and one day I discovered that I could read the writing on bits of paper if they were placed just right at the top of the basket when it was full. It was always full between three and four o'clock, the time of our daily spelling lesson. Why not, I thought, write out the list of words I would be asked to write from memory and have it there on the wastepaper heap for quick reference in case of trouble? I wrote the words and placed them just right for easy reading, but Miss Mathinson caught me. My penalty was to stay after school until I had written each of those words ten times. Miss Mathinson sat patiently as I wrote, but Sister Ruth was less patient as she waited for our long walk home. This was another occasion for embarrassment in the eyes of the family, but it left a thoroughly lasting impression of Miss Mathinson, whose lecture on the evils of cheating seemed to come from the heart and to be spoken in my own best interest.

While Miss Mathinson didn't figure in it, there was another episode involving my integrity in which her beans did figure. A boy named Ernest Souders sat behind me, and one day he

217

placed one of the beans in my right ear. I plucked it out, looked at it and replaced it. On the way home that night I casually told Ruth there was a bean in my ear and that Ernest had put it there. After supper that night Ruth rather casually told Mother I had a bean in my ear. Mother spotted it, but her maneuvering to remove it only pushed it farther into my ear. Father was summoned from the bunkhouse, and somewhat reluctantly he called the doctor at Iliff, who suggested bringing me to his office immediately. The bean would be swelling, he warned.

And so there was a nine-mile trip in a buggy, some painful experience in the doctor's office and a decision, finally, that I had to be placed under an anesthetic. Father's good friend, Tom Moore, who lived in Iliff, got out his car and we headed for Sterling where there could be a second doctor in attendance as state law—or medical ethics—required when an anesthetic was administered. We got back to Iliff about three a.m., and Mrs. Moore provided a bed for Father and me for the rest of the night. Our horse was put up in the livery stable.

As we neared Proctor the next day about noon, we met Ernest Souders' father, driving a team to a wagon. Father pulled up and greeted him with an abrupt statement that because his boy had put a bean in my ear, he (Father) had been up most of the night before and had spent about $15 on doctor bills. Mr. Souders was a bit startled, but said he would inquire of Ernest. The latter, of course, explained that the final placement of the bean had been my own action. In any event, I had some explaining to do when I returned to school next day. And the whole incident was confused—more or less to my advantage—by the fact I could make a case for Ernest's having started it all.

At the end of the year at Proctor, Miss Mathinson returned to Nebraska and was married shortly thereafter to Arthur Swanson, for many years a well-known grocer and community leader at Holdrege. She died in 1974 at the age of 89.

W. L. Strickland had come to Colorado from Iowa and was living in Iliff and editing that town's weekly newspaper, the *Independent,* when he was employed to succeed Miss Mathinson. For the first several weeks of his first term he walked from Iliff to Proctor and back each day. Mr. Strickland had previous teaching experience, also, but his style differed materially from that of Miss Mathinson. Being a man, he gave the impression of being a strict disciplinarian, but in truth he was less demanding in many ways than his female predecessor.

Miss Mathinson had played the organ to help us learn some songs that she recited from memory or wrote on the blackboard, but Mr. Strickland went further. He ordered some songbooks and proceeded to familiarize us with their contents. He couldn't play the organ, but he brought his brass cornet to school and, with cheeks bulging and face reddening, he led us in singing "Love's Old Sweet Song," "Flow Gently Sweet Afton," "Sweet and Low," and other selections. By the time he had taken us through a couple of songs, his horn would be dripping saliva, and we were about as much interested in the widening wet spot on the pine floor as in the gesturing hand with which he kept time.

One of the many books Mr. Strickland added to our school shelves was one called "Foolish Dictionary." It was something of a disappointment to me, but I went through its definitions of a hundred or more familiar words. One of the first words, if not the very first one, was "athlete." There was an illustration, as I recall, showing a man with bulging biceps. The definition ran something like this: "A person with powerful muscles who can lift heavy objects, run fast, jump high and accomplish many other feats, but who shies away from such chores as the sifting of cinders." In some vague way I related that definition to Mr. Strickland. He was a wiry individual, but not especially athletic. He could not have been termed lazy, either. But he was obviously uninterested in caring for the big sheet-iron stove that sat in the middle of the schoolroom.

For months on end, it seemed, he neglected to remove the ashes, and I recall distinctly a time when they had accumulated to the point of filling the firebox and extending up into the heat chamber. How he managed to keep a fire going on top of that thick bed of cold ashes remains a mystery. I don't recall that we ever were cold to the point of suffering, but somebody at some stage pushed a poker through a seam in the stove opposite the door, and this seemed to provide a draft that kept the fire going without benefit of any air through the grates. With or without a thick bed of ashes, the stove often was red hot and it seems almost a miracle that no pupil ever fell into it or that a fire was not started from the hot coals that often popped out of that hole in the seam or out of the door.

Mr. Strickland's interest in adding new books to the school's meager library turns out to have been extremely important to me, because I was ready to read just about every volume he ordered. He was an intellectual in the sense that he had an interest in what went on at state and national levels and in ideas generally, and he was, as previously mentioned, an extensive reader. After two and a half years, he resigned his teaching job to become operating officer of the Proctor State Bank.

B. R. Church followed Mr. Strickland, but after about a year and a half he, too, was lured from teaching into Proctor's expanding commerce. He became an employee of the Lamb store. My memories of the Church era were of a period of relative tranquility. Mr. Church's resignation, though, was an act that set off what might well have been termed a reign of terror in the Proctor school.

It was not easy to find replacement teachers in mid-term, but somehow Father and his colleagues on the school board managed to have a third male teacher on the job the day after Mr. Church left. His name was G. C. Ashbrook, and he wrote it on the blackboard in his marvelous Spencerian style for all of us to get acquainted with that first day.

He had taught in other states, but the only one I can recall from his references is Oklahoma. He probably was past 50 and he seemed to belong not only to a different generation, but to a world we pupils could not understand. His actions, his manners, his orders, established a gulf between him and me—and most of the rest of the pupils, I am sure—that seemed almost beyond my capacity to bear. I longed for Mr. Church and his generally cheerful outlook, his ability to smile, his readiness to encourage.

Mr. Ashbrook seemed more determined to torment than to teach, though his knowledge of subject-matter was probably as good or better than that of any of his predecessors. He reigned over his huddled charges as though he were the devil and we were the condemned. I cannot recall his ever smiling or putting a humorous twist to any remark. He could have been haunted by a great personal tragedy or disappointment, but no one seemed to know anything about his private life.

He was hung up, obviously, on the importance of discipline. Our conduct was everything. What we might learn under him seemed secondary. He was given to lecturing us on how good the boys and girls had been in other schools he had taught. One day he told about a boy he had had in school for two or three years. This boy, he said, had never in all that time been caught whispering to another pupil, never had looked over his shoulder even in any moment of distraction from his studies. "And when you see him today on the streets of Tulsa, he's looking straight ahead, all business, a great success," he said.

For some reason, though, Mr. Ashbrook failed to convince any of us that he was indispensable. Ruth, Dave and I carried our complaints home. Al and Ruth Stewart were telling the same stories to their parents, and Jesse Stewart was one of the three members of the board. I am sure our parents were sympathetic, but by the time our case was fully understood there were not more than six weeks of the term left. Mother and Father advised patience, but we felt we had already exhausted that. Then came word that schools in some part of the county were closing because of some kind of epidemic. The decision to close the Proctor school came in short order, and I am convinced that it was hastened more by pupil unrest than advice from the medical profession. Father had work laid out for us boys during those early spring days, but we faced it almost enthusiastically. Anything seemed better than what we had just experienced.

The history books we studied gave much more than passing attention to that early period of our nation's history that was known as the "era of good feeling." If ever there was an era of good feeling at the Proctor school it was in the fall of 1917, when our new teacher was Lucille Reynolds. While there had been no cause to think unkindly of Mr. Strickland and Mr. Church, there was a definite prejudice against male teachers that seemed to stem from those months under G. C. Ashbrook. Miss Reynolds came on the scene, therefore, with everything in her favor. She had auburn hair, a few freckles and a most friendly disposition. She and other members of her family had come from Shelton, Neb., and she liked to tell us about how people in Shelton thought of Proctor as the prototype of towns pictured in wild-west movies.

Miss Reynolds was followed by Alma Calvert, whom I remember as an innovative teacher and one who seemed to give the proper respect to her eighth graders, of whom I was one.

Because we were going to have to go into Sterling to attend high school, our parents required that the three older Hamils spend two years in the eighth grade. Miss Calvert allowed me to take the county examinations in geography and physiology, but my final examinations in other subjects were postponed until I had completed that second year in the eighth grade. The teacher that year was Norah McGuire, who had come from Kansas and lived with her sister, Mrs. Glenn Davis, wife of the Union Pacific agent.

Miss McGuire had taught one or two years in Kansas, and she introduced some Kansas books and methods. She seemed even more respectful than Miss Calvert had been toward eighth graders, but she kept us working on our arithmetic, grammar and history, reminding us now and then that our grades in the final examinations would measure her abilities as well as ours.

The final touch of that good relationship with Miss McGuire was a souvenir folder that she prepared at her own expense. It included her picture and a list of all the pupils at Proctor in that 1919-20 term. There were 23 of us, and the last day of school was marked by a picnic lunch at the school, with some of our parents joining us. Al Stewart and I were the only graduates, and Miss McGuire invited us to go for a walk of a half mile or so in what seemed an especially appropriate gesture for a big day in our lives.

In Sterling High School the next year, I would ponder the good and the bad of having had my first eight years in that one-room school at Proctor. I was a little lost in the high school gymnasium. I had never done calisthenics, had never seen a basketball. Algebra was a somewhat mysterious field, but I never had any feeling of inferiority in history and English classes. As a matter of fact, I finished highest in American history and general information when interested students were tested for a competition in academic subjects with other Northeastern Colorado high schools. This was in my senior year but I always felt the groundwork was laid during those hours when there was nothing to do at Proctor but read books of my own choosing. Professional educators were recommending this sort of free-time experience 50 years later, and many of them treated it as something new.

### Epilogue

I saw Mrs. Minnie Mathinson-Swanson at Holdrege one hot night in the mid 30's and again in the late 50's. I visited frequently with Mr. Strickland on my trips to Sterling in the 1930's. He died in late middle age. B. R. Church returned to teaching and was honored eventually for 50 years of school work, most of it in Logan County. Alma Calvert-Marks lived for many years in the Fleming community, and we exchanged letters a time or two in the 1960's. Norah McGuire-Thompson was living at Hill City, Kan., when I renewed contact with her in 1971 and later visited her home. Her memory was clear on many details of her year at Proctor and she helped me reconstruct some incidents of that period. I have no information as to what Lucille Reynolds did after leaving Proctor. G. C. Ashbrook disappeared as abruptly as he came on the scene back in 1917.

# 20. SWIMMING ON SUNDAY

## ... And Other Issues Involving God and Mammon

The spiritual climate in which we grew up at Proctor was a lot like the physical climate of the region. It was fitful, inconsistent and defiant of easy description.

At home we were subjected to the Presbyterian tradition in which Mother and Father and their ancestors for several generations had been reared. There was more emphasis on custom than zeal. There was no public praying, beyond the bedtime ritual through which we were put as small children. There were no confessions of having been in two-way communication with God and no expressions of conviction of His having rescued anyone from trouble.

Still, there was a powerful feeling that a powerful God ruled the universe and that His judgments generally prevailed. In both parents there was a strong belief in the virtue of diligence and a tendency to blame some individuals' difficulties on their own laziness or bad conduct. Though Mother was more inclined than Father to put her explanations in religious terms, both seemed to recognize the jealous God of the Old Testament and to subscribe to the so-called Puritan ethic that had come with their forebears from England and Scotland. Hard work and thrift were viewed as effective antidotes to temptation.

Mother quoted the Golden Rule and the Ten Commandments in criticizing our conduct in given situations. Her attempts to inspire us to rise above prejudice or greed and live what she called the Christian life brought out lines from songs and verses she had committed to memory. She had several quotations to warn against judging people by their looks. One of these was from a song about "Sweet Marie," for whom the singer had affection "not because (your) face so fair I love to see . . . but your heart is pure and sweet, it makes my happiness complete . . ." We were reminded often that pride "goeth before a fall."

In our family circle, therefore, there was a tendency to relate religion to ethics and vice versa, without, in fact, any attempts to argue philosophical fine points. Good people had religion, generally, and those who didn't have it were a bit suspect. There was some question, of course, as to whether we were to accept Catholicism as religion, and for me this was a matter of recurring concern. My classmate—the only one most of the time—was Al Stewart, and his family was Catholic. Since there was no Catholic church in the vicinity, Al's exposure to doctrines and forms was as limited as mine. Without tested and approved ammunition, therefore, there was little reason for our getting into arguments over religion. And besides that, Al was bigger and stronger than I was, and I was not going to lead off even when I might have been able to make some convincing points in favor of Protestantism.

As much as Mother strived to teach us tolerance and understanding, she was less tolerant than Father in her attitudes toward those around us who chose ways of life different from hers. Father's confidence in his ability to manage his own affairs in his own way was no small factor in his marvelous capacity to get along with people generally. He had knocked around enough in his single years to understand the great diversity of talents and personalities he had to deal with in a new and struggling community. He got along because of a rare combination of affability and reserve.

He was careful not to use profane and vulgar language in the presence of us children, but we knew that he knew the words when he heard them. During the prohibition era he often was invited to duck into the back of somebody's barn to sample some home brew or even stronger stuff at times. When he declined these invitations—as he did often in the presence of us boys—he did it in tones from which the inviter could take no offense. On one or two occasions, I can recall that he made the gesture of acceptance with a stern admonition that I stay in the car or on my horse. And I could read between the lines that I was expected not to try to explain the incident to Mother.

Men on assignments from the home missions of several religious denominations appeared on the scene within a short time after we arrived at the ranch. I have only vague recollections of their visits, but I can speculate on fairly safe grounds that only when they identified themselves as Presbyterians did they get much encouragement at our house. In due time one of these succeeded in organizing a Sunday School and attracting from 15 to 20 adults to listen to him preach in the school house on Sunday mornings. This first missionary, a young fellow who may still have been in seminary, came with his own saddle horse, and this fact alone must have been of considerable help in a neighborhood where a good horseman had extra points on his scoreboard even before the game started.

Through this fellow's efforts and some later work by another man in the mission field, a Presbyterian church was organized at Proctor in the summer of 1912. Those attending the organizational meeting assembled in front of the school house for a picture that took in some pretty high alkali weeds along with more than 40 persons. Mr. and Mrs. Ramsey and their two daughters were there, Grandma Colburn and her granddaughters, members of the Fedder family, Mr. and Mrs. Charlie Morton, J. J. Skinner (who would soon sell out and leave the community), Mrs. J. B. Spears and her daughter, Stella, and at least five Hamils.

Mother always referred to the founding membership (adults only) as being 28, and the figure didn't change much over the years when she struggled to keep the congregation alive. In due time it was agreed in the proper Presbyterian circles that the Proctor church wasn't worth saving. The records were transferred to Crook, where another new church, with more people to draw on, had shown more vigor and growth.

The vicissitudes of the church at Proctor bore importantly on the routines of our lives at the ranch. Sunday was the only day when field work was suspended. During the frequent spells when there was no one to lead worship at Proctor, the Sabbath became a free day for us boys, so to speak. There were many things we preferred over changing into knee-length pants and attending Sunday School and church. We welcomed the recurring news that the Rev. So-and-So had decided he could no longer tend the flocks at Proctor and Crook—a joint operation for several pastors in succession—and we waited for Mother to decree that without a preacher it would be hardly worthwhile to try to keep the Sunday School program alive.

For several years within my memory those no-church Sundays were not so free as we would have preferred. Mother and Father had grown up in communities where Sunday was literally a day of rest. And rest among those East Tennessee Presbyterians had not meant recreation. People dressed up, went to church, and except for a little visiting among relatives and neighbors, that was it. Or so at least Mother reminded us as we sought to expand our Sunday pleasures.

Father was not so firm in his keeping of the Sabbath that he did not on occasion decide to move his personal mule herd from one pasture to another on a Sunday afternoon when I was available to help him. There were, in fact, some occasions of tension between him and Mother as to just what should and could be done on Sunday. Field work shut down on Sunday, without exception.

We boys liked to play in the blacksmith shop on Sunday afternoons in winter, and I recall my sense of having embarrassed the family when visitors from Sterling came one Sunday and found us with the forge going and other evidences that we were "working" on Sunday.

Ultimately, there was a sort of break-through, and I recall

vividly my long and serious conversations with Mother that preceded it. She had laid down a rule against going swimming on Sundays. This hadn't seemed an impossible restraint until I began to sense that I was working full-time, six days a week, in the hayfields through most of the summer. One could make a quick run to the pond about the time the sun was going down, but there was often a chill in the air that took the fun out of the experience.

We longed to be free to spend Sunday afternoons at our favorite dipping place. It was a pool about 20 feet in diameter and six to seven feet deep at its deepest. It had been washed into shape by the discharge from a spillway pipe that served three irrigation ditches at the point they came into ranch property at its western boundary.

The top of the corrugated steel pipe was our diving board, and the perpendicular banks hid the surface of the water from persons passing by on a road that was not more than 50 feet from the pool. This road, of course, was a constant hazard. Nobody in the neighborhood owned a bathing suit, and there were reports now and then of persons who saw some impropriety in the fact we were caught naked on our diving pipe by persons in cars, buggies or wagons that could sneak over the hill from the north without much notice. Dressing and undressing within sight of the road was a problem we sometimes solved by leaving our clothes behind an abandoned steam engine that stood near the pool for several summers. There was still the necessity of streaking across some 80 feet of open ground between the engine and the pool.

Despite the hazards of exposure, this was a wonderful place to spend a hot afternoon, and after Mother and I came to agreement as to the legitimacy of such activities on a Sunday, our afternoons there were the high points of summer.

One Sunday afternoon in the mid-teen years, the whole family journeyed some six miles to observe an event in which irrigation water and religion figured quite differently than in the case when we Hamils were finally authorized to swim on Sunday.

There was a new Baptist congregation that met in the Sunny Slope School. It was holding its first public baptism service, and the site was a point on the new North Sterling ditch near the Otto Fallidori farm. I can't recall how many persons were immersed on that cloudy and cool afternoon, but I recall Father's having observed that it was a pretty dangerous proceeding because of the treacherously steep banks and the possibility of slipping into deep water.

I can't recall that Mother said anything, but she had some thoughts surely about how this new Baptist organization was just another force she had to contend with in her efforts to nourish the feeble sprouts of Presbyterianism in the same community. She was already aware of the fact that Roy Kohler, one of the few hired men she might have expected to join her in her church effort, was traveling many extra miles to be among these Baptists, one family of which had a daughter who had caught his attention.

In the founding picture of the Proctor Presbyterian Church, one hired man, Charlie Brecht, appears. In his later years he recalled that he was the only one in the bunkhouse who went to church regularly, but he went on to explain that he acted under Father's orders, more or less, at a time when Father was his legal guardian. Besides that, it was mighty convenient, from Father's point of view, to have Charlie harness a team and hitch it to the surrey (two-seated buggy) for the drive to church.

Our first exposure to a truly fervent and devout Christian family came when we went to Sterling to attend high school. We roomed and boarded with Mr. and Mrs. R. L. Thompson. The Thompsons were members of the Church of the Brethren, and religion with them was a primary and active concern. It was a practice of their church to eschew ornamental dress of any kind. Mr. Thompson's Sunday suit was cut with a simple upturned collar not unlike the military blouses of the period.

He wore no necktie, and Mrs. Thompson wore a simple bonnet rather than anything resembling the hats most women wore.

Each morning, before breakfast, Mr. Thompson read a passage from the Bible, and everyone knelt for prayer. The walls of the living room were adorned with colorful silk and velvet plaques with verses from the Sermon on the Mount that stood out in bright letters. In later years I found myself remembering several of these in their King James phrasing:

"Judge not that ye be not judged."

"For where your treasure is there will your heart be also."

"No man can serve two masters; for either he will hate the one and cling to the other; or else he will love the one and despise the other. Ye cannot serve God and mammon."

As rules for living, they have seemed hard to beat, and hard to abide by at times.

The very life style of Mr. and Mrs. Thompson was assurance to our parents that there was a minimum of risk in sending us away from home to attend high school. They were quick to sense that we loved Mrs. Thompson's cooking and that we would tolerate her rather strict discipline in return for the food and the comforts she provided. She did not permit smoking in her house, but made exceptions when Father would stop by to pick us up. If he carried a cigar, she insisted he smoke it in the house. It was something her potted plants could benefit from, she would insist, and then reassure Father that none of her roomers was ever invited to take the liberties he was enjoying.

Her ability to smell smoke was such that we went through a regular routine on our way home after our occasional stops at one of Sterling's pool halls, where the smoke was always thick. Regardless of how cold it was, we would remove our coats and jackets or sweaters for the last couple of blocks of our walks home to let the wind get to the inner folds and remove any trace of tobacco scent.

Sister Ruth and her classmate from Proctor, Ruth Stewart, had stayed one year with the Thompsons before Al Stewart and

I joined them in our freshman year. Brother Dave and Al and I were the only boarders the year following the girls' graduation.

As a matter of fact, Mrs. Thompson, with grandchildren approaching high school age, was becoming less and less active and she had decreed that when she got Al and me through high school she would take in no more roomers or boarders.

During our senior year, and her year of transition, so to speak, it was arranged that I should do the breakfast dishes and the dinner dishes and help prepare the evening meal. Beyond that I would pay $16 a month. Dave and Al each paid about $30, as I recall. In any event, I had their help most of the time with the dishes.

Al helped me sometimes with preparation of supper, and his job often was that of turning the grinder through which we ran the leftover beef roast, raw potatoes and onions in the making of hash. Mrs. Thompson's formula for hash had been very carefully explained to me, and I followed it. Never has hash tasted so good as at her evening table.

I could flatter myself and conclude that Al and Dave hung around the kitchen because of my company. It was obvious that Al viewed his pre-meal presence as a means of making sure we ate on schedule. And he wanted to make sure also, I suspect, that there was plenty of hash.

Mrs. Thompson laid down strict rules for more than making hash. I was to use one dishcloth for the dishes and another for the pots and pans. I took her to mean what she said and was so careful with each so-called "good" dishcloth that it remained white and stainless until it wore out. It was a matter of some embarrassment to me when word got back to Mother that Mrs. Thompson was telling friends that there was one thing about a boy in her kitchen as opposed to a girl: he kept a clean dishcloth. And when she got to that point in her conversation, she would go into the kitchen, take that cloth from the hot water pipe and show it to her guests.

Life with the Thompsons was so satisfying that when it was

interrupted for a few months in my junior year, the effect on us boys was little short of trauma. Mrs. Thompson's sister and family had come from Canada after hard times on a farm and would be settling, they hoped, in the Sterling area. Mrs. Thompson, trying to help in the only way that seemed open to her, took the parents and four children into her home. She and Mr. Thompson retired to a corner bedroom, set up their own temporary cooking facilities there, and turned her three boarders over to her sister.

It was our immediate conclusion that without Mrs. Thompson's touch our meals were definitely below the standard to which we had become accustomed. Especially did we miss her home-made jellies, jams and the like—particularly among these her piece de resistance of the canning season—apricot butter. She put up dozens of pint jars of it each year, and while we were not seeing any on the table, we were confident that it filled rows of jars in the basement. Al, Dave and I talked a lot about apricot butter—or the need of it—and in some vague way we agreed that at the right moment we should go to the basement and, just for old times' sake, take unto ourselves at least one small jar of this delicious concoction.

The day came. We got home from school one afternoon to find everyone gone and the probability of no one's returning for at least half an hour. Al and Dave were to go to the basement. I was to stand guard. In an emergency, we had agreed, anyone trapped in the basement could get out through a small rear window at ground level. The two of them had barely got through Mrs. Thompson's little apartment and down the stairs, when the doorbell rang. I went to the door and did my best to encourage the caller, a next-door neighbor, to accept my explanation and leave. She loitered long enough that Dave and Al—having heard the doorbell—went for the prearranged escape route. When I finally got around to informing them that the coast was still clear, Dave was outside the basement window and Al, much larger in size, was stuck in it. Eventually, he extricated himself, and we covered our tracks. For the life of me, I can't recall whether they got out with a jar of apricot butter, or whether the expedition was literally fruitless.

Mrs. Thompson had great faith in us, I am confident. I have often wondered, though, if her trust would not have been sorely shaken if she had known of this escapade. One thing she surely would have offered, I am certain, is a biblical admonition, and in the spirit of Christian charity, which she exemplified as faithfully as any human ever did, she undoubtedly would have offered full forgiveness.

# 21. STERLING

## ... An Oasis, A Babylon

The population of Sterling when I first took note of such things was about 4,000. That made it almost 80 times as big as Proctor and some 20 times as big as Iliff or Crook. From our point of view, it was pretty big.

Father and Mother had developed a familiarity with the town and had made many acquaintances there during the several years they lived on the Frost farm north of Sterling. My own attitude seemed to be that it was a city of strangers, a place where people lived and dressed differently from the way we did on the ranch at Proctor.

Men in Sterling wore white shirts, stiff collars and ties, and their faces were usually free from more than a day's growth of beard. Most men I was accustomed to were in work clothes most of the time, and by the end of the week their faces were covered by a heavy stubble.

Most Sterling women we saw were dressed for shopping, for clerking in stores or for greeting callers in their homes. I was more accustomed to women in aprons or sunbonnets, fully recognizing, I must presume, that Proctor women dressed up to go to Sterling and for the occasional social affairs of our community. Everybody in Sterling seemed dressed up all the time.

What probably suggested a difference between people of Proctor and people of Sterling more than anything else was the seeming absence of boys in bib overalls on the streets of Sterling. I always wore knee pants for a trip to Sterling, but I was uncomfortable in them and envied the way town boys seemed to take to their knee pants and look casual and at ease. There was something of a dilemma in the fact that if Mother had permitted me to go to Sterling in overalls, I would have felt conspicuous and fully as uncomfortable, I am sure, as I was in my knee pants.

About the only home we seemed to visit was that of the W. S. Hadfields. Mother and two or three of us children stayed all night there once when I was possibly four years old. Two things about that home fixed themselves in my memory: The black oblong knobs with which one turned on electric ceiling lights and the bathroom toilet tank, covered with wood veneer and affixed to the wall a foot or so below the ceiling. The rush of water that was set off in the bathroom by a pull on a dangling chain seemed almost deafening. Those electric lights and that indoor toilet very definitely seemed to set all who lived in Sterling apart from all who lived in and around Proctor, where there was no electricity and no indoor plumbing until after World War I.

Despite our awareness of differences between life in Sterling and life on the ranch, we took for granted that Sterling figured prominently in our lives. It was where we went to buy ready-made clothes and most of our shoes. Mother got to Sterling on an average of once every two months perhaps, and she almost always came home with packages from Mentgen's, from Glass and Bryant's or from the Golden Rule (the original name of the Penney store). She bought practically all of her groceries at the Proctor stores, but when in Sterling she often stopped at the fresh fruit and vegetable store to buy grapes, celery or whatever happened to be in season.

Father's stops were usually at the First National Bank, whose president, George Henderson, was also president of the Proctor State Bank, at the Sterling Hardware and Implement Company, and the courthouse.

For four years, starting in 1913, Father went to Sterling at regular intervals for meetings of the board of county commissioners, to which he was elected in November, 1912. About once each summer during that period he took me with him. On several occasions it had been arranged that Cash Morris of Fleming would bring his son, Arthur. The two of us made a real day of it. We lolled on the cool grass around the courthouse. We watched the goldfish in the pool at the rear of the building. We stood at the iron bars outside the windows of the basement jail, sniffed the ammonia-scented air and sometimes attracted words of greeting from unseen men within. We toured the echoing corridors of the courthouse and admired the mounted antelope that stood on an especially-built frame that spanned the rotunda on one floor. (The story was that the county gained the carcass after the killer was fined for his illegal act.)

Going to lunch with the commissioners was often the highlight of those days in Sterling. They went to the dining room of the Southern Hotel, between Second and Third on the west side of Main Street, or the Annex, on Front Street, across from the railroad station. Among my memories of wonderful tastes is the soup at the Southern (with little round crackers such as we never saw at home).

There were at least three memorable trips to Sterling in those early years to attend circuses. The first of these was to see Buffalo Bill's Wild West Show, in 1911 or 1912. Bill himself was there, riding a white horse and breaking glass balls with shots from a pistol. Cynical writers in later years insisted that Bill was almost blind at that time and that the success of his act depended on the use of fine birdshot against very fragile balls.

The next circus—probably Hagenbeck-Wallace—we saw was more traditional, with elephants, lions, tigers and a full assortment of acrobats, clowns and so forth. What I liked best was the parade along Main Street, and the four-, six- and eight-horse teams on the big gilded wagons seemed to impress me more than the elephants, the caged animals, or the acts under the big tent.

The county fair had more than passing interest for us. The

grounds were at the edge of town on the road we traveled when we went to Sterling by car. Father's first term as county commissioner brought him into some involvement in financing the fair and governing its policies. About 1919, Brother Dave and I had joined a pig club (we were the total membership), and, as a matter of course, we showed our animals at the fair. My first gilt was weak in the shoulders and didn't place. Dave's got something better than honorable mention.

One of the most attractive aspects of being a member of one of the many agricultural clubs (forerunners of 4-H) was that the county fair was the climactic event of the club year. We came in by the dozen from Iliff, Crook, Fleming, Merino, Peetz and other communities, some to show corn, some to show calves, some to show poultry, etc. If we brought sheets, pillows and blankets, we were entitled to sleep in a makeshift camp at the back of the high school. There were some tents, as I recall, but the main shelter was a large shed that was used during the school year for horses and an occasional automobile. Along with the sleeping quarters, we were provided with meal tickets that enabled us to get breakfast and dinner at a downtown restaurant.

Six or seven years later, when I was in college and Father had got back on the board of county commissioners, he arranged with A. P. Berkstresser, the fair manager, for me to be clerk of the horse races. The job paid several dollars a day for each of the four days, and I needed the money. Several times during that four-day ordeal, though, I wished I were on a buckrake in the hayfields rather than in the judges' stand of a race track.

The harness races, run in heats, seemed to require a lot of bookkeeping and offer all sorts of openings for error. I soon learned that any error on my part could mean trouble with high-strung drivers, riders and horse owners. There was one race, though, that seemed very simple to record. That was the relay race, in which one man rode two miles and changed horses three times. It was a sure thing that Tom Propst of Atwood

*Logan County Courthouse (New)* -

would be one of the riders and either Fred or Bryson Van Gundy of Logan would be another. Because these men of the county were regular contenders for first place, the men's relay race engendered as much interest as any event. For the racing clerk the big break was in the fact that there were rarely more than four entries.

To recall the fair without recalling Sterling's town band would be a grave oversight. The band, for many years directed by C. W. Seymour, a druggist, and later by Dick Smith, who had come into the school system, played regularly one night a week, in summer, on the courthouse lawn. But the highlight of the season was its playing at the fair. Three tunes I first heard at the fair were "Barney Google," "Yes, We Have No Bananas," and "Beautiful Ohio."

The Sterling I first knew was without paved streets. The downtown buildings seemed to be mainly of red or yellow brick with flat roofs and generally square lines. There were a few frame buildings, including one with landmark status that stood back from the walks at Third and Main and was cleared to make way for the Simon Raabe Building and its neighbor, the A and M Building. The town had the looks, one must presume, of scores of county seats in the Great Plains, especially those in irrigated valleys with sugar factories. But we always approached it as a quite uncommon place. It was our Rome, our Paris, our London, our Babylon.

It was when we went to Sterling that we began to sense, rather vaguely, the greater complexities of our civilization. Its courthouse symbolized the legalities and formalities of government, the basic intricacies of an organized society. Sterling's commerce suggested more than the subsistence economy that seemed to dictate so many practices at the ranch.

Sterling offered a sort of microcosm of the general disjointing of our national economy as it started in the wake of World War I and extended eventually through the Depression years of the 1930's. Between 1920 and 1924, several Sterling banks went into receivership, and the families of several of my high school classmates were hard hit.

J. D. Blue, most active of the Cedar Rapids, Iowa, officers of the Logan County Development Company (which owned the Proctor ranch) sensed a booming spirit in Sterling and decided in about 1919 or 1920 to come to Colorado and go into business there. He purchased a farm immediately south of town, named it Blue Bird Acres and started subdividing it. He built a fine house for himself as a sort of starter, but Blue Bird Acres languished through most of my four years in high school, and Mr. Blue and his family eventually moved to California. By that time the Proctor property was for sale, and the Logan County Development Company was at or near its end.

Looking back, I am amazed, almost, that my four years of high school were hard years for Logan County. Things seemed pretty good for me, and while Father was complaining about cattle, wheat and hay prices and his troubles with the ranch ownership, his was no voice of despair. My fellow high school pupils seemed to eat and dress well and engage in a minimum of complaint about hard times. There was much talk in our senior year about going to college, about the high cost of living in college towns, mainly Boulder. I made no boasts of what I would do, but deduced that if I went to college, it would be a low-cost project, and it turned out that way. Watching the pennies just seemed to be our way of life.

Except for what happened to the banks, things in Sterling seemed to go along quite well during those early 1920's. The Graham Hotel was opened, and the city completed a far-reaching storm sewer and paving project. Some retail stores closed, but others opened, and the increasing use of automobiles meant an expanding trade territory.

The town was literally strewn with temptations. The soda fountains near the front doors of all the drug stores beckoned our nickels and dimes. There was a variety store that kept toys on display the year around. (Other stores displayed toys only at Christmas time.) And a popcorn wagon was a tantalizing presence on the sidewalk south of the First National at Second and Main for many years, in good weather and bad. For those who developed a thirst after eating a bag of popcorn there was, in summer, a drinking fountain right beside it. This fountain and the one at Third and Main flowed constantly in good weather and struck me as an ultimate in convenience.

Those bubbling fountains created deep impressions. They symbolized perhaps the fact that Sterling was a sort of haven from the bright sun and heat of summer. Most certainly the courthouse lawn had that effect. The caretakers seemed always to be mowing the grass. And the smell of that had a pungency which, because of the altitude, I suspect, was different from that of most freshly cut bluegrass I have smelled through the years (at lower altitudes). As a result, I cannot smell a new-cut lawn in Sterling or other Colorado cities without a rush of memories of those hours of treasured leisure on the courthouse lawn. The contrast of the coolness, the freshness, the seeming cleanliness of that green oasis with the dry heat, the glare and the dust of the hayfields of Proctor was powerful and lasting.

The south end of Main Street on the east side seemed dominated by pool halls. At least three separate establishments operated there at one time. Across the street was where Mr. Appelbaum sold Father our first Ford. The building later housed the Stickney cycle shop.

There was a livery stable west of Main near Front Street, and we left our horses there one night after delivering a bunch of cattle to the Harris feedlots on the road between town and the river.

Going into Sterling by car, our first glimpse was of the top of a water tank that seemed to stand on a direct line with the road as it paralleled the Union Pacific tracks about five miles north of town. On our left we would soon see a Bull Durham ad covering the whole side of a barn. By either car or train, the last mile or so took us past vast strings of railroad freight cars. These were on storage tracks, many of them waiting for repairs at the Burlington shops. They included many cars of the kind the Burlington used to haul iron ore. As we got into town we passed within a block of the Burlington roundhouse. It and the adjacent car repair tracks were important to the economy of Sterling in the World War I era. Many high school-age boys worked on the "rep track" in summer.

Just south of the business district (across the tracks) was a small Union Pacific roundhouse which seemed to serve mainly for storage and maintenance of the local freight engines whose runs originated at Sterling. The Burlington's roundhouse usually was occupied by several locomotives, because it was headquarters for all the equipment that made runs each day to Holdrege, Neb., on the east, and Cheyenne, Wyo., on the west, as well as some used on runs through Sterling on the Alliance-Denver line.

Sterling was a lot of things to those of us who grew up at Proctor. But even after four years in high school there, I never felt that I belonged. When I boarded the train to go to Hastings,

Neb., and enter college, there was no question in my mind as to the finality of this farewell to Colorado. After my graduation from college, Father came to Hastings to try to persuade me to accept a job in Sterling. I had no interest, and because I had viewed Sterling from Proctor as a place of infinite variety in attractions and diversions, this is something I have never been able to explain to my own satisfaction. It could be there was a subconscious resentment of the fact that Sterling's growth and seeming permanence related in some way to Proctor's gradual fading into oblivion.

As for relating my future with Denver, as some classmates did, I must have heeded the wisdom of the time that Denver was a low-pay city, where people seeking relief from tuberculosis would "work for nothing."

# 22. STERLING HIGH SCHOOL

## ... And Some People There

The high school in Sterling was the center of a county-wide system of high schools that was still in the process of formulation during my first years there. The branches, in 1920, were at Merino, Fleming, New Haven, Dailey, Willard, Graylin, Crook and Peetz. The branch at Iliff was organized during my second year in school. My 1921 yearbook reports that there were 65 graduates at Sterling and 11 at all the other schools combined.

In Sterling itself the system included a relatively new junior high school, two elementary schools and the high school. Presiding over this, as superintendent, was John A. Sexson. He had supervised the building of the junior high school and the establishment in Sterling of the so-called 4-4-4 plan of school organization—four elementary grades, four junior-high grades and four senior-high grades. In many places the junior high schools were coming into being as three-year units between six years of elementary education and three years of high school.

Sexson, a jovial, round-faced fellow who had spread the word of his 4-4-4 system at Sterling via Columbia University's Teachers College and other institutions, left Sterling to be superintendent at Bisbee, Ariz., a booming copper town. He eventually was superintendent at Pasadena, Calif., where his innovative spirit resulted in something unique in American public school systems—one with a 6-4-4 breakdown. The final 4 included two years of conventional high school and two of junior college.

Sexson's 4-4-4 system was ideal for Sterling, where many pupils were coming from one-room country schools, as we from

Proctor did. Except for the fact we had not been in organized gym classes and had not been segregated from pupils of lower grades, we were pretty much on a par with our classmates. It was quite a change, though, to attend classes in 45-minute periods and move from room to room.

I can't help thinking that John Sexson's reputation as a progressive educator attracted good teachers to Sterling. Some were better than others. Most were fairly young. Several went on to bigger and better jobs. It was my good fortune to be in classes under several men and women who were true professionals. The lasting recollections of a few individuals provide a framework on which I can hang most of the formative experiences of those four years in the Logan County High School at Sterling.

### Beulah Christopher

She was petite, blond, in her second year out of the University of Colorado, when she came to Sterling to teach history. Her first year was my first year, and the fact that she was getting acquainted with the ways of a bigger high school after one year of teaching in a small rural high school may have contributed to her seeming understanding of me and my general insecurity during those first few weeks in her class. Her mobile features were quick to transmit moods and attitudes. She was essentially cheerful and friendly. She was besieged by various classes and groups to serve in sponsorship roles. She was popular in the pure sense of that word. But she was also a good teacher.

She gave little tests now and then that seemed to have minor bearing on our grades, but they served to give her new insights into the interests and abilities of those in her classes. At some stage in my freshman year I found myself rating high in a general information test she sprang on the class. In my senior year she was involved in the process whereby I qualified to represent our school in a regional academic competition—and my subjects were American history and general information.

Because the regional contest, held at Sterling, came on the

day our track team was to leave for Boulder and the state meet, I entered the history event (in the forenoon), but gave way to a substitute in the general information test (scheduled for late-afternoon).

When we got back from the track meet, Miss Christopher advised me I had won first in American history and persuaded me to come to her room after school and see how I might have scored in general information. (She had kept a copy of the questions.) After she had graded my paper, she advised me that my score would have made me a double winner if I had chosen to compete in general information at home rather than go to Boulder, where I had not won a single point for Sterling in the sprints and high jump.

I remember her for the hours she spent drilling and quizzing me to make sure I could list the presidents in order, give dates of all the United States' wars and sum up issues in each of the conflicts. But as much as she emphasized history, her specialty, she encouraged my interest in general knowledge, and for that I remain grateful.

## K. C. Morse

Keith C. Morse was somewhere beyond 30 when I entered high school. Whatever his age, he seemed mature, experienced and tough. One of the worries of my freshman year was over how I could manage to stay alive in his class in general science that was everybody's fate as a sophomore. Among other things, he required that everyone maintain a notebook, the size and general nature of which he carefully prescribed. There was hardly a day when he did not specify that a certain illustration, a maxim or a definition (heat is energy) go into the notebook. At regular intervals he asked that all notebooks be turned in for his inspection. In a matter of one or two days we got them back, and the evidence was clear that he read them, because he graded them and wrote critical comments. His idea, obviously, was that fifteen-year-olds were more likely to understand the principles of a water pump, a fulcrum or an inclined plane if they had to draw pictures of such things than if they merely took their information from a textbook.

Looking back, I am convinced that he was a sort of paper tiger. He was actually shy. But his insistence on discipline, his extreme thoroughness, his demand that each pupil do something every day on his own (keeping the notebook) was good pedagogy. After my year of general science, I rather welcomed going back to his room for physics in my junior year. There was a feeling that what he taught had meaning and could stand one in good stead someday. In about 1922, he assembled a radio receiver—with a huge horn—at the rear of his large classroom, and I was a bit envious of classmates who could talk with him about the basic principles of radio transmission and reception. K. C. seemed to turn on an entirely different personality on those occasions and when talking about other special interests—which included baseball.

He knew his subjects. He knew how to communicate, and he had developed his own techniques for making sure there was reception in those rows of seats in front of him. Nothing about him caused me ever to want to look him up in my later visits to Sterling. But he stands in my records as an outstanding teacher.

### Vera Thompson

She was tall, slender and sharp-featured. Her bachelor's degree was from the University of Michigan. She was my English teacher in my freshman and senior years. She was not so relaxed and chatty as Beulah Christopher, but she knew how and when to transmit the feeling that she had confidence in a pupil and expected top performance. She had spent a weekend on our ranch with other teachers and some of my Sister Ruth's classmates, but I was not conscious of her having singled me out for special attention until my senior year. There had been trouble the year before with publication of the school yearbook. The principal, R. R. Knowles, had decreed that there should be firm faculty intervention in what had been largely a student-

247

directed activity. Instead of popular election of the yearbook staff, it would be by faculty appointment, and direct responsibility would rest with one teacher, Miss Thompson. One of the troubles the year before was that the project lost money.

Miss Thompson kept me after our English class one day in September and said she wanted me to be business manager of the book. She wanted someone who would keep good records, sell advertising and make sure that the finances were handled in such a way as to bring the project to conclusion in black ink. I was stunned, but flattered, and flattery prevailed. That vote of confidence by this rather reserved and timid woman is hard to discard from any list of key events of my life. I set up a simple set of books, trudged the downtown streets to solicit advertising and pressured the editorial staff to get work done in time to earn maximum discounts on our photo-engraving bills.

Miss Thompson was my sole adviser and guide, and she performed with a minimum knowledge of the processes of photography, printing and engraving. The book came out on time and in the black, but I had made up my mind that next time I would rather be editor—and that's what I was in college.

Meanwhile, I attended Miss Thompson's senior English class and memorized the prologue to Chaucer's "Canterbury Tales" (in old English), Milton's "Sonnet on his Blindness", several passages from Shakespeare and more. I also got my first real lessons in writing, and they were not based on the theory that the way to write is to sit down and place words together the way one would in conversation. Miss Thompson was a bear for correct sentence structure. One of our textbooks had an appendix of about 100 pages of sentences—all incorrectly written. For most of that senior year she made regular assignments of five to ten of those sentences to be rewritten and turned in as the next day's "written work."

Memory work and syntax. I have wondered sometimes what has happened to them. And I have thanked my lucky stars for Miss Thompson's emphasis on them. They contributed to the shaping of my career almost as much as anything I was exposed to in high school. Vera Thompson taught many years in the Denver school system, and after retirement operated a shop in Aspen. I regret not having looked her up in her later years to express my appreciation. She pushed me into a sort of lifetime love affair with the English sentence.

## Camille E. Werling

I often have wondered how this man ever got to Sterling and why he stayed as long as he did. A native of Belgium, with a doctor's degree and credit for having studied at Lausanne, Lille, Paris and Munich, he taught French and Spanish and probably could have taught two or three other languages. He was the super-scholar of the faculty, a bachelor, a loner and, by the popular standards of measurement, a complete misfit. I dreaded the opening of my junior year when I would have to face him in Spanish or French or meet my language requirement by studying Latin. I was genuinely interested in Spanish, but he made it appear the worse of two evils. (I had tried Latin as a freshman, but got out after one week.) Still, I took my chance on Werling and Spanish. For several months I never entered his classroom without the sense of a rising flow of adrenalin, but I learned more in two years of his classes than I learned in any two years under any teacher in high school or college.

We started first-year Spanish with a class of about 30. By the end of the second year there were not more than 16 of that original group eligible for the two years of credit required in college preparatory courses. Werling stuck stubbornly to the belief that it was his job to teach Spanish and ours to learn it. He was aloof, impatient and almost scornful of anyone who came to class prepared for less than a flawless recitation. Early in our first year he placed on the blackboard with a mixture of colored chalks his personally-devised outline of all the irregular Spanish verbs. This we were supposed to memorize—and, with hope for survival, we put it in our notebooks and went to work.

Ralph Hays, a good friend and classmate, shared my anxieties, and the two of us engaged in many hours of team study. We stole time from physics lab during our junior year to quiz each other on the irregular verbs and the new words we were supposed to add to our vocabularies with each day's lessons.

Toward the end of our first year Werling supplied each of us with copies of a new book, "Veinte-Cinco Episodios Biblicos" (Twenty-Five Biblical Episodes). It came as a shock, almost—a shock with satisfying overtones—that we could recognize most of the words and could, with a little effort, get the sense of a story written in a foreign language. Our responsibilities for given days were to come to class prepared to translate one of these stories from Spanish to English. The story of Ruth, the story of the sale of Joseph by his brothers—these and others came through with a clarity and meaning I had never gained in Sunday School. All of a sudden, I sensed the fruits of Camille Werling's discipline and his insistence on high standards of performance. With the end of the first year I went back to Proctor and started practicing my Spanish on the Mexicans who were coming into the community in increasing numbers as beet laborers. There were few who could not speak English better than I could speak Spanish, but they were gracious and enthusiastic in their responses to my questions and comments in a halting version of their mother tongue. They provided, among other things, some translations of English four-letter words and various vulgarities with which I introduced a sort of back-room, or extra-curricular, aspect of Spanish study to some of my friends in our class the following fall.

Werling was given to occasional lectures on subjects quite outside the study of Spanish. We welcomed these, because they meant shortening of the time in which he might ask a question and discover someone had come to class unprepared. One of his most memorable talks was on the importance of personal hygiene—especially as it could prevent some unpleasantness in the atmosphere of a poorly ventilated basement room such as the one in which we met. He talked about wearing the right kind of underwear, implying that there were garments that would contain odors. All in the class were puzzled, but nevertheless fascinated and transfixed by the delicacy, the ambiguity and the feigned humor of his lecture. Among other things, he was using English words we had never heard from him before, and his accents were intriguing. Nobody knew for sure what he was driving at, but three or four of us got our heads together and concluded that Werling was not aware of the tragic health problem of one of our classmates. It was referred to sometimes as "rotten lung," but whatever it was, it forced him to live with a breath that was almost intolerable at times to those around him. So far as I know, nobody ever explained the situation to Werling.

Another of his lectures was on the evils of interscholastic athletics. If the idea was to provide exercise for young men, he argued, there were gymnastic programs far more beneficial than football or basketball. This lecture he repeated from time to time—with variations.

He got his own exercise (in good weather) parading up and down the sidewalk in front of the home of Mrs. Gatewood Milligan, where he roomed—always with a book in front of his eyes. About 25 years after our graduation, I saw him standing at a bus stop in downtown Denver, and he was reading a book. I accosted him, explained who I was and was ready to launch into a sort of thank-you speech for all he had done for me in high school. I barely had identified myself when a bus rolled up. He excused himself with more impatience than apology and rushed for the bus.

He was at that time—and had been for 20 years or more—on the faculty of the University of Denver. There were many things about him that I never understood. Among them was the fact that on his arrival from Europe after World War I he had to do time at an ordinary high school, when his qualifications and temperament seemed to dictate that he belonged in a university atmosphere, where he could isolate himself from the

251

athletic locker room—which was within smelling distance of his Sterling classroom—and keep as far away as possible from the dull and non-scholarly among colleagues as well as students.

### Harvey E. Turk

If he had been teaching in a high school during the 1970's, his principal concern, I am sure, would have been drugs. There were no drugs around Sterling in our day, but cigarettes were available, and some of the boys used them. But nobody smoked in the presence of Harvey Turk, the physical education teacher, part-time coach and a sort of self-appointed monitor of masculine morals.

His office was a nook that the architects must have considered an unfortunate surplus space when they designed the boys' toilet and washroom. He looked out on a row of washbowls and soft-soap dispensers and on all traffic to and from the toilet room beyond.

When not in class, he seemed always to be holding court in his crowded and smelly quarters. When discussing anything which might be defined as a "problem," he put on a most serious look and plunged into long discourses on the ultimate price men paid for their deviations from prescribed procedures in all sorts of things besides care of the body. He was a moralist with a coach's ambivalent approach to such questions as whether it's right to use the elbow when the referee isn't looking. (He coached basketball one or two years.)

Sometime in my four years in school he organized a club along lines prescribed by the Y.M.C.A. There was a certain exclusiveness about it, and when I was invited to join, I jumped at the chance. At our last meeting of my senior year, we had dinner together at the Annex and retired to the lawn of the railroad station for a very "serious" discussion of life and its problems. I can't recall that we reached any conclusions, but we seemed to feel good when Harvey Turk lectured us on the importance of being good.

## Others

Louise Hagen had come to Sterling as a teacher of German. During World War I, however, all German teaching was halted, and she ended up as registrar and librarian. From her cage at the rear of the big central study hall she dispensed books, certain credentials related to enrollment and a sort of free-lance discipline. In reference to a book, I once said "don't" when I should have said "doesn't." Her insistence on my rephrasing the sentence stayed with me better than any lecture on that particular point I ever got in an English class. She probably knew the entire student body better than any teacher who met classes.

R. R. Knowles advanced in 1922 from mathematics teacher and football and track coach and assistant principal to principal. Ted Long, fresh out of Drake University, coached football and track one year. A. P. Berkstresser came into the system in my senior year and was the coach during my only successful track season. A graduate of Morningside College in Iowa, he encouraged me to attend a small college and may have influenced me on this point as much as any individual. His recommendation was that I go to Grinnell, but I found that one year's tuition there was more money than I could come up with.

It was puzzling to some of our friends that I—Brother Dave in my footsteps—gave no thought to the possibility of enrolling in the new Smith-Hughes vocational agriculture program that headquartered in the room adjacent to Mr. Werling's room. The man in charge of agriculture my first year in school was Herman Sandhouse, with whom I had had an enjoyable relationship when he supervised our extension service-sponsored pig club.

There was a presumption on the part of both our parents that we had plenty to learn outside the field of agriculture. While Father had seemed tolerant toward the first county agents in the county and had developed a congenial relationship with Jim Morrison, one of the agents, and with Herman Sandhouse, he seemed to harbor the notion that education was something outside and beyond the development of knowledge and skills strictly applicable to the operation of a farm or ranch. He didn't challenge the research results that came to his attention through the extension service. He respected the college-trained men's ability to select good breeding stock, but he never quite equated their learning with the learning of a lawyer or doctor or of what he would describe as a "well-read" individual. And so both Dave and I took college preparatory courses. In my case it was, to some extent, blind flying. That I should go to college was more hope than aim, more speculation than ambition, but when I got my diploma, it was a certificate of preparation for college for which I had not yet formulated definite plans.

# 23. ABOUT SOD HOUSES

## . . . And the Ants on Cousin Minnie's Syrup Pitcher

The years of my youth were the twilight years of the sod house—one of the distinctive institutions of pioneer days in the Great Plains.

I can't recall seeing or hearing about a sod house under construction, but many that had been built in the 80's and 90's or later were still around. The Fred Gothorp family lived for several years in a sod house northeast of Proctor.

There were two sod houses southwest of Proctor, both of which were occupied during the early years of my memory. One had been the temporary residence of the Powell and Blair families during construction of the big stone house into which the Hamil family eventually moved. The land on which this stood was part of a homestead of a J. W. Iliff employee and was part of the original land sale by Powell and Blair to the Logan County Development Company. In 1913 this land was turned back to Powell and Blair, and Uncle Bob Hamil farmed the place for several years. The second sod house in the area was not far to the south and east, on the edge of the river. I recall visiting there when a Mrs. McMurray, a widow, was the occupant.

The remains of a two-story sod house were part of the landscape south of the railroad, east of Iliff, on land once a part of the J. W. Iliff domain, that was owned by F. H. Blair during my boyhood years.

I have vague recollections of houses that were partly sod and partly frame. The impression was that the frame portions represented additions made several years after the original construction. Somewhere in the vicinity there was a two-story frame house that had been built against a sod unit that remained as a sort of kitchen lean-to.

The sod house that I came to know best, however, was not in the Proctor community. It was southeast of Atwood, on a farm that Father acquired during World War I. The house had been lived in for from 10 to 20 years when Father bought the place, and it was the home for at least 12 more years of Mr. and Mrs. Will Logan, who farmed the land on a share and rental basis. (Will, a first cousin, had accompanied Father to Colorado.)

My residence in the "soddy" probably added up to five months during summers when I was in college. Father, as owner of the farm, tended to become impatient with Cousin Will's reluctance to hire a man for rush seasons, and when Will implied he couldn't find a man at a given time, Father would counter with the suggestion that one of us boys was available. And so it was that during three successive summers I was assigned for periods of several weeks to the little bedroom just off the kitchen in a sod house that was lived in long after sod construction had gone out of style.

Most everything about this house bespoke the builder's determination to erect more than a temporary shelter. It was not until the late 20's that anybody talked of abandoning it. By the standard of the times, the floor plan was radical, imaginative and almost colossal. Built on an L pattern, the walls embraced an area of at least 1,500 square feet. The big living room was in the center of the building, with windows on the east and west and no exposure to the southern sun in summer or to the northerly winds in winter. The hips in the roof design were to be duplicated in smart ranch houses of the 1950's, 60's and 70's. The roof was covered with tar paper that had to be repaired or replaced after severe hailstorms.

There was no basement, no central heat, no electricity. A crude sink in the kitchen was served by a so-called pitcher pump that brought water direct from a shallow well. A pipe from the sink carried waste water through the wall to a spot on an unused side of the house. There was no bathroom. In these regards, the house was about on a par with farm dwellings of the neighborhood. A high-tension electric line ran within 100 feet of the house, but the power industry of that day discouraged farm hookups with transformer installation charges that farmers considered prohibitive.

The interior walls were plastered, but their surfaces were irregular and given to crumbling in spots, especially around the door and window frames. There had been attempts to plaster the exterior walls with lime and cement mixes, but nothing stuck for more than a year or two.

The vulnerability of the walls to the exploratory digging of insects and rodents led to frequent little crises for most families who ever lived in a sod house. The sod for the house in question had been cut from the valley floor, where the native grasses tended to grow to heights of two feet or more. This meant that every layer of sod included a heavy compaction of stems and roots. These had deteriorated over the years, and the process created soft places and pockets that seemed to make the walls attractive to burrowing pests. Ants were especially active and they sometimes sneaked into the house undetected.

*Sod house near Atwood*

Will Logan's wife—we called her Cousin Minnie—was a good cook and a neat housekeeper, and she carried on a running battle with her insect enemies without benefit of the many chemicals that would simplify matters for women of a later generation. Vigilant though she was, she was victim now and then of a sneak attack or a flanking action.

One mid-summer morning, after bringing the work stock from the night pasture and harnessing at least six animals, I arrived at the kitchen to find that Cousin Minnie was going to treat us to pancakes. This was something special. Pancakes were on the breakfast menu not more than three or four times during a summer, she would explain each time she served them. They were more trouble than the usual cereal, eggs, ham or bacon and toast.

The infrequency of pancakes on the table meant that Cousin Minnie's syrup pitcher often sat unused for two or three weeks in her walk-in pantry. Everybody took for granted that when the pitcher came off the shelf there would be an encrustment of sugar crystals from syrup that clung to the spout after the last using.

On the morning in question the spout seemed to carry an unusually heavy burden of dried sugar, and just as I had finished saturating my pancakes with syrup I detected that the solid mass around the spout included dead ants, dozens of them, that had dried with the sugar. I quickly brushed one or two ants from my pancakes, handed the pitcher to Cousin Will, and proceeded to eat.

It was on his second helping, as I recall, that he spotted the ants, and the apologies began to fly. It came out that Cousin Minnie had known for several months that she needed stronger lenses in her glasses. She had failed to detect the trapped ants, of course, when she brought out the syrup.

By that time I had eaten five or six pancakes and was quite well satisfied with the breakfast. As I reconstruct the incident, I am sure that I had at least two thought flashes at the moment

I discovered the ants: First of all, I was desperately hungry, and ants always had struck me as being among the cleaner insects. Secondly, I had a sneaking suspicion that the syrup in the pitcher was all Cousin Minnie had in stock. When she found out about the ants she would want to discard all the contents of the pitcher. I was too hungry to run the risk of getting no pancakes or taking what I got without syrup.

While life in a sod house included many brushes with varmints of one kind or another, there were some advantages. These thick-walled houses were amazingly cool in summer and amazingly easy to heat in winter.

But every time I think of sod houses, I am reminded of that summer when the ants came out of the earthwork and died on the spout of Cousin Minnie's syrup pitcher.

# 24. THE YEAR OF THE KLAN

## . . . And My High School Graduation

When members of our class of 1924 at Sterling High School got together for our 50th anniversary reunion, we could claim at least one distinction. Ours was the only class ever graduated at Sterling with hooded members of the Ku Klux Klan joining in the services.

There were many, of course, who looked upon the Klan as an intruder rather than a participant, but the drama and tension of the occasion could not be denied. This was one aspect of our commencement weekend that everyone seemed to recall in detail after more than 50 years.

Those who have dug into the history of the Klan say that 1924 was the year of its largest national membership. The surge of enthusiasm for the organization was apparent around Sterling, and some of the talk in school corridors had suggested that fathers of some members of the class of 1924 were active in the local unit.

There was a baccalaureate service at the First Presbyterian Church the Sunday evening before the actual graduation program at the high school. We seniors, some 80 of us, sat in our caps and gowns in the front pews.

At a point about midway in the service there was a commotion at the rear door and concerned looks on the faces of members of the choir who looked out on all that went on.

The presiding pastor, somewhat awkwardly and uneasily, tried to carry on as though nothing was happening. Glancing over our shoulders, we ultimately caught the outlines of peaked hoods in the rear doorway.

I could never believe that the appearance of these Klansmen, about eight in number, was a complete surprise to everyone, but it was obvious that nobody had tipped off the ushers. They had taken a firm position against any interruption of the program, and therefore the commotion. Finally, though, somebody passed the word along, and the intruders marched in single file to the front of the church and lined up before the pulpit.

The minister asked if any member of the group had something to say, and one came forward and handed him an envelope. There was a mumbled exchange, and if the minister had been taken by surprise, what he heard seemed to answer all his questions. The visitors marched silently to the exit; the minister put the service back on track, and all of us relaxed.

While the Klan engaged in all kinds of double-talk as to its ideals and purposes, there was a general presumption that its prime concern was to press the interests of white Protestants over those of Negroes, Catholics and Jews. (I was to learn many years later that some of the Protestant German-Russians in Logan County felt the Klan was antagonistic toward them.) There were no Negroes in our class and, to the best of my recollections, no Jews. But there were a half-dozen or more Catholics, and I could detect an obvious uneasiness on the part of a Catholic girl in my pew. If the truth were known, though, the uneasiness was shared by most everyone. This was our first view of the Klan in action. One could not help pondering the ability of such performers to strike terror into the hearts of persons who knew they were on the "enemies" list.

There was much talk around school the next day about our unexpected guests. The minister, as I recall, made known that the envelope he received contained a cash gift and a note of appreciation of his services to the community. Classmates were calling off the names of persons who might have been behind the hoods. One was of a very large man and one was of a fellow with a missing finger.

Most members of the faculty indicated disgust with what had

happened. But one teacher, T. L. Girault, was openly scornful. He denounced the Klan and all it stood for. At the moment he seemed to make more of the incident than it deserved. Some of us, I am sure, were inclined to think it would have been a pretty dull evening if the Klan hadn't appeared.

About six weeks later, a black touring car drove into the hayfield where Father, two hired men and I were working. Four men, all in white shirts, got out and went into serious conversation with Father. They stayed for about an hour. On the way to the house that evening nothing was said about the visitors. But when Father started off to care for the hogs—a chore he reserved for himself—he asked me to join him. This was unprecedented, almost, because I was supposed to milk cows.

As we dipped half-bushel buckets of corn from the granary and spread it on the concrete feeding floor, Father explained that his afternoon visitors had come from Sterling to suggest he be a candidate for the Republican nomination for sheriff. They had known, perhaps, of his plans to leave the ranch and of his hankering to get back into county politics after one term as county commissioner. They had brought assurance of powerful support for his candidacy. But he would have to agree to join the Klan. And the question he finally put to me, in tones that carried a surprising hint my decision might be binding, was whether he should accept the offer and the conditions.

I surprised myself with the promptness of my reply. I told him I was opposed to the Klan and what it stood for in words that I had not repeated since hearing them from T. L. Girault and other teachers following our baccalaureate service. All of a sudden, I realized that I was subscribing fully to opinions I had heard but hadn't taken the time to consolidate into my own thinking.

Whether Father was merely asking me to confirm a decision he already had made is a secret he took to his grave. He didn't run for sheriff.

I went off to college in the fall and was not around to witness other activities of the Klan in Logan County, but I did observe a big Klan rally at Hastings, Neb., that fall. Delegates came from a large section of Nebraska and staged a parade that stretched for at least a mile. There were hooded men on horseback and floats depicting little red schoolhouses and other symbols of solid American tradition.

Those who have traced the history of the Klan say that what we witnessed in 1924 was the high water mark of the organization. It remained, but never enjoyed the widespread popularity that it enjoyed for a brief period in the mid-1920's.

T. L. Girault, who taught for many years in the Denver schools before retiring, came to Sterling for our 1974 reunion, and I couldn't help telling him about how his forthrightness helped me make up my mind on what seemed to be a pretty important issue back there in 1924.

# 25. WATCHING THE TRAINS GO BY

## . . . And Eventually Riding Them

The economy of early Proctor depended heavily on the Union Pacific Railroad. And the lives of us young people were tremendously enlivened by its inescapable presence.

The passing trains were a part of each day and night. We saw them, we heard them, and when we were anywhere near the tracks we smelled the pungent smoke that gushed in opaque columns from the locomotives' stacks during those frequent intervals when the firemen had to lay down new beds of coal. We always suspected that some firemen delighted in creating especially heavy clouds when the wind was such that these would slump down over a field where we were working.

Black smoke on the horizon signaled the approach of every train, and when we were on the rim of the valley above the ranch buildings we could keep a full train in view for five or six miles.

The U. P. hauled away the cars we filled with hay, with sugar beets, or with fat hogs and cattle. The "local freight" that made a round-trip between Sterling and Julesburg each day brought in most of the merchandise for the general stores, including machinery parts. It dropped off a carload of lumber or posts every now and then, coal from the mountain areas, and an occasional car of Nebraska corn for the feeding operations at the ranch.

Rarely did a passenger train stop without a rattling transfer of cream cans between the station agent's four-wheeled hand truck and the baggage car. Farmers with cream to sell were free-enterprisers in the purest sense. Some sent theirs to

Sterling or Denver; some shipped to points as far east as Omaha. Thus there was a movement of filled and empty cans in both directions.

We used every excuse in the book to be at the station for the arrival of a train. And when the non-stopping "flyer" was picking up mail, we liked to stand on the platform and watch a hook from the mail car grab the sack the agent had hung from a gallows-like device that stood about 50 feet from the station.

The coming and going of trains broke the monotony of long days in the fields, most of which were in view of the railroad. The more regular trains gave an indication of the time of day. The westbound "five-o'clock" was especially punctual and most welcome. Its passing meant there was just one more hour of work.

Father, a light sleeper, often reported on nocturnal activities at the Proctor siding that he could reconstruct from the sounds of whistles and locomotive starts. "The eastbound passenger was late this morning," he would observe. "It had to wait for the westbound train at Proctor and there was a freight on one of the sidetracks at the same time."

There was special fascination in the passenger trains that ran only in summer and carried vacationers from the East to Denver and points west. A boy speculated on what kind of people, with what sources of income, were those who sat under the canopies along the brass railings of the observation cars as they streaked by at 45 miles an hour. He would learn years later that those observation platforms were often caught up in whirlwinds filled with smoke and dust, and were more ostentation than luxurious comfort.

But the real personality train was the "local freight." One saw it on the way out from Sterling in the morning and on the way back at night. Its schedule depended pretty much on the volume of business and how often it had to stand on sidings to let the passengers and through-freights pass.

For most of the years of my memory, the "local" had the

same engine and the same engineer. The latter was sometimes referred to as "Yorky." I knew his face well from countless opportunities to watch as he sat in obvious impatience on his throne, while others of the crew were unloading merchandise from the LCL (less-than-carload) car. But it seemed beyond hope or expectation that I should ever get close enough to speak. By some quirk of circumstance, I once was invited by the fireman to climb into the cab and look into the white-hot firebox. "Yorky" said, "Hello." That was a big day.

This engineer was a sort of hot-rodder of the rails. His usual engine had high wheels and probably had been in passenger service at one time. With a light load, it could pick up and get out of town faster than either of the passenger trains that stopped regularly. And with "Yorky" at the throttle, it did.

During the sugar beet harvest, the sleek, high-wheeler often gave way to a plodding creature with half-solid drivers, clanking eccentric rods and absolutely no class in its looks or movements. Those were dull days for train watchers along the route, but probably bright in the railroad accounting office where tonnage charges were being figured.

If one suspected what was under the cloud of smoke down the line four or five miles, one waited for confirmation in the first audible whistle, because the "local" whistle made music all its own. And the engineer—or at least we so suspected—enjoyed seeing saddle horses jump at a sudden blast, or testing the life in a span of flop-eared mules by letting off steam at just the right moment.

For a while after the United States had declared war on Germany in 1917, an American flag flew from the caboose—just one of the many flourishes that gave character to this particular train.

Later, the caboose gave way to a combination baggage and passenger car. This was the high-water mark, more or less. Trucks began dropping off the items that once moved in the LCL car. The daily-running local freights were passing out of the picture by the time the diesels came along. But even if they had stayed around, they couldn't have been the same. No steam!

The ease with which we likened those old trains to personalities can be explained, in my opinion, by the animation that was characteristic of most engines utilizing steam power. Streaking across the countryside, leaving a trail of smoke as it went, a steam locomotive was suggestive of a running child with hair in the wind, a greyhound, or a racing horse kicking up dust. There was something very lifelike in the groans and puffs of an engine bucking a stiff grade with a long train behind it. Even when they stood idle at stations, the monsters sweated and dripped, breathed and sighed, belched a little and voiced impatience through their pop-off valves.

The romantic fancies of youth almost inevitably must take a beating now and then on the rocks of reality. My love affair with trains probably was at its height when in August, 1918, a month or so prior to my 12th birthday, I spent six days and five nights riding in chair cars and sitting in crowded stations. This was reality, but it was exciting, nevertheless, and memorable.

Uncle Bob Hamil had to make a business trip to Tennessee. For Mother, that was a chance to get before the eyes of our three living grandparents and various uncles and aunts the only one of her children they had not seen in recent years. For me, it was a two-week reprieve from the wild hay harvest and untold opportunities for adventure.

We boarded the eastbound train about seven o'clock on a warm evening and spent an almost sleepless night crossing Nebraska. This was wartime, and the trains were crowded. At Grand Island, about 3:30 a.m., the station platform was brightly lighted, and a crowd of several hundred was on hand to cheer the arrival or departure of somebody. Word had passed through our coach to the effect that it was a local man who had distinguished himself in France.

At Omaha we were to change to the North Western and go

through Chicago. But the Union Pacific had lost time across Nebraska, and the North Western train was gone when we got to the station gate. Uncle Bob did a little checking, and in due time we had our tickets changed and were boarding the Missouri Pacific that would take us by way of Kansas City. We got out of Omaha between 8 and 9 a.m., as I recall, but even with such a late start, it was the beginning of what, in retrospect, was to be one of my longest days.

The town names were mostly new. Plattsmouth suggested that it bore some relationship to the river that ran along the home ranch. We pulled into Union with the announcement that here was where one changed trains for Lincoln, a place I knew about from conversations of hired men and the masthead of the *Nebraska Farmer*. Of Nebraska City, Auburn, Falls City, Hiawatha, I had never heard. There was some familiarity with Atchison and Leavenworth and, of course, with Kansas City.

By noon we were keenly conscious that the heat of August in that part of the country was accentuated by a humidity factor we were not accustomed to on the plains of Colorado. Every window of the chair car was opened high, and gusts of coal smoke and stinging cinders came in with the heat.

The spirit of high adventure with which I had started the day began to wilt under these conditions, but an even more distracting aspect of the trip had to do with Uncle Bob's insistence on getting off and pacing the station platform at every stop.

He was in his early 30's and a very active farmer. It was only natural that he be restless on this first day away from hard work. But he was also a victim of what someone has called the tobacco chewer's syndrome—an intuitive search for open spaces, bare ground and favorable wind directions.

I was confident that sooner or later the train would leave him, and I would be alone among strange surroundings. In any event, he persisted in catching an open door after the train had started moving. But finally came the kind of trouble I had anxiously anticipated.

The train was moving after a rather long stop, and I heard Uncle Bob calling from outside my window to go back and open the door. When I got to the door, I could see him beyond it, hanging to the handrails. In a matter of seconds I learned where to trigger the rather complicated release on the trap door that covered the steps, and it was simple then to get the other door open and let him in. We were fortunate that the incident took place at a station where there was a considerable expanse of paved platform. At one of the smaller stations there would have been no running room for Uncle Bob while he was getting my attention.

As we filed off the train in Kansas City, we passed a mirror at the end of the coach. I was startled to see a black face; I hadn't seen one among the passengers. A second glance and I realized I was looking at myself after seven hours of exposure to coal smoke.

But filth, fatigue and the day's anxieties were soon forgotten. We came out of the semi-darkness of the track level into a wonderment of massive columns, sparkling chandeliers, vast spaces and the rolling echoes of a thousand voices and twice that many tramping feet.

It was entirely proper, I guess, and possibly portentous, that of all the things I would see on this trip none would leave quite the impression of Kansas City's Union Station, still new at the time, still talked about as an architectural wonder of the Middlewest. Some 50 years later, its cycle of service completed, the grand old building would be a topic of many conferences, a center of concern, during my years on the City Council of Kansas City. The big question: How could it be saved for posterity?

It never occurred to me, back there in 1918, as it seems to have occurred to many rural folk on seeing the Union Station for the first time, that it would hold a lot of hay. But I marveled that there was a complete drug store within the walls, a complete restaurant, a barber shop, a dozen other establishments, yet plenty of room for the marching and countermarching of as many people as I had ever seen at the county fair.

We had left home the night before with boxes of fried chicken, sandwiches, apples—enough food, as it turned out, to meet our needs for the whole trip. But after we had washed up and taken a walk along a street where Uncle Bob left me briefly while he stepped through some swinging doors, we decided to eat at the counter of the Fred Harvey restaurant.

The restaurant as well as everything else about Union Station was busy. And because of government rationing, there were no sugar bowls. The man next to me at the counter asked the waitress for sugar. She noted that all she had served him was cantaloupe and asked what he wanted the sugar for.

"To put on my cantaloupe," he replied.

This seemed to be shocking information, and the waitress said something to the effect that she wasn't getting sugar for anyone who wanted to use it on cantaloupe. The only thing that exchange did for me was stir my curiosity to the extent I tried sugar on cantaloupe at the first opportunity and have used it off and on ever since—especially when the cantaloupe is a little short of flavor. My memory of that occasion was vivid enough that when I came to live in Kansas City in 1951, I could point out the exact stools where I sat and where the man with the cantaloupe sat.

Back to the trip: We got out of Kansas City shortly before midnight and slept in our seats all the way to St. Louis, where we changed to the Baltimore and Ohio. We took due note of Olney, Ill., when the train stopped there. It was where Grandfather Hamil had sat out the Civil War and where Father had spent a year or two before going on to Colorado. We saw pumping oil wells around Lawrenceville, Ill., and tomato canneries at Vincennes, Ind. But mostly, we were conscious of another day of intense heat, humidity and coal smoke. Uncle Bob, much to my satisfaction, was not getting off at every stop, but he was spending a lot of time in the smoker, where spittoons were handy.

Our third night out was spent on a Louisville and Nashville train between Cincinnati and Knoxville. I was disappointed that we couldn't make this leg in daylight, because I wanted to see more of the mountains and because there was more drama in going in and out of tunnels in daylight than after dark.

I recall much less about the trip home. We traveled by way of Louisville and Chicago, where we caught a train operated jointly by the North Western and the Union Pacific that was ours all the way to Proctor. We started with an ample supply of food again, including nearly a peck of green pears from Grandpa Walker's orchard. The first of them became edible somewhere around Chicago. The real staple of these carry-on lunches, of course, was fried chicken, and I recall having the last of the chicken and pears for breakfast somewhere around North Platte, Neb., on the trip home. Never once did we patronize the dining car, and despite all my curiosity about the luxuries some people enjoyed while riding the trains, I never once thought we should.

The new school term opened a few days after we got back to Proctor, and the new teacher, Miss Calvert, sought to learn something about her charges by asking each of us to tell how he or she had spent the summer. When she came to me, I explained that I had worked in the hayfields, had gone swimming a lot and took a trip to Tennessee. This, she concluded, was the most exciting experience anyone had reported, and when she started drawing me out, my responses were two- and three-word sentences. Somehow, it just didn't seem proper to dwell on those two weeks of travel. For one reason, the others in the room hadn't shown any interest, and I was suspicious, I guess, that they wouldn't believe me if I had tried to tell them all I had seen and done.

271

During our high school years we rode the trains often between Proctor and Sterling. I rode to Denver once with Father to attend the National Western Livestock Show. During my senior year in high school I traveled to Denver with Miss Vera Thompson, my English teacher, and Marjorie Campbell, editor of the annual yearbook. I was business manager of the book, and the three of us were en route to Boulder to attend a conference of high school publications staffs.

That ride with the two women included an incident that seems to illustrate a sort of propriety gap that lay very wide then between the sexes in so-called polite society. I may be a bit gauche in recounting it, but there must be some significance in the fact it ranks high among incidents of my adolescent years in which I found myself completely without the capacity to react with any sense of decorum.

When we entered the chair car at about 3:30 a.m., we saw in the half-light that passengers from farther down the line had deployed themselves in such ways as to take up practically all the seats. Mostly men, they had tended to spread arms and legs into any unoccupied space. The dispersal of distorted bodies was not unlike a movie scene of the interior of a saloon just after a shoot-out. The trainman in charge eventually managed to shuffle a couple of grumbling individuals and place the three of us in two pairs of facing seats.

When the train stopped at Merino, all was quiet, except for a low chorus of snores. We had been talking in muted tones as the train moved along, but sat silent when the train was silent, out of respect, I suppose, for our slumbering companions.

Suddenly from the direction of a fellow in front of us who lay cramped in two seats with a foot over the back of the seat ahead of his came the sound of a relaxing passage of gas. It was abundantly obvious and painfully prolonged. This hit me as something close to a personal disaster. It would have been humorous and entertaining, I am certain, in the right situation, but there could be no display of amusement, no wisecracks, in

272

the presence of two ladies. Neither of my companions offered any comment, of course. Both seemed to sense, as I did, that a quick launching of fresh conversation at this moment would fairly ring with irrelevance. Just as Miss Thompson finally saw fit to venture a remark—about the weather or our annual, or something—the train jerked into motion, and we seemed to relax together.

I went through a whole cycle of suppressed emotions in the next few minutes, including extreme anger with that guy in the white shirt and dark trousers with one foot over the seat ahead of him. When the train came to a stop at Fort Morgan, I excused myself and said I wanted to get some fresh air. As the train crew moved things in and out of the baggage car ahead, I stood on the platform and suddenly noted I was laughing out loud with an audience of one—myself. What the ladies may have said in my absence, I never knew. One thing for sure, I never asked.

In the early dusk of a September evening in 1924 I boarded the eastbound train at Proctor. I was on my way to Hastings, Neb., where I would enroll in college. I had bidden goodbye to my home of almost 18 years and felt I was saying goodbye to

Proctor, too, because Mother and Father would move to Sterling in a few months.

The farewells at the station were dry-eyed and tight-lipped, in the pattern Mother and Father had pretty well established for such occasions. Nobody spoke of any doubt or concern as to the wisdom of my course. But inwardly my doubts and uncertainties ran deep. I was committing myself to four years of college. Nobody in my family, all the way through a long list of uncles, aunts and cousins had done this. The train ride was the first leg of a long journey, and I was dreadfully uncertain as to where it was taking me. With nothing else to think about, nobody to talk with, I kept those doubts and anxieties at the front of my mind through the long night. I dozed occasionally, but on the double-track main line below Julesburg every crossing signal was equipped with belligerent bells that broke into my naps with what began to seem like a warning to me as well as to the motorists they were designed to protect. Bells of that kind are still around, and they still seem to convey a melancholy message.

# 26. ODDS AND THE END

Writing memoirs is a lot like loading the goods of a big household into a moving van. Many of the bits and pieces are pushed aside in the hope that at some stage in the loading process there will be just the exact spaces into which they will fit. But the loaders often end up having to force such things into the space available, sometimes awkwardly. A few things finally may be tied on the tailgate.

In any event, it seems proper that I review here some flashes of memory that have recurred from the day I wrote the first paragraph of the opening chapter. They merited attention, but seemed never to fit.

I remember myself in Father's arms looking down on Mother and Brother David Alexander, a few hours old and some 26 months younger than I. There must be something special about the infant mind to explain that through our boyhood years I always thought of him looking exactly as he did when we were introduced to each other.

I remember in less detail when Sister Daisy Edna was born in that same room. But memories are vivid of the word a few months later that Mother was sick with typhoid fever and Edna would have to go live with the Spears family in Proctor. I remember that Father rode Old Tom past the Spears home almost every day and took the baby of some three months for a ride. He felt she needed more fresh air than she was getting.

I remember a late evening when Father asked Sister Ruth and me to walk with him beyond the barn, around the upper garden to the main headgate in the big irrigation ditch. On the way he prepared us for the worst by saying that Mother, in periods of delirium now for several days, was getting no better, and the doctor had told him she might be dead in a day or two. If seemed like a miracle—Mother insisted it was her prayers—that within two days she had passed the crisis and the doctor was predicting her recovery.

Mother's nurse for several weeks was Miss Margaret Seibert, recently come to Sterling from Pennsylvania. At or about the time she went back to Sterling she started caring for Mrs. W. S. Hadfield, and we always presumed that Father probably had talked with Mr. Hadfield and recommended her. In any event, Father came home one day, some time after Mrs. Hadfield's death, and said Miss Seibert or Mr. Hadfield, or both, had talked with him about the possibility they would be married, and in due time they were.

I remember a night in January, 1914, when my sleep was broken by unexplained activity that included my being moved from my bed to a hastily arranged one in the parlor. I lay still, but awake, through the clock's striking of the hours from one to five. I heard Father crank the telephone and talk with the doctor. I heard the doctor's car drive up an hour or so later. Suddenly, there was a strange sound from the bedroom. It was all a surprise to me, but I accepted without question the announcement when Father got me out of bed that I had a new baby brother. It was my early suggestion that he be named for two uncles, Robert and Roy. It would be simple, I explained to Mother, to shorten these to Rob Roy, the name of a popular coffee. But Mother went ahead and named him Donald Walker.

Mother's next pregnancy, five years later, when she was in her 43rd year, was fraught with difficulties. As the time of delivery neared, Dr. Houf insisted she be taken to a Denver hospital. Arrangements were made for her and Father to board the morning train at Proctor and Dr. Houf to join them at Iliff. Some of the difficulty, it turned out, was in the fact that there were two babies instead of one. Mildred Lorie was born on the train at Ft. Lupton, in Weld County, and Margaret Louise was born at the next stop, Brighton, in Adams County. Besides making for some news in papers across the country, this situation made confusion when birth certificates were required. These show both born at Denver. My memories of the occasion are mainly of my role of driver of the Model-T with which I delivered Father and Mother to the station on the way in and met them and the babies upon their return.

Edna was three-and-a-half years old when she fell from the windmill tower and suffered breaks in a thigh and wrist. Dr. J. H. Daniel set the bones without benefit of x-rays and then had Father construct a frame and pulley arrangement at the foot of the bed with which he could keep a constant pull on the leg. He measured the leg on each visit. Sometimes he would add sand to the gallon jug that was at the end of the rope. Sometimes he would remove sand. In later years it could be said that the result was as near a perfect restoration of both limbs as anyone could have expected.

I have a vague recollection of Father's lifting me in his arms somewhere near the railroad station at Sterling and rushing along with a crowd trying to get near a train. The occasion was a visit either by William Howard Taft or Theodore Roosevelt. Were it the former, he would have been president at the time. Were it the latter, he would have been on a tour to cultivate Republican support for the 1912 nomination.

Somebody staying with us temporarily at about this time had a phonograph with a large tin horn through which I heard screetchy renditions of a Roosevelt campaign song, the repeated phrase of which was, "Oh, Theodore." Another record in the collection was of someone singing "Red Wing."

We didn't have our own phonograph until about 1919. It was ordered through the Lamb store from Beebe and Runyan at Omaha, and the initial records included "Beautiful Blue Danube," "Voices of Spring," "Tales of Vienna Woods," "My Isle of Golden Dreams," and "Missouri Waltz."

There was a special song in 1916 for Charles Evans Hughes in his unsuccessful bid for the presidency. Father and Mother had something to do with a Republican rally at the Proctor school, and the party leaders from Sterling brought along a quartet whose repertoire included a ditty with a line saying, "We'll vote for Mr. Hughes on election day."

There was a snow in 1912 or 1913 that stopped everything. We children stayed home from school. Father and the hired men checked on the livestock they could get to and then holed up around the stove in the bunkhouse. During the afternoon, Brother Dave and I got permission to put on our coats and step outside. The wind caught Dave and swept him around the house and out of sight. I reported to Mother. She rang the dinner bell, and Father came running from the bunkhouse. In a minute or two Dave was found huddled in a corner, and everyone was newly conscious of the ferocity of a storm that eventually took a tremendous toll of cattle, including a hundred or more owned by Charlie Simpson, who lived on that portion of the ranch known as the "lower place."

Drifts of that snow remained for weeks. Ruth and I found some with a crusted surface on which we could walk to the top of the chicken house. The mulberry hedge along the west side of the lower orchard must have been 15 feet high at the time, and there was snow that buried all but the highest twigs in one spot.

In April, 1920, there had been two days of almost constant rain before the wind changed and the temperature started falling. The rain changed to snow and that fell for at least 24 hours. The snow was wet and heavy, but it drifted nevertheless, and it tended to blind cattle and send them to wandering aimlessly for shelter.

The morning after the weather had cleared, Father assigned me to join others who were checking cattle losses along the Union Pacific right of way between Proctor and Iliff. J. P. Dillon was designated as the railroad's representative, and the job at hand was to count and identify, by brand, between 150 and 200 carcasses that were strewn along the track—some under several feet of snow. The story was that an engine and caboose had made the run between Sterling and Julesburg at the height of the storm and that the engineer thought he was hitting snowdrifts when he was running through bunches of cattle that had drifted onto the right of way. We found many live animals with broken legs that were buried under two or three feet of snow. A man with a gun took care of them.

What all of us neglected to consider as we spent that day in the snow was that the April sun was coming down with considerable intensity and reflecting into our faces. I got the worst sunburn of my life, and all through the following summer I encountered men in the neighborhood who were still nursing skin troubles attributed to the day after the April blizzard.

From some experiences of my boyhood I was lucky to escape alive and whole. Once when Dave and I were grabbing the tails of the milk cows and letting them pull us in their excited runs around the corral, we failed to take note of a mare that became concerned about the welfare of her small colt. I did not see her coming, but Dave did. She ran at me, wheeled and kicked. I went down, and Dave started for the house to alert Mother. In a minute or so I regained my senses and got on my feet while blood streamed down my face. The mare's hoof had grazed the top of my head and turned back a two-inch triangle of scalp. If she had aimed an inch lower, I most certainly could not have survived.

On a Sunday afternoon one October, I was alone on the back porch and came upon some .38 caliber cartridges. At hand was a large pumpkin, resting on a five-gallon can of honey and at eye level. I undertook to push the rounded bullet into the pumpkin. The pumpkin was tough, but I persisted, and reached for the iron wrench with which we dismantled the cream separator each day for washing. I struck the cartridge on the firing pin side and broke the pumpkin's skin. This was progress. I had driven the cartridge pretty well into the pumpkin when the whole thing blew up in my face. My wrench had hit just the right spot. There were pumpkin seeds and pulp all over me and the porch floor. The pumpkin had a black-edged hole about six inches in diameter, and there was a small dent in the honey can where the bullet had been deflected.

One thing I had succeeded in doing was to clean the pumpkin of all seeds and pulp. No one seemed to appreciate that, though, and I got considerable criticism for destroying a pumpkin as well as for having displayed a horrible lapse of judgment. I was about 10 years old and should have known better.

When Brother Dave was much younger, he had made a casual plaything of a .30-.30 cartridge. He placed it in the end of a new Christmas popgun and sent the bullet ricocheting around the kitchen.

There were lessons in these incidents in the possibility of accidents that the very presence of guns tends to create. There were guns on every hand at our house, but they were little used. The .22 caliber rifle was on hand primarily for the shooting of hogs at butchering time. There were at least two shotguns with it on hooks in the porch, but only when we boys started shooting ducks at high school age did they get much use. The .38 caliber revolver was one Father had carried while managing Mr. Hadfield's cattle on Lewis Creek. The .30-.30, stored in a closet, was fired not more than two or three times in my memory. Most of the shooting that went on around the ranch was on the occasions when Mr. Blue or others came out from Cedar Rapids and hunted ducks or prairie chickens.

There had been cattle roundups in the county since the days when J. W. Iliff, Jared Brush and a few others controlled most of the cattle ranging up and down the South Platte. They were still being conducted in the fall on a modest scale during the years of my earliest recollection. Men talked about each one as possibly the last one, and their talk reflected a feeling that here was an institution they would miss. And for me, of course, there was the regret that something romantic, or at least appealing, would be gone before I could take part.

Father may have sensed this when he announced one Friday night that I could join him and others, including my cousin, Clarence Lane, about 14 years old, who was visiting from Tennessee, and attend the roundup that was progressing across the county on a line generally above the level of the new North Sterling irrigation ditch.

It was early fall—probably in 1912—and there was heavy frost on the alkali grass as we picked up 15 or 20 critters that had strayed into our home pastures from the herds of those ranchers who still turned cattle loose in the spring to graze the unfenced areas, some of which were about to come under irrigation.

We traveled about seven miles to the northwest, moving on a diagonal course most of the time and lowering wires so we could stay on course across a fenced section. We crossed the freshly dug North Sterling ditch and pushed our little herd into the roundup area at about 11 a.m.

Cattle were spread over 30 or 40 acres and surrounded by horsemen. Owners or their representatives were moving in and out at several points, picking animals carrying their brands and moving them out to assembly points where helpers could hold them together or start them moving toward home pastures.

There was a definite impression of competitive daring on the part of the men on cutting horses. I was a bit startled to see our neighbor, J. W. Ramsey, ride on the dead run in pursuit of a stubborn calf, his long coat and gray beard making him look as I thought Robert E. Lee would have looked on a running horse.

The real highlight, though, was dinner, served from the rear of a chuck wagon and cooked in kettles over an open wood fire. There was beef, of course, but what impressed me most was the massive serving of stewed tomatoes with which everything else was drenched.

This day at the roundup was a sort of homecoming for Father, I am sure. He didn't talk much about his experiences as a cowboy for W. S. Hadfield. He never boasted of having stayed astride a bucking horse longer than other men might have. He was a competent roper, but no exhibitionist. His leather chaps hung in the back porch, and it was a great day when I discovered I was big enough to fit into them. The chaps, the canvas tarpaulin with which he had covered his bedroll, the .38 revolver—these were memorabilia of the day when over-night duty with cattle was routine. The chaps dried and cracked over the years. First the cuffs fell off and then some of the bits of leather fringe, but I recall wearing them once on a long, cold ride during my senior year in high school.

The tarpaulin was used to cover tender plants and flowers against late frosts, but it finally fell to pieces. It is amazing, as I think back on it, that there were these mementos of Father's cowboy days with so little conversation about experiences with which they might have related. I do recall once that Father referred to the revolver as assurance, in case of an accident, he could kill his horse rather than be dragged to death. He recalled shooting rattlesnakes with it, but indicated he never thought it necessary for protection against other men.

While he did not talk much about his days on the range, he loved the company of men he had come to know as young ranchers or employees of ranchers. As he approached the age of 50, he started attending old-timers' reunions of one sort or another, mainly those held in conjunction with the county fair. This for a man still in middle age seems now to have been a somewhat hurried interest in re-living the days of his youth. I can't help thinking that Father sensed the likelihood of an early death from the heart condition the doctors had discovered when he took an examination for insurance in his early 40's.

On a hot night in July, 1931, I returned to my desk at the Hastings *Tribune*, worked an hour or so and was at the front door when the phone rang. It was Brother Dave in Sterling with word that Father was in the hospital and that he might not live through the night.

I had been on the road about seven hours when the sun came

up behind me. The air was clear and sparkling clean. The sky was blue and cloudless. It would be a hot day, and a sad one, but there was cause to reflect on the attractions of these open lands where Father had chosen to live out his years. There was a faint smell of sage in the breeze that blew across the sandhills west of Fleming. Meadowlarks sang above the put-put of my four-cylinder Plymouth and the grate of its tires on gravel. Through a break in the hills to my right I caught glimpses of the South Platte Valley, the trees, the green fields and the uplands beyond.

Through the last few miles of that long ride a lot of things seemed to come into focus. I came a little closer to understanding Father and his love of the high plains. This seems a proper note to close on. It was because of him and his decisions that I was there.

# The Family

James Newton Hamil      Ada Gertrude Walker-Hamil
1875-1931           1876-1960
Clara Ruth Hamil-Williamson
1905-1944
James Harold Hamil, Kansas City, Mo.
1906-
David Alexander Hamil, Washington, D.C.
1908-
Daisy Edna Hamil-Gaines, Sterling, Colo.
1911-
Donald Walker Hamil, Sterling, Colo.
1914-
Mildred Lorie Hamil-Schroer, Albuquerque, N.M.
1919-
Margaret Louise Hamil-Brittain, Lakewood, Colo.
1919-